Passion and Craft

Michael Szenberg, Editor

Passion and Craft
Economists at Work

Foreword by Paul A. Samuelson

Ann Arbor

THE UNIVERSITY OF MICHIGAN PRESS

2001   2000   1999   1998   4   3   2   1

*A CIP catalog record for this book is available
from the British Library.*

Library of Congress Cataloging-in-Publication Data

Passion and craft : economists at work / Michael Szenberg ; foreword
by Paul A. Samuelson.
     p.   cm.
   Includes index.
   ISBN 0-472-09685-0 (cloth : alk. paper). — ISBN 0-472-06685-4
(paper : alk. paper)
   1. Economists — Biography.   2. Economics — Philosophy.
I. Szenberg, Michael.
HB76.P37   1999
330'.092'2 — dc21   98-27739
                                                                            CIP

B'H
To my precocious adorable sextet:
Elki, Batya, Chanoch, Devorah, Ephraim, and Ayala
May they go from strength to strength
and fulfill their promise.

Come to the edge, he said.
    Come to the edge, he said.
    they said: we are afraid.
Come to the edge, he said.
    they came.
He pushed them . . . and they flew.
          —GUILLAUME APOLLINAIRE

One ought only to write when one leaves a piece of one's
own flesh in the inkpot each time one dips one's pen.
          —LEO TOLSTOY

I give you the end of a golden string,
    only wind it into a ball:
It will lead you in at Heaven's gate,
    Built in Jerusalem's wall.
          —WILLIAM BLAKE

Contents

PAUL A. SAMUELSON

Foreword

Most people think of scientists as dull people who spend their time in doing boring things — things boring possibly even to themselves. That is not the view of us scholars. We deem ourselves lucky: the system pays us to do what we'd like to do for nothing. For pure pleasure, boring research beats playing tennis, or dancing, or eating at four-star restaurants. It ranks up there with teaching your child to tell time.

I am speaking, of course, about successful researchers. If you spend your life in the doomed quest for a proof of how to trisect an angle, there's not a lot to look back upon with nostalgia and pleasure. That explains why the biologist Peter Medawar could say that scientists narrow down to focus on *tractable* problems. It is the rational coward's way, just as those darn sensible rats are the first ones to leave the sinking ship.

Usually it is only elderly celebrities who get to publish their autobiographies. *Passion and Craft* is an exception in that it sought deliberately to recruit active scholars in the active phase of their lifetime career. Some sage has said, "Science advances funeral by funeral." (Actually it was the creator of quantum physics, Max Planck, in his own scientific biography; but I confess to having polished for English its more guarded German wording.)

Passion and Craft is both exciting and valuable. If you are at the beginning of a possible calling to scholarship and teaching, it can help you decide what career is truly best for you. And at any stage or station in life, reading what lively minds remember and want to say is fascinating and rewarding. In my experience a collection like this is not best read at one or two sittings. You wouldn't gobble up the best box of chocolates all at once. Stretch out the fun. Leave the volume on your desk or beside your bed and dip into it as fancy tempts you. Lest you lose track of the best parts, underline and make checkmarks. After all, it's *your* book.

No one has written a really successful novel about what makes a Newton or Darwin or Mozart or Keynes tick. Only Leibnizes or Wallaces or Beethovens or Adam Smiths will understand — and they will understand without having to read it in a book. (When Mozart was asked how old you had to be to write your first symphony, he replied: "eighteen." "But," came the protest, "*you* wrote your first one at eleven." "Yes," he replied, "but I didn't have to go around asking people when it was OK to do that.")

Passion and Craft is a collection of accounts about how successful younger economists do and have done their creative work. It is like the famous interviews in the *Paris Review* with authors and poets. Do they use ball pens or word processors? Do they revise endlessly like Balzac or write it all down perfect the first time like Verdi? (The style of Henry James was comparatively simple in his *first phase* when he wrote his drafts with a pen; later, because of writer's cramp, he came to dictate; when his catty brother William (the philosopher) was asked about H.J.'s famous second phase, he more or less averred: "There is no *second phase*. It's just that his new secretary leaves in all that guff." Bill never understood that Hank would have been bothered rather than pleased to write what would command his brother's approval.)

Who cares about another chap's work habits? Well, I do, even though it is late in the day to benefit from the account. And I did when I was just entering into my studies of economics. Wolfe Boy in the jungle goes whole hours not thinking about the best way to discover scientific breakthroughs. But we must not forget that Einstein and Bohr and Watson-Crick were all young once. Except for the chance encounter with the biography of some earlier scientist, they might have become violinists or brokers or plumbers rather than mere Nobel laureates.

Do I exaggerate? Maybe. Fifty years ago Paul de Kruif wrote *Microbe Hunters,* a sparkling vulgarization of the history of biological science. Its pages tell how Pasteur, searching for better fermenters of wine, stumbled on the Pasteur vaccines to keep alive children who are bitten by rabid dogs. He wrote about Lister's crusade for sterility in operating rooms and told how Jenner infected folk with cowpox in order to ward off the more virulent smallpox. In the same vein, and at about the same time, the novelist Sinclair Lewis wrote *Arrowsmith* to describe how Dr. Arrowsmith took a vow to work unselfishly toward the distant goal of new knowledge and the saving of lives. Those books sold well—even if not to the senior faculty. Hans Zinsser (author of *Rats, Lice, and History* and of his own exemplary scientist's autobiography, *As I Knew Him*) sniffed snobbishly at de Kruif and Lewis, writing, "When a real scientist reads Arrowsmith's prayer and oath, it makes him [*sic*] want to throw up."

Sorry. Zinsser was quite wrong. I have read short autobiographies of many Nobel Prize winners. A surprisingly large fraction of them report: "It was reading *Arrowsmith* or de Kruif or Darwin's aw-shucks autobiography for his grandchildren that first drew me into the realm of research and science." Once again we see how cynicism and sophistication are the enemies of enthusiasm. And it is enthusiasm that is the gasoline that drives us to accomplishment and to self-fulfillment. No medal or promotion or pay raise can stand comparison with self-fulfillment: that's the coin worth working for.

Shaw was wrong: Youth is not wasted on the young. Nor is it a matter of arteries and brain circulation. Thus the great Swedish economist Knut Wicksell didn't come into economics proper until he was forty: at forty-eight he had to take a Ph.D. in order to get his first chair. But still, at whatever chronological age, he had his glorious first decade of youth in the subject. And well into his seventies he wrote works that we still study today, works that of course benefited from contributions that younger Swedish and world economists (Heckscher, Ohlin, Keynes) were then making.

I must not quit without warning against a misunderstanding. Scholarship is not an invariable delight. Disappointments abound. Writer's block—this really means a period when nothing good occurs to one to write about—can occur and reoccur. Experimenters—empiricists in our case as economists—can more easily overcome this drought. Always there is something fascinating to investigate, describe, and measure. Charles Darwin, at his peak, took years off to describe barnacles. Small beer? Not to Charles D. or to his scholarly posterity. And his findings, in the end, contributed much to our understanding of the grand and abstract principles of evolution.

In my own case I fall back on the least unimportant problem left in my inventory of useful questions. Moving down curves of diminishing returns is the rational thing to do between great Schumpeterian shocks and innovations.

Autobiography has one advantage over biography. In a prior book edited by Michael Szenberg, *Eminent Economists: Their Life Philosophies*, as interesting as authors' claims for their successes were to my mind their confessions of failures and complaints that some of their genuinely important contributions have, as yet, not been given their due by contemporary scholars. That has the authenticity of real life.

And this leads to another, and final, correction that will be reassuring to neophyte scholars. A worthy contemporary of mine, who accomplished much that was unique, was hounded all his life by a sense of nonfulfillment. Why? His brilliant father, a noneconomist acquaintance of the brilliant Joseph Schumpeter, told him early in life: "If you can't be a Schumpeter, the scholarly game isn't worth the candle." What nonsense! Schumpeter himself was never the transcendental genius. The corpus of science does not trace to Nobel laureates and off-the-chart IQs. Science is a beehive to which we all add our bits. Carlyle's Great Man theory of History, to my mind and on the evidences of all experience, is a 10 percent truth — even less true in science and scholarship than it is in politics and war.

Fortunately young humans have evolved to believe in the worth of their works. If cave people had not developed a slight overestimation of their own achievements, they would never have survived in the incessant struggle for existence. One does one's best. One cuts one's losses. And satisfaction comes whether directly sought or not.

Preface

The underlying notion in this volume is that understanding what economists actually do and what they think they do when they engage in research is important. Thus, the economists presented in this volume have been asked to reflect introspectively on their methods of working and to offer us details about their private revelries, discoveries, and ravishing illuminations, if any. The contributors were free to determine their own approach, though I did ask them to explore whether their work proceeds according to the scientific method.[1] Their essays unravel much about the characteristics of greatness, whatever the difficulties, uncertainties, and hazards, although there is still much in the creative process, which Samuelson views as "a fluid that wants to get free," that is indecipherable.

This book was a delight to compile, for it gave me cause to ponder innumerable questions again. I am an economist by profession and a student observer of human behavior and reader of biographies by avocation. Because the human lab is forever intriguing, I hold the subject of biographical inquiry close to my heart. I hope that readers will find the material in this volume not only instructive and thought provoking but entertaining. To paraphrase Dylan Thomas, their pieces sing their own song and will, I hope, evoke applause. Furthermore, these autobiographical vignettes reveal the human context of economists — their passion and spirit — besides the evidence and logical rigor that are the ingredients of craft.

This book is a natural extension of the editor's previous volume, *Eminent Economists: Their Life Philosophies* (Cambridge University Press, 1992), which focused on the older generation of economists and has been translated into several languages. The editorial director of Cambridge University Press then was Colin Day, an enthusiastic supporter of the book who shortly afterward became director of University of Michigan Press. It was only natural therefore that I publish these solicited essays with Day's publishing house. As with the previous volume, several essays appearing here have been published in the *American Economist*. These essays have generated widespread interest, and overseas journals have requested permission to translate them.

In the several years that have elapsed between the conception of this book and its publication, I amassed an enormous volume of debt. It is a delight to discharge it here. My first vote of thanks must go to Paul A. Samuelson, who extended to me many kindnesses in the past and unhesitatingly agreed to pen the foreword to this volume, and to the contributors who graciously produced their essays and commented on my introduction while being ferociously engaged in other projects. I must, second, express my gratitude to Arthur L. Centonze, Dean of the Lubin School of Business, for his ongoing research support and advice. He exemplifies the dictum of the Chinese military strategist that the true leader is one who leads in a way that makes followers feel it is they who initiate and direct the activities.

My list of intellectual debt is far longer. Professors Mary Ellen Oliverio, Joseph T. Salerno, and Thomas J. Webster made valued observations on this volume. Professor Barbara Adams gave my introduction a good critical reading and helped me to resist the stubborn efforts of each footnote to achieve chapter-length proportions. It was Noel Coward who humorously likened being interrupted by a footnote in an essay to the telephone ringing in the midst of lovemaking.

The collegiality at Lubin of William C. Freund, M. Peter Hoefer, Burton Leiser, James Russell, Lynette Wailoo, Diana Ward, and Philip K. Y. Young was a constant source of encouragement and affection. Professor Dian Seiler offered many useful suggestions, and Elizabeth Birnbaum, the librarian, was extraordinarily supportive. The center's administrative staff—Debbie Ash, Yvonne Rosario, and Amy Thomas—and Natalie Marcus, my graduate assistant, have all assisted me enthusiastically with this project. My deep gratitude for their generosity is extended to all these individuals.

Special appreciation and thanks are owed to the members of the Executive Board of the Honor Society in Economics for being a source of support: Professors Stanley L. Brue, Kristine L. Chase, William D. Gunther, Alexander J. Kondonassis, Shirley Johnson-Lans, Vincent R. McDonald, Patrick O'Neill, Charles F. Phillips, Jr., and Harold F. Williamson.

Turning to the publishing end of the book, I want to thank Dr.

Colin Day for lending his warmth to incubating this egg from the beginning.

Finally, my special debt and gratitude is extended to Sandy Franklin, a longtime editor and an outstanding student whom I picked to be my graduate assistant and who also became my close friend. While retaining my voice and style, Sandy braved many drafts to improve the manuscript. Imbued with unremitting kindness and concern, she did the job with humor, exactitude, and patience.

I regret that David Gordon died on March 16, 1996, of heart failure before he could read his words in print.

NOTE

1. B. F. Skinner claimed the following: "The notes, data, and publications which I have examined do not show that I ever behaved in the manner . . . described by John Stuart Mill or John Dewey or as in reconstructions of scientific behavior by other philosophers of science. I never faced a problem which was more than the eternal problem of finding order. I never attacked a problem by constructing a hypothesis. I never deduced theorems or submitted them to experimental check. So far as I can see, I had no preconceived model of behavior — certainly not a physiological or mentalistic one, and I believe, not a conceptual one. . . . Of course, I was working on a basic assumption — that there was order in behavior if I could only discover it — but such an assumption is not to be confused with the hypotheses of deductive theory. It is also true that I exercised a certain selection of facts, but not because of relevance to theory but because one fact was more orderly than another. If I engaged in experimental design at all, it was simply to complete or extend some evidence of order already observed" ("A Case History in Scientific Method," in *Cumulative Record,* 3d ed. [New York: Appleton Century, 1972], 122).

Introduction

Plato is said to have inscribed above the entrance to his Academy: "Let no man ignorant of geometry enter here." Readers of this volume need no similar warning, unless, of course, they are among the geniuses who have nothing more to learn or those at a total loss whose mission is to extol ignorance. By getting to know other scholars and their research experiences, we enhance our understanding of the true nature of art and science and of ourselves. The contributors of these essays remind me of the monks who proclaim, "Ora Labora" — to work is to pray. The economists' dedication and emotional attachment to scientific work can be likened to the monk's spiritual missionary zeal for prayer. Indeed, scholars feel a mystic sense, a calling to give their best when they engage in difficult, meticulous work.

Plato proposed that we produce geniuses by breeding them, much as we breed animals.[1] Having established scholars stroll beside aspiring researchers is a more congenial path. If the mind of a human being can be compared to an ember, then the purpose of these essays is to fan the smoldering coals of young scholars so that their cognitive and imaginative faculties are not only exercised but propelled ever forward. Frederick Mosteller, the eminent statistician, once complained about a cookbook to a master chef.[2] The chef responded that the most one can expect from a cookbook is one good recipe. I am certain, however, that once exposed to these essays, readers will find in them more than one thing they can adapt to their specific scholarly needs in research, teaching, and life. As for regrets that may arise, the nineteenth-century poet John Greenleaf Whittier wrote the following memorable and evincing lines:

> For all sad words of
>   tongue or pen,
> The saddest are these: "It
>   might have been!"

I am sorry that a number of economists who had agreed to pen an essay for this volume were unable to contribute, for they or their spouses joined the top ranks of the Clinton administration, and as one of them wrote, he was not able to "deliver on my promise that [he] made when [he] had time to think!" Another claimed that he had become enslaved by time units no longer than ten minutes.

Before going on to meet the economists in this volume, a word about the rationale for their selection. Several criteria were applied, including leadership in the field as exemplified by election to prominent positions in various learned societies, scholarly awards, citations, and diversity. Obviously my personal preferences and tastes led me to include certain economists and exclude others; that was unavoidable.

Although the previous collection of essays was devoid of female voices,[3] I am pleased that this new volume has them in fruitful representation, a trend increasingly found in other fields as well.

Since the essays by the distinguished economists in this volume focus on introspective activities rather than on scientific papers, I have taken the liberty in this introduction of expanding on some of the thoughts of the contributors. I beg the indulgence of those readers who find this approach by the editor — and a lesser-league economist — inappropriate.

The Query and the Answer

The 1957 Nobel laureate Albert Camus made a distinction between people who have all the answers because they look backward and those who have all the questions because they look forward. It is for the scientist to integrate both worlds by religiously and unrelentingly casting doubt upon, and undermining the validity of, the answers and conventions of yesterday and positing new questions that arise from the scholar's quest for knowledge. In this way, hopefully, the scientist will reveal some new relationship, some new pattern of which we were previously unaware.

The passion for creating and advancing knowledge is aptly amplified by Aristotle's opening line in *Metaphysics:* "All men by nature desire to know."[4] Just consider the fate of Adam and Eve.[5] Our common ancestors were given not only the Garden of Eden but physical immortality. Only one prescription was handed down to them. They were forbidden to eat from the Tree of Knowledge. Yet the human craving to penetrate the boundaries of the unknown, the concealed, and the mysterious was too enticing for Adam and Eve to resist, even at the cost of their lives.[6] Adam and Eve must have concluded that a life characterized by certainty is unsatisfying because it is filled with a sense of ennui.

In the scholar's intellectual probing for knowledge, the centrality of the query must be recognized. As such, a superior student evolves into a skeptic. To paraphrase Isaac Bashevis Singer, the Nobelist in literature, scholars can be called "the people of the book" who, with their intellectual probing and restlessness, "do not sleep themselves and do not let others sleep." It is not surprising then that when the Nazi or Soviet regimes occupied another country, one of their early tasks was to eliminate the intelligentsia. Neither is it surprising that England was the first country forced to decolonize, while Portugal was the last one. Whereas Britain established educational institutions in the colonies that produced an intellectual and therefore more sensitive class that challenged and rebelled against the foreign rulers, Portugal's policy in education was benign neglect.

In the words of the poet Rainer Maria Rilke, one has "to love the questions themselves." A manifestation of this passion to plumb the depth of an issue for questions is seen in the Talmud. Samuel E. Edels (known as Maharsha), an eminent sixteenth-century Talmudic scholar, ended many of his commentaries with the word *vdok* (examine), thereby instructing readers to research the subject further, since no detail is beyond challenge.[7] This exhortation suggests that the analysis of any subject is tentative and open-ended, and that a searching mind should practice reverent irreverence.

Flaubert advised a fellow writer in a letter that only "superficial, limited creatures, rash featherbrained souls, demand a conclusion from everything. . . . The day on which the answer is found will be this planet's last."[8] Without final truths there is always room for further debate, argument, and questioning. Although with time some reach the status of a master, one must remain a perpetual student. Yet the scientist must retain childlike qualities besides. These qualities convey curiosity, discontent, a tendency to ask questions, adventurousness, an eagerness to unravel puzzles, and especially naïveté. In the face of strong opposition and frequent ridicule by parties with vested interests and entrenched minds, a sense of daring naïveté is required to advance what then may look like far-fetched or even absurd alternative explanations for existing phenomena.

A recent example related by Donald L. Bentley illustrates the importance of focusing and defining questions.[9] The high quality and phenomenal success of the Japanese auto industry are attributed to its adoption of W. Edward Deming's Total Quality Management (TQM) system. Adopters of Deming's TQM initiative like to point out that, in the 1980s, if a problem arose in the industry, the Japanese automakers would devote 90 percent of their time to discussing the problem and 10 percent to finding a solution. By contrast, their counterparts in the United States would allocate 10 percent of their time to the problem and 90 percent to the solution.

The Aesthetics of Research

Words that express aesthetic values, such as *beautiful, ingenious, simple, graceful,* and *elegant,* appear increasingly in the writings of scholars, including economists. Although aesthetic criteria are hardly clear, for some, these qualities are expressed by the dictum "less is more."[10] Jaroslav Pelikan, at the other end of the spectrum, holds that any research project by which " 'What?' can lead to 'How?' can then lead to 'Why?' is ineluctably aesthetic in its nature and scope."[11] Such a broad definition of aesthetics would encompass the processes of artistic creation and appreciation that spring from the scholar's ideology and vision. It is the scholar's grasp of the central issues of the period, especially in social inquiry, that determines the selection of research areas; the design, identification, and framing of the questions to be broached; the right blending and flow of the constituent parts of the project; and, ultimately, the research results.

Whether a narrow or broad approach is adopted, scientific activity has the great potential of offering aesthetic joy.[12] At the heart of scientific activity is the discovery of universal laws of nature that bring order and unity to a diverse, uncertain world, and purpose, direction, and meaning. Thus, Coleridge's definition of what is beauty — "unity in variety" — is appropriate. Some researchers even contend that scientific curiosities alone have the capacity to lift us onto the highest perch of human development. For example, Isidor Isaac Rabi, the physics Nobelist, appears to argue in a sense (though unconvincingly in my view) that art is the antithesis of science, as if thinking and feeling, and truth and beauty, can be easily separated or even distinguished.

The arts are certainly central to life, yet they are not the kind of thing that will inspire men to push onto new heights. Suppose we were to become a nation of poets and were taught in school, as the Japanese are taught, that every good citizen should write a poem. Some would be very good and people would read and enjoy them. But what would anybody talk about? Only everyday things—love, sorrow, life, and death. If men want to go beyond these everyday things to a grand theme, they will find it only in science. . . . I mean, after Shakespeare and others, how many more persons can say the same things? They can say it in different ways, they can say it in beautiful ways and in other contexts, and I hope they will never stop. But just the same, where do we find the really new thing, the moving thing, the thing that will show the glory of God and the originality of nature, the profundity—and where do we find the imagination that delves into the mysteries of life, into the existence of matter? That imagination, I would say, will be found only in science.[13]

A number of scientists have addressed the important relationship between aesthetics and intuition. Dirac's reaction to Schrödinger's decision to delay publishing his wave equation because it conflicted with the data (which cost Schrödinger priority to what is now known as the Klein-Gordon equation) is noteworthy: "I think there is a moral to this story, namely that having beauty in one's equations is more important than to have them fit the experiment. . . . It seems that if one is working from the point of view of getting beauty in one's equations, and if one has really a sound insight, one is on a sure line of progress. If there is not complete agreement between the results of one's work and experiment, one should not allow oneself to be too discouraged, because the discrepancy may be due to minor features that are not properly taken into account and that will get cleared up with further developments of the theory."[14]

Communicating one's research contents and findings is likewise an art that embraces aesthetic dimensions, however tortured and lonely the process of composition may be. Words can be as enchanting, as captivating, as uplifting, and as sensuous to the listener or reader as musical notes because the paths of language and music are very much connected. Both are steeped in affect and can inspire human emotions. Tolstoy, the author of one of the epigraphs to this volume, would have been pleased to hear that Flaubert rolled on the floor for hours until he found just the happy turn of phrase he was groping for, or that Ernest Hemingway is said to have revised the last page of *A Farewell to Arms* sixty times.[15] The objective then is to wield the writer's tools in a way that grabs the reader and makes for zesty reading. This involves clarity, precision, and the economical use of words.[16] Before Bill Moyers assumed the position of commentator on *NBC Nightly News,* he approached John Chancellor, who had served in that capacity for several years, for some advice. Chancellor advised Moyers to start reading the first chapter of Genesis. "A minute and a half (the time allotted for a commentary) gets you to the afternoon of the third day; if you cannot say what you need to by the afternoon of the third day, then you are not a commentator."[17]

Equally important is the realization that no paper will ever be perfect. Take the illustrative case of Lord Acton. He planned to write a masterpiece on the history of liberty that he titled "The Madonna of the Future." The work was never completed, however, because each time Lord Acton encountered new materials related to the subject, he felt compelled to redraft his findings. This anecdote underscores the importance of creating a balance between one's writing and reading. The two compete with one another. Similarly, a balance between a critical attitude toward one's own work and a sense of self-confidence must be developed, lest the research project reach oblivion rather than what Henry James called (upon publishing his first piece — a book review) "the incredibility of print." For those who ask where to find interesting research projects, besides the practical advice offered by the economists in this volume, Isaac Bashevis Singer has a delightful, metaphysical answer: "There are powers who take care of you. If you are a doctor, you get sick people; if you are a lawyer, you get cases; if you are a writer, the Almighty sends you stories, sometimes too many."[18]

Finally, when the principle of "publish or perish!" makes a game of the citations and peer approval that are supposed to certify the scientist's standing in the scholarly world, the game takes on an aesthetic dimension for scholars.

The Vista of Knowledge

If there is any truth about power, it is this: The only way to retain it is to pass it on to others. Pablo Picasso, who had great difficulty in dealing with his mortality, did not attend his mother's funeral and told his teenage son he was no longer welcome and should not visit him again because "I am old, and you are young." Picasso, great artist though he was, was deadly wrong. The way to extend the life horizon and indeed gain immortality is to delegate and transmit the insights and wisdom one has gained to the younger generation. To change Robert Frost's couplet, we can continue walking the miles even after "we go to sleep" by relaying the life baton to our children, students, and colleagues.

Already in ancient times sages argued whether vast knowledge and erudition take precedence over brilliant depth and sharp dialectics. The argument was inconclusive and ended in a draw.[19] Archilochus, the pre-Socratic philosopher, expressed this enigmatically: "The fox knows many things, but the hedgehog knows one big thing." Several of the economists in this volume can be placed, as it were, among the hedgehogs of economists who delve for scientific insights by turning their critical lens toward few areas. The others, being more foxlike, drive their talents into many directions. Whatever group the economists presented here belong to, as experimenters they must share at least one important trait: that is, a desire, in each new work undertaken, to do something that goes beyond the ordinary, or in John Dewey's phrase, "be an adventurer." Otherwise, a scholar "repeats himself and becomes aesthetically dead."[20]

Still, there are certain economists, such as John Stuart Mill and Paul A. Samuelson, who have reached immortal stature in the history of economics. These individuals, embraced by God, possess a genius that covers in its depth and breadth many areas besides economics. Their life of buoyant precocity, brilliant, unsurpassed talent, astonishing intelligence, and dazzling, prodigious scholarship sets them so far apart from other economists that their achievements dwarf us. As such, they cannot serve as role models. They are members of the pantheon who deserve to be revered and worshiped.

Still, economists can get a sense of fulfillment in the grove of academe or consulting without being a Mill or a Samuelson. When the violinist and composer Fritz Kreisler heard Jascha Heifetz play the violin for the first time, Kreisler told Efrem Zimbalist, who then was the first violinist of the New York Philharmonic, that they should both break their violins over their knees and stop playing. Both, of course, continued to plod forward. Similarly, in economics, there is still much work left and satisfaction to be gained from being "a tail to lions," as the ancient sages say, or a twig on Samuelson's branch.[21]

Of greater pedagogical and nourishing significance are the individuals with ordinary intellectual endowments who succeed in producing astonishing work. These individuals show an enthusiasm, ambition, and extraordinary capacity for endless (but often fruitless) toil with which they acquire remarkable skills and develop their potential talents to the fullest.[22] In short, they are very extraordinary ordinary men and women possessing what Plato called a "fine frenzy."

Among the economists of the older generation who embody those traits are two exemplary figures whom I would like to name: Theodore Schultz and Victor R. Fuchs.[23] These are individuals with whom young economists can identify. Both started with small problems that did not attract attention and in no way intimated these individuals would grow to full stature and reach the top ranks of their profession. It was not until their forties that both started to blossom and produce practical, critical studies, which broadened the vista of conventional economics to include ethical, philosophical, and sociological dimensions. Since their scholarship is not overwhelming, they can easily, together with the economists assembled in this volume, serve as role models and thus snatch what Rachel McCulloch calls "ordinary, garden-variety students" from the jaws of mediocrity and even oblivion.

Pondering the doctrine of selection, Henry Roth, the author of the 1934 classic *Call It Sleep,* noted that there were writers more original and brilliant than he who didn't quite make it. In his last autobiographical novel, Roth (who suffered from writer's block for nearly forty-five years) attributed his success to an accidental stroke of luck. He "deserved very little credit. Only that of striving to develop the most preeminent, if not the only gift he had . . . which was what the others did . . . those more gifted than he, who failed to win universal appeal. It was a Calvinist fluke."[24] One might also argue that greater familiarity with the innermost precincts of scholarship would reveal that from unexpected experiences great insights or ideas frequently emerge. James Buchanan relates that a chance browsing in the library stacks at the University of Chicago in 1948 led him to stumble upon Knut Wicksell's unknown and untranslated 1896 dissertation on taxation, which had a profound and everlasting effect on his career.[25]

Such assertions make good copy, but they miss an enduring truth: the character of the individual and the inner connections of character and action. One measure of an individual's character is his or her reaction to what appear as impassable barriers. One might draw creative energies from the resultant tensions. Take Victor

Fuchs and Kenneth Boulding, for example. Fuchs was denied tenure at Columbia, and Boulding was told by the department head at Edinburgh University that he would never make a good teacher. Yet each was unshakable in his pursuit of a fruitful scholarly life.[26] These individuals exemplify Descartes's observation that character consists of "raising your soul so high that offense cannot reach it."

At a symposium held on November 10–11, 1995, for Fuchs's retirement from teaching, and the windup of his presidency of the American Economic Association, several economists, including Fuchs, referred several times to one praiseworthy quality that a productive scholar must possess — courage. This is exemplified when the scholar is willing to take on difficult and unfashionable problems and offer bold conclusions if the facts warrant them. Gardner argues that for breakthroughs to occur, creative minds must have emotional and cognitive support.[27] For Fuchs, whose significant books reel with a pulsing force, support spanned the range from A to Z and came from Kenneth Arrow and Richard Zeckhauser with Gary Becker sandwiched between, besides his loving, warm family.

Imagination and Morality

As for imaginative talents, Kant said it beautifully: "The imagination is a powerful agent for creating, as it was, a second nature out of the materials supplied to it by actual nature."[28] Obviously, scholars wish to exist in this second nature, because the sense of freedom they obtain in it enables them to conceive new forms, new experiences, new patterns, and new order and coherence.

When we speak about imagination, we spontaneously associate it with artistic or scholarly ideas and endeavors.[29] But there is another form of imagination that extends the boundaries of knowledge and is too often disregarded. It is the type of imagination that illuminated the moral outlook of the ancient prophets. It is the type of imagination that the poet Percy Shelley considered "the great instrument of moral good." How else but through imagination can we "form any conception of what are [another's] sensations?"[30] It is the type of imagination that fosters the righting of wrongs and virtuous conduct, including teacher-student relationships, and by that leads to more equitable outcomes. Unfortunately, far too many scholars strike a Faustian bargain that involves sacrificing the most basic human virtues for work. Far too often those possessed by creative sparks are drained of a measure of noble human behavior. Observers of the scientific scene hold that this is expected of scholars in order for them to reach the front ranks of the profession.[31] In the words of the poet William Butler Yeats, "The intellect of man is forced to choose perfection of the life or of the work."

Major ideas advanced by the founders of the social sciences have contributed to the belief that scientists exhibit hostility toward and distance themselves from moral concerns.[32] Consider, for example, Machiavelli's argument that states should base their decisions on power relations alone, Adam Smith's claim that the "Invisible Hand" based on individual self-interest is a most reliable and efficient system for economic interaction, or Karl Marx's insistence that his predictions of the collapse of capitalism were based on the "scientific" law of the falling rate of profit and class conflict. Consider too the "immoral" ideas of Darwin and Freud on the survival of the fittest and the unproductiveness of guilt, respectively. These teachings explain human behavior by reference to how it *is* rather than what it *ought* to be (Hume's famous distinction) and thereby contribute to the powerful and influential notion that moral sensibility has no basis in science or logic.

In recent years, however, there has been increasing recognition that no economy can function effectively without cultural traits such as trust, that a better balance is needed between the acquisitive and pleasure-seeking instincts and those of benevolence and moderation, and, more important, that economic analysis must find ways to incorporate relevant cultural sensibilities, particularly the moral dimension. How this is to be done is eminently expressed by Hirschman: "Morality . . . belongs to the center of our work. It can get there only if the social scientists are morally alive and make themselves vulnerable to moral concerns — then they will produce morally significant works."[33] To be "morally alive" means to be aware of the distinction between means and ends and to foster intellectual honesty when engaged in the pursuit of knowledge.[34]

Some of the departed economists I have mentioned — Mill and Boulding, for example — were as prodigious in human decencies as in scholarship. Their vitality and vigor did not wane even as they advanced in age, and they exhibited an undeviating adherence to moral standards. The same is true of Samuelson, Schultz, and Fuchs. Of such figures a verse says: "A righteous man will flourish like a date palm . . . will be fruitful in old age, vigorous and fresh."[35]

These are individuals who lead a balanced life and, therefore, a very aesthetic one.

Generalizations and Details

David Berlinski, the mathematician, is not entirely right when he argues that a novelist is the opposite of a scholar.[36] True, the novelist has an eye for elaborate detail upon which he or she expands. However, also true is that literary works constructed totally on facts fast retreat into melodrama. As for scientists, many do not accumulate facts but instead distill them, focusing on the general, the abstract. Numerous theoretical scholars construct their models irrespective of concrete evidence. Solow notes that "theorists hope that their particular make-believe world can tell us something . . . about the world we actually live in. . . . The made-up world has an advantage. . . . It is possible to understand it completely. The real world is much too complicated for that."[37] They even feel that it is the virtuosity with which their models are constructed that gives them an independent value and truth.

However, whether the sphere of interest is fiction or economics, the authors of masterpieces display a flair not only for trenchant and colorful writing, but in painting for us a large, rich canvas as impressive in its sweep as in its intricate details. As one insightful observer of creative individuals notes, "The scientist, as the artist, must live on several planes at once. . . . All great geniuses of science were endowed with this particular dualism of their faculties: a head for generalizations and an eye for minute particulars."[38]

There are two extreme styles in which to conduct research: the theoretical and the empirical. The theoretician works from the top down; the empiricist from the bottom up. The former deduces mathematical laws guided by criteria of simplicity and elegance and then tries to generalize and fit real phenomena to them. The latter induces laws from data and details that have been sought out, accumulated, and observed. One eminent physicist classifies scientists as unifiers or diversifiers: "Unifiers are trying to reduce the prodigality of nature to a few general laws and principles. Diversifiers are exploring the details of things and events in their infinite variety. Unifiers are in love with ideas and equations; diversifiers are in love with birds and butterflies."[39] However, the essays in this volume suggest a remarkable separation of economists into three groups: applied theorists, empiricists, and those who feel a deep affinity with the latter but who have taken upon themselves an additional task of being the profession's critics at large or detached observers of the scene. The contents of these pieces also illustrate Paul Valéry's statement that "there is no theory that is not a fragment, carefully prepared, of some autobiography."

Who Are the Contributors?

The applied theorists, personified by Avinash Dixit, Elhanan Helpman, Paul Krugman, Roger Myerson, and Hal Varian "build," as Dixit writes, "mathematical models to address specific issues and contexts of economic interest, rather than abstract systems of general and overreaching significance." The empirical economists included in this volume are Francine Blau, William Darity, Jr., Benjamin Friedman, Claudia Goldin, William Landes, Rachel McCulloch, and Gavin Wright. These economists, who work from the bottom up, view themselves as detectives working with data because, as Blau relates, "the data has secrets to tell . . . and it's [our] job to unlock them." N. Gregory Mankiw and Richard Schmalensee have strong interests in both theoretical and empirical work.

The third group of economists presented in this volume includes David Colander, David Gordon, Deirdre McCloskey, Philip Mirowski, Susan Rose-Ackerman, and David Warsh. These economists have an affinity for the empirical and are endowed with the acute critical sense that is a mixed blessing for the scholar as well as artist. The contributions of this group are not without their own theatrical flourishes, which serve as an important dimension of their competence as critics and compel our attention because they coax and shame complacent economists. This group's vote is cast with those economists who are becoming more fashionable today than one or two decades ago: the political economists, who factor in their work observation, reasoning, and experience with its innumerable, unpredictable, and inassessable details of human behavior, rather than relying on equations with their finality of results.

Two of our critics write of times past when antipathy reigned among the groups. Mirowski reminisces about members of the Yale faculty advising graduate students to stay away from his projects when he was a visiting professor. Colander observes in his essay: "A while back I went to dinner with some economics professors. I was describing the reasoning behind the market anti–inflation plan that Abba Lerner and I had been working on. An MIT-trained economist asked me if I had a formal model of iι, and when I said no, he said that he couldn't discuss it. For him . . . understanding had to go through a prism of a formal model."

Dixit in private correspondence with the editor states, "Theorists like formal modelling because it imposes logic or discipline on the reasoning that all economists must do. Neither assumptions nor equations are 'final'; assumptions are 'working hypotheses' and the model is simply the quickest way to see what follows from adopting a particular set of such hypotheses. In the absence of the model, it is just too easy to think that something is a valid inference from the premises when it isn't. . . . Where [empirical economists] look and what they notice is itself powerfully influenced by their prior beliefs or, in other words, the 'theories' they implicitly hold."

I must note, however, that recent years have witnessed substantial changes in the discipline. Nowadays leading theorists rarely linger in ivory towers. Almost all of our applied theorists have been involved in policy debates, and some have even served on the Council of Economic Advisers or have assumed high administrative positions. There is now much greater recognition of the need "to bridge the gaping gulf between beautiful economic theory and ugly economic reality"[40] and greater acceptance of the inescapable presence of a multiplicity of styles. Applied theorists understand that investment in empirical or policy-oriented issues will not necessarily rob them of theoretical occasions but rather add to their intellectual vitality.

As for comparisons with the older generation of economists, as reflected in the volume *Eminent Economists,* the 1930s theorists exhibited an enormous range of interests and moved freely between the natural and social sciences. In this sense they have been Renaissance figures. As for the younger generation's breadth of scholarship, William Darity has this to say: "To do a Ph.D. at MIT in the late 1970s required reading very little, if anything, published before 1960 or 1965. . . . you could do a Ph.D. without reading anything written by Adam Smith, David Ricardo, Joseph Schumpeter, Karl Marx, or, for that matter, Maynard Keynes. . . . this pattern of training . . . is pervasive in the United States."

A recent survey of graduate students in economics from top American universities showed that only 3 percent of them believed it was very important to have a thorough understanding of how the economy works in order to gain prominence in the field.[41] The dominant position expressed by exemplary figures of the older generation of economists is that a mere positivistic economics discipline devoid of relevance would have little impact on the major problems affecting our society. Their work and outlook suggests that the analytical tools of economics can and indeed should be offered in the social interest.

The evolving demarcations among the polarized sides in this intellectual fracas have much to do with the maturation of the economics discipline and the resultant narrowing of interests and greater specialization of the chief participants. That recent Nobel Prizes in economic science have been awarded to individuals who have strayed from highly abstract mathematical models and who have immersed themselves in the practical and operational side of the discipline indicates a greater appreciation for a broader approach.

A lesson from the annals of physics is instructive here. A historian and past White House aide for national security relates the importance of cooperation among the American theoretical and experimental physicists in the speedy construction of the first atomic bomb. The German failure to build the bomb is attributable to the tension that existed between the two groups in that country. The Nobelist Werner Heisenberg, of principle-of-uncertainty fame and Germany's leading nuclear theorist during World War II, was not interested in the experimental side of physics. He almost failed his doctoral orals at the University of Munich because he was unable to explain simple practical questions such as how a battery functions. In the United States, Robert Oppenheimer, director of the atomic program at Los Alamos, had been an experimentalist before becoming a theoretical physicist; as a condition of assuming the leadership at Los Alamos, he insisted that an experimental physicist be assigned to assist him.[42]

This suggests that a more intimate dialogue between the diverse camps in economics is needed for the purpose of mutual support and enrichment.

NOTES

1. The Nazis' little-known program of breeding and raising perfect Aryans based on physical traits failed dismally.

2. Frederick Mosteller, "Classroom and Platform Performance," *American Statistician* (February 1980): 17.

3. At the time *Eminent Economists* was published, Joan Robinson was already deceased, and Irma Adelman was younger than the male colleagues solicited. Adelman's essay, "My Life Philosophy," was published in the *American Economist* (fall 1990): 3–14.

4. However, Gregory Chaitin, the eminent IBM computer scientist, feels that society is blessed by having only a few people who pursue "the greater questions. If everybody were trying to understand the limits of mathematics or do great paintings, it would be a catastrophe! The plumbing wouldn't work! The electricity wouldn't work! Buildings would fall down! I mean, if everyone wanted to do great art or deep science, the world wouldn't function!" (qtd. in John Horgan, *The End of Science: Facing the Limits of Knowledge in the Twilight of the Scientific Age* [Reading, MA: Addison-Wesley, 1996], 241). Martin Buber argues that humanity by nature is destined to commit injustices. One has to wonder whether the human desire to know is linked to our readiness to commit injustice.

5. See the intriguing ancient passages Genesis 2:15–18, and Chulin, 139B.

6. John Shattuck, in a witty interpretation of Milton's *Paradise Lost,* casts Adam as pleading before the Almighty that his inquisitiveness was caused by a wish to find "better ways to glorify God" (*Forbidden Knowledge: From Prometheus to Pornography* [New York: St. Martin's Press, 1996]).

7. A fascinating Talmudic story, told in a legendary form, depicts a remarkable assertion of the independence of the human mind. The idea advanced is that although the source of law is God, it is for humans, for the community, to interpret and to determine the direction of the law. Remarkably, it is God himself who heartily approves of the arrangement that the majority rules (Baba Metzia, 59B). It is worth contrasting this view with that of the last Iranian shah. When the shah was asked in a TV interview by Barbara Walters, a short time before he was overthrown, why he forbade the public to question his rulings and decrees, his response was that no one should be allowed to criticize or to challenge the source of law, meaning himself.

8. Gustave Flaubert, *Gustave Flaubert, Selected Letters,* trans. M. J. Cohen (London: Weidenfeld and Nicolson, 1950), 108.

9. Donald L. Bentley, "My First Day's Lectures: Past and Present," in *Education in a Research University,* ed. Kenneth J. Arrow, Richard W. Cottle, B. Curtis Eaves, and Ingram Olkim (Stanford: Stanford University Press, 1996), 221.

10. Originally, *aesthetics* referred to the domain of human sensation rather than the intellect. Immanuel Kant noted that, in our perceptual experience, there is a difference between the conceptual-logical and the sensuous. "Concepts, thoughts without factual content, are empty senses; intuitions without concepts, are blind. . . . The senses cannot think. The understanding cannot see. By their union only can knowledge be produced" (*The Critique of Pure Reason,* trans. Norman Kemp Smith [London: Macmillan, 1929], 41).

11. Jaroslav Pelikan, "The Aesthetics of Scholarly Research," in *Sesquicentennial Lecture, Tulane University,* September 21, 1984, 7. Leonard B. Meyer, in *Music, the Arts, and Ideas* (Chicago: University of Chicago Press, 1967), 58, holds that of the cultural beliefs that determine aesthetic criteria, the belief in

causation is the most significant because it suggests that creation is a "purposeful act of human will."

12. Many scholars have concluded that along with self-discipline and analytic rigor, aesthetic values are crucial in significant scientific research. See Judith Wechsler, ed., *On Aesthetics in Science* (Cambridge, MA: MIT Press, 1978). However, the 1986 Nobelist, James Buchanan, argues that aesthetic criteria should play little role in the social sciences. See Michael Szenberg, ed., *Eminent Economists: Their Life Philosophies* (Cambridge: Cambridge University Press, 1992), 102. For other contrarian views, see David Lindley, *The End of Physics* (New York: Basic Books, 1993).

13. I. I. Rabi, "The Interaction of Science and Technology," in *The Impact of Science on Technology,* ed. A. W. Warner, Dean Morse, and Alfred S. Eichner (New York: Columbia University Press, 1965), 20.

14. Paul A. M. Dirac, "The Evolution of the Physicist's Picture of Nature," *Scientific American,* May 1963, 47. John Dewey notes that James Clerk Maxwell, the discoverer of the electromagnetic field, once introduced a symbol to make an equation symmetrical and thus aesthetically more attractive and only later sought and found a meaning for it. See his "Art as Experience," in *Philosophies of Art and Beauty,* ed. Albert Hofstadter and Richard Kuhns (New York: Random House, 1964), 637.

15. Mark Twain once remarked that in writing, the gap between the perfect adjective and the next-best adjective is the difference between lightning and lightning bug.

16. When reminiscing in January 1997 at the American Economic Association New Orleans meetings about Walter Heller's tenure as chair of the Council of Economic Advisors during the Kennedy administration, Roger Porter, a former White House official, attributed Heller's increasingly decisive influence over President Kennedy to the persuasiveness of Heller's writing and the clarity of his exposition.

17. *Wall Street Journal,* March 13, 1995, A12.

18. Herbert Mitgang, *Words Still Count with Me* (New York: W. W. Norton, 1995), 228.

19. Horajot, 14A

20. Dewey, "Art as Experience," 629.

21. The following anecdote illustrates that for some, less than sublime work in others won't do. A story is told of the great but erratic conductor Otto Klemperer, whom a French fan once asked what he thought of Francis Poulenc's new piano concerto. Klemperer, who just finished conducting the piece, turned to a German-speaking concertgoer and asked him: "How do you say 's. . .' in French?" (Peter Heyworth, *Otto Klemperer: His Life and Times* [Cambridge: Cambridge University Press, 1996] 2:225). It is worth noting my experience with two excessively self-demanding and self-destructive students. One with an undergraduate record of straight As dropped out of a doctoral program after one year because she received her first B. The second involved a Juilliard graduate who, failing to become a concert pianist, turned into an accountant and decided never to touch a piano again. What an impoverished and a pathetic life to lead if one is satisfied only with perfection. Beatrice Webb's description of Oswald Mosley is very apt: "So much perfection argues rottenness somewhere." It is instructive to

note that at one of the most selective colleges in the United States — Deep Springs, California (enrollment twenty-four; emphasis on classical studies and work on the college's cattle ranch) — one of the most valuable lessons students are supposed to learn is that "it's impossible to do a perfect job." Most Deep Springs students continue their studies at Ivy League schools (Ellen Graham, "Isolated, All Male Deep Springs Is Free, Student Run, Rigorous," *Wall Street Journal*, March 6, 1997, B1). On the links between music and mathematics and numbers, see Edward Rothstein, *Emblems of Mind* (New York: Times Books, 1995).

22. Frederick Brown, in *Zola: A Life* (New York: Farrar, Straus and Giroux, 1995), put it colorfully well: "[M]en brought to learning the same monstrous appetite and digestive capacity they displayed around the banquet table." When Pablo Casals, the cellist, was asked why he continued to practice four hours a day at the age of ninety-three he said: "Because I think I can still make some progress."

23. A recent conversation with Julian L. Simon about a new series for the *American Economist* turned to role models. Simon suggested Schultz; I, Fuchs. We both agreed with the choices of each other. Only upon further reflection did I come to realize several common features in their intellectual development.

24. Henry Roth, *From Bondage*, vol. 3 of *Mercy of a Rude Stream* (New York: St. Martin's Press, 1995).

25. James M. Buchanan, *Better Than Plowing* (Chicago: University of Chicago Press, 1992), 5. Or consider what Koestler called "the most important dream in history since Joseph's seven fat and seven lean cows," a dream that led to the most important discovery in organic chemistry that organic compounds are "closed rings like the snake swallowing its tail" (Arthur Koestler, *The Act of Creation* [New York: Macmillan, 1964], 118). Erwin Schrödinger, the physics Nobelist, was right when he astutely observed that the conscious mind is an outpost of the unconscious.

26. Szenberg, *Eminent Economists*, 69–83, and Victor R. Fuchs, "Education and Its Consequences: My Philosophy of Life," *American Economist*, fall 1993, 17–24. The experimental psychologist K. Raaheim reached the following simple but very insightful conclusion concerning successful individuals: "The ultimately successful subjects make more unsuccessful attempts" (in John Radford's *Child Prodigies and Exceptional Early Achievers* [New York: Free Press, 1990], 176).

27. Howard Gardner, *Creating Minds: An Anatomy of Creativity Seen through the Lives of Freud, Einstein, Picasso, Stravinsky, Eliot, Graham, and Gandhi* (New York: Basic Books, 1992), 44–46. See also Ira I. Mitroff, T. Jacob, and E. T. Moore, "On the Shoulders of the Spouses of Scientists," *Social Studies of Science* 7 (1977): 303–27.

28. Immanuel Kant, *Critique of Judgement*, trans. James Creed Meredith (Oxford: Oxford University Press, 1952), 176. Another author claims that the imagination is deeply linked to beauty because it flourishes when people love work. I can't agree with this "conjecture" since despair and pain are equally important in releasing imagination because they spur reflection and insight (Robert Grudin, *The Grace of Great Things* [New York: Ticknor and Fields, 1995], 55).

29. Claude Lévi-Strauss, the noted anthropologist, maintains that in primitive societies imagination exceeds knowledge, whereas in modern societies knowledge overwhelms imagination.

30. Adam Smith, "The Theory of Moral Sentiments," in *British Moralists,* ed. L. A. Selby-Bigge (New York: Dover, 1965), 258.

31. Gardner, *Creating Minds,* 362. See also Rothstein, *Emblems of Mind* (New York: Times Books, 1995), 13, and Paul Johnson, *Intellectuals* (New York: Harper and Row, 1989).

32. Social scientists note that this view holds for poets as well. Charles Baudelaire, the French author, in his "The Didactic Heresy" had this to say about the matter: "I say that if the poet has pursued a moral end, he has diminished his poetical power; and it is not risky to bet that his work will be poor. Poetry cannot, on pain of death or dethronement, be assimilated into science or morality" (in Richard Ellman and Charles Feidelson, eds., *The Modern Tradition* [New York: Oxford University Press, 1965], 101).

33. Albert O. Hirshman, "Morality and the Social Sciences: A Durable Tension," Acceptance Paper, The Frank E. Seidman Distinguished Award in Political Economy, Rhodes College, 1980, 13. In history it is the perception of the concepts and not their actual meanings that shapes our actions. For example, Adam Smith's narrative portrays self-interest or self-love as only one facet of human behavior, notwithstanding Smith's famous and oft-quoted classic expression in *The Wealth of Nations:* "It is not from the benevolence of the butcher, the brewer, or the baker, that we expect our dinner, but from their regard to their own interest." This is Smith's remark with its unshakable ring of truth: "Concern for our own happiness recommends to us the virtue of prudence; concern for that of other people, the virtues of justice and beneficence — of which the one restrains us from hurting, the other prompts us to promote that happiness. Independent of any regard either to what are or to what ought to be, or to what upon a certain condition would be the sentiments of other people, the first of those three virtues is originally recommended to us by our selfish, the other two by our benevolent affections" (Adam Smith, *The Theory of Moral Sentiments* [New York: Augustus M. Kelley, 1966], 385). Smith recognizes, then, that the butcher, the brewer, and the baker have the capacity to embrace benevolent passions.

34. Jaroslav Pelikan, "The Individual's Search for Truth — and Its Limitations," in *Individualism and Social Responsibility,* ed. W. L. Taitte (Dallas: University of Texas Press, 1994), 226–31.

35. Psalms 92:18.

36. David Berlinski, *A Tour of the Calculus* (New York: Pantheon Books, 1995), 62.

37. Robert M. Solow, *Learning from "Learning by Doing"* (Stanford: Stanford University Press, 1997), 69.

38. Koestler, *The Act of Creation,* 706. Nat Wyeth, an engineer and inventor, has this to say on his brother, the artist Andrew Wyeth: "Andy did a picture of Lafayette's quarters near Chadds Ford, Pennsylvania with a sycamore tree behind the building. When I first saw the painting, he wasn't finished with it. He showed me a lot of drawings of the trunk and the sycamore's gnarled roots, and I said, 'Where's all that in the picture?' 'It's not *in* the picture, Nat,' he said. 'For me to get what I want in the part of the tree that's showing, I've got to know thoroughly how it is anchored in back of the house.' I find that remarkable. He could draw the tree above the house with such authenticity because he knew

exactly how the thing was in the ground" (in Kenneth A. Brown, *Inventors at Work* [Redmond, WA: Tempus Books of Microsoft Press, 1988], 375).

39. Freeman Dyson, *From Eros to Gaia* (New York: Pantheon Books, 1992), 280.

40. Tibor Scitovsky, *Human Desire and Economic Satisfaction* (Brighton, Sussex: Wheatsheaf Books, 1986), viii.

41. David Colander and Arjo Klamer, "The Making of an Economist," *Journal of Economic Perspectives* 1 (fall 1987): 95–111.

42. See McGeorge Bundy, *Danger and Survival* (New York: Random House, 1988), 16–17, 20. Also see Gerald Holton, *The Advancement of Science and Its Burdens* (Cambridge: Cambridge University Press, 1986), 160. The lack of both coordination among physicists and mustering of resources for the construction of the atomic bomb in Germany was helped, to the great fortune of humanity, by none other than Hitler himself, who mistrusted nuclear science because he considered it as "Jewish physics" (Leon Lederman with Dick Teresi, *The God Particle* [Boston: Houghton Mifflin, 1993], 166). However, Thomas Powers in *Heisenberg's War* (New York: Alfred A. Knopf, 1993) argues that Heisenberg's conscience led him to try to slow Germany's efforts to build nuclear weapons, a position disputed by David C. Cassidy in *Uncertainty: The Life and Science of Werner Heisenberg* (New York: W. H. Freeman, 1992).

FRANCINE D. BLAU

On Becoming and Being an Economist

Becoming an Economist

While our models often deal in rational decisions made with full information, I regard my entry into the economics profession as at least in part the result of some happy coincidences. By this I mean that it was the outcome of a process launched before I had any clear idea what economics was or that I would like to make it my career, although it is certainly possible that had I selected a different route I might nonetheless have arrived at the same destination. When I was a high school student in Queens, New York, most of my friends were planning to attend one of the City Colleges. I was always extremely academically oriented and got the idea that I would like to explore a new environment and go away to school. This ambition was not easily gratified since financial resources were not abundant in my family. Cornell University came to my attention not only as an excellent school, but also as a university that had both public, low-tuition colleges and private, high-tuition ones—a combination that I think is unique nationally. In exploring Cornell, I learned of the New York State School of Industrial and Labor Relations there.

In honesty, I initially was not sure exactly what "industrial and labor relations" was, but with a little research I found out more, and it sounded interesting. This was the mid-1960s and girls were supposed to think primarily of marriage and family rather than careers. A predominantly male field like industrial and labor relations was

I am indebted to Lawrence Kahn, Jody Sindelar, Marianne Ferber, and Rebecca Blank for helpful comments and feedback.

20

particularly outside the pale. But I came from a rather unusual background and always wanted a career.

My parents were both teachers, and my mother worked outside the home from the time I was three or four years old. In fact I recall that in New York City at that time kindergarten and first grade were offered on a split session due to the overcrowding of the schools. My parents received special permission for me to attend both sessions — an informal child care arrangement. My parents were divorced when I was six years old. That experience plus the urban apartment we lived in probably alienated me, at least on a subconscious level, from the *Ozzie and Harriet, Father Knows Best* model of the ideal family and women's roles (such families always seemed to live in a private house with a white picket fence), even though at another level I longed for it. After five years in which my brother and I lived in a female-headed, single-parent family, my mother's illness resulted in our going to live with my father. From the age of eleven until I left for college, I was in a male-run household. My father encouraged my career aspirations from a very early age, even when they included "unfeminine" professions like law. (He was very pleased when I went into economics but always a bit disappointed that with all my studies I never learned how to make a lot of money on the stock market.) I also relied a great deal on my older brother, who gave me considerable support in a family setting that was rather unstable.

In some respects, then, I was not overly concerned with what was considered socially appropriate for women. On the other hand, since this all predated the modern feminist movement, I never thought explicitly about these issues, nor did I consciously reject the prevailing norms. Indeed, I often regretted that I was not more conventional, but didn't feel there was much I could do about it. As I considered studying industrial relations, I was influenced by the pioneering role of Frances Perkins, Franklin D. Roosevelt's secretary of labor throughout his administration and the first woman to ever serve in a Cabinet position. FDR was a larger-than-life figure in my family — I was actually named after him; my initials are FDB. So taking Perkins as my exemplar, I applied to the ILR school and was one of the ten to fifteen women (out of one hundred students) in the freshman class. The number of women admitted to the ILR school was determined by a strict quota (an upper bound, not a lower one). This was allegedly due to limited space allocated to the ILR school in the dormitories for women, though it may have crossed our minds that that constraint was suspiciously endogenous.

Despite these constraints on the admission of women, I did not find the ILR school to be a sexist place, although some of the male students groused that women were taking up positions at the head of the class and lowering their ranking. Most important, I found my professors, especially my mentor Robert Ferguson, enormously supportive and encouraging of my evolving interest in economics and academia. Under their tutelage I began to look at economics as a field that I was perhaps especially well suited for. It didn't seem highly significant to me or to them that it was an overwhelmingly male field. None of my professors ever for a moment scoffed at the idea of a woman becoming an economics professor or expressed doubts about my capability to do so.

Given these beginnings, I regard it as somewhat remarkable that my vocation was so successfully determined so early. Not only was I led into the economics profession, but for nineteen years I had a joint appointment in economics and at the Institute of Labor and Industrial Relations at the University of Illinois. In the fall of 1994, I returned to the ILR school at Cornell as the first Frances Perkins Professor of Industrial and Labor Relations.

But we are perhaps moving too quickly here. I have a few more observations regarding my entry into economics and what it felt like to be a woman in a predominantly male field. When I entered graduate school at Harvard, there were only four women out of a class of sixty-three students. In some respects I was very well prepared for the experience. As I mentioned above, I was always very career oriented, even though at the time most social pressures were for women to think in terms of marriage and family. I also had the advantage of previous experience in predominantly male environments, my own family as well as the ILR school. But even I was unprepared for the subjective feeling of being a member of a small minority in an overwhelmingly male environment. There weren't many female students, and virtually no female faculty.

Moreover, I found myself facing this situation with essentially no awareness of the broader issues of gender. Although the modern women's movement is often dated from 1963, when Betty Friedan published *The Feminine Mystique,* I was almost completely ignorant of feminist ideas when I entered graduate school in 1966, having just turned twenty. And I doubt that I was unusual in this respect. Thus, I had no tools to analyze the problems caused by what we now identify as an absence of role models and a feeling of being on the outs of the "old boy" network. I was left with a sense of unease, exacerbated occasionally by overt discrimination. Some of the latter incidents are even somewhat humorous in retrospect. For example, there was the time when a fellow graduate student echoed the old refrain by asking me what I was doing in graduate school, taking up a spot that could have gone to a man. Not entirely unfamiliar with this complaint, I drew myself up and said, "I imagine I am here for much the same reasons you are"—a pretty good response, I thought. He replied, "I'm here to avoid the draft!"

Less humorous was my first day as a teaching assistant in introductory economics at Harvard. Each of us had primary responsibility for one section of the course and was, with the exception of some group lectures, the primary instructor for the semester. I had arrived early and, as I nervously awaited the start of class, was writing on the blackboard an outline of topics I would be covering. The bulk of the students, most of whom were male, had arrived, and one of them took exception to me. As I wrote on the board, he made loud remarks: "Who's she?" "What's she doing up there?" "What does she know about economics?" Meanwhile, as I continued to write, I wondered to myself: "What *was* I doing there?" "What *did* I know about economics?" I was totally unprepared for this behavior and initially hoped to ignore it. But that was impossible when a student poked his nose in the door, asking if this was introductory economics, and my heckler said, "No, sex education!" Without thinking it through, I whirled around from the blackboard, looked straight at the offending student, and said severely, "Did somebody say something?" Much to my amazement, his bravado collapsed entirely, like a punctured balloon. He shook his head no as he looked to his right and left for the person who might have been responsible. He never gave any trouble after that.

But incidents like these, even if handled successfully, take their toll. Often the situation isn't an easy one to begin with, for example, your first class. (Some friends at another prestigious economics department reported that their professor in graduate macroeconomics as he handed out their first exam said that it would "separate the boys from the girls.") And the ideal retort or reaction usually occurs to you only much later. Moreover, any overt difficulties are built on a foundation of minority status. It takes an exceptionally self-confident individual not to be assailed by doubt when confronted by an almost complete absence of women. This is not to say, of course, that others don't feel self-doubts in these challenging situations. But minority status adds an additional layer, making difficult situations even more so.

What eventually helped me a great deal was my growing awareness of the women's movement. This gave me a frame of reference to see that from time to time I would encounter inappropriate sexist behavior of one type or another and to realize that it was not my fault. (Believe it or not, prior to that I tended to see myself in some way responsible for the incident, no matter how egregious.) It was also comforting to seek mutual support from other women in similar situations. Through national meetings and the formation of the AEA Committee on the Status of Women in the Economics Profession, in which I played a part as a graduate student, I got to know established women economists like Barbara Bergmann, then of the University of Maryland, Carolyn Shaw Bell of Wellesley, and Barbara Reagan of Southern Methodist University, who could serve as my role models, as well as other female graduate students and junior faculty. Later, at the University of Illinois, I benefited from my close collaboration and friendship with my colleague Marianne Ferber. Moreover, one does become accustomed to being a woman in a male field, and it is not something that I particularly notice now. I am comfortable with myself, at least in this respect, and that is much of the battle. At the same time, I have formed many close friendships and good working relationships with my male colleagues in the profession, and that adds to my feeling of comfort.

My Evolving Interest in Gender Issues

My growing interest in women's issues also turned out to be of enormous importance to me intellectually. I initially read widely on the topic, not only the relatively little that had been written at the time in economics, but also in fields like sociology and history. Exposure to a new set of issues of great social importance, combined with the dearth of previous work by economists on women, was extremely stimulating. This became the area of my dissertation research and much of my subsequent work. The decision to work in this area was not, however, without its costs. At the time, research on women was generally not seen as central. For a member of a "marginal group" to work on a "marginal" subject was risky. In addition, a woman working on women, especially one known to have feminist leanings, was suspected of bias. The latter point, the role of values in social-science research, is an interesting and important one. But it has always seemed illogical to assume that, for an issue like gender, women are likely to be ideologues and men neutral, or that an individual, regardless of sex, who favors social change is less objective than one who upholds the status quo. Obviously, either person might be tempted to fit the facts to their views. I have always endeavored to benefit from the insights that concern over gender inequities gives me into problems to study and explanations for observed outcomes, and, at the same time, to be as objective as possible in reporting my results, even if they do not accord with what I would have liked to find. Indeed, one quickly learns that a source of great excitement — and great frustration — to the empirical economist is how often the data fail to confirm a priori expectations.

In the long run it was certainly the right decision to stick with my interests. I have been reasonably successful and work on topics that I find engaging and important. While not all have related to gender issues, many have. I have also been lucky in that circumstances have become more favorable to research in this area. With the continued evolution of women's roles, topics related to gender have become of greater interest to economists in general, and the notion that women can do important and evenhanded work on gender has become fairly well established. The fundamental lesson I draw is that, in research, you have to follow your interests, without undue concern for the current status within the profession of your topic or approach. Only in this way will you do your best work. The topics that most engage you stimulate your best ideas and insights and enable you to perform at the highest levels of your ability. And in the long run, doing your best work, regardless of the topic, contributes most to your success.

A few years back I was present at an AEA session where two women economists took opposing views on whether women ought to research gender issues. The first argued that it was the moral obligation of all women economists to do some work on gender because of its enormous social importance. The other said that she advises all her female students to eschew this area because of the problems that I described above. I disagree with both of them. You have to follow your interests. It is as counterproductive for a woman who has no interest in gender issues to work on them as it is for a woman who has a burning interest in the subject to avoid it.

The experience of Avinash Dixit, which is recounted in another essay in this volume, lends support to my position. Under the influence of the demand for social relevance that was so dominant in the 1960s, he investigated issues that he identified as socially relevant, and he notes that he does not consider this among his best work. I, on the other hand, another child of the sixties, have just indicated that an important social issue was and remains a moving force behind my work and stimulates my best endeavors. How can we reconcile these conflicting views? Again, it seems to me you have to follow your interests. Tastes differ. As my husband and fellow economist, Larry Kahn, is fond of saying, "You have to follow your nose." This doesn't mean following your nose off a cliff. You cannot afford to close your eyes to a variety of important factors. Some economists need funding to pursue their research at any depth. Whether a critical mass of others share your interests is also of relevance. I should point out that in the early days there was never want of interest in research on women. The issue was the status accorded the work. Moreover, a desire not to become a prisoner to the latest fad in the profession — to follow one's own drummer — must not become a justification for failing to keep up with major developments. But giving appropriate weight to these considerations, one does have to follow one's interests.

After I had read widely in the area of gender, the issue that captured my attention in my thesis work was the male-female pay differential.[1] I was intrigued that substantial differentials existed even within narrowly defined occupational categories. Influenced by some early work by Barbara Bergmann[2] that modeled the impact of segregation of blacks and women by occupations on their pay as well as literature in sociology that emphasized the importance of occupational segregation, I developed the idea that even within occupational categories, gender segregation — in this case by establishment size — would play an important role in difference in pay. Drawing on the insights of institutional labor economists, I posited an internal wage structure that constrained the employer to pay the same base rate to all workers within an occupational category, as well as a wage hierarchy of firms for potentially equal productive labor that was consistent across occupational categories. I further assumed that employer tastes for discrimination against women à la Becker (1971) were widespread, but the ability to exercise them was constrained by the firm's position in the wage hierarchy. That is, the wages offered by the firm for each occupation were determined by a variety of institutional and market forces and could not easily be altered to accommodate preferences for male over female employees.

The model predicted that there would be considerable establishment segregation by sex within occupations. Moreover, women would be concentrated in firms that paid lower wages to both men and women, and conversely men would tend to be employed at the firms that paid higher wages to both sexes. The gender pay differential within occupations would be due primarily to pay differences among firms rather than pay differences within firms. These predictions were all strongly borne out by the data.

On Being an Empirical Economist

My thesis work started me off in an eclectic approach to economics. I gleaned insights from other disciplines and adopted important ideas from institutionalists but did not renounce mainstream or neoclassical economics. Since that time the notion of interfirm wage differentials has become much more generally accepted within mainstream labor economics, and theories like efficiency wage models and the impact of employer and employee search have been developed to explain this phenomenon.

New theories that capture additional features of labor markets and the increasing importance of empirical work make this an exciting time to be an empirical labor economist. When I began studying economics, the climate in the profession was less favorable for empirical economists. The emphasis on new models or econometric approaches was often so great that empirical work was regarded as a way of illustrating the contribution of a new theory. My own development as an empirical economist and my views about the seriousness of empirical work were influenced by Richard Freeman, one of my thesis advisers. He instilled a considerable respect for empirical findings, my own and others', whether or not they accorded with prior expectations or the conventional wisdom in the profession.

The rise in interest in empirical work within labor economics is in part the outcome of the greater ease of computing, which enables researchers to process more data in a shorter period. This means, for example, that researchers can more easily check results across a number of data sets and weed out nonrobust findings. Freeman (1989) was an early practitioner of this "collage" approach. This technique heightens the self-esteem of empirical economists and gives us the feeling that we are uncovering "true facts." The greater speed of data processing also means that we can rapidly analyze important trends in a fairly sophisticated manner. A decade or two ago, it was not uncommon for five or ten years to pass before the first respectable study of a new economic development. The ability to speak to current issues adds excitement to contemporary empirical work.

As an empirical economist I view myself as rather like a detective. When launching on a new study I feel the excitement of Sherlock Holmes when he is called onto a new case and says to Watson, "The game is afoot!" The data has secrets to tell me and it's my job to unlock them. The process of empirical research is far more complex and interactive than one is led to imagine, and the best empirical work changes our way of looking at a problem or an issue. Asking the right questions is of course crucial. And it is important to formulate hypotheses in advance. But sometimes the early results only deepen the mystery, and solving the puzzle may call for new insights, techniques, or data. Or initial findings may suggest an even more interesting question to pursue.

In getting both initial ideas and breaking out of the logjams that may develop as you pursue a project, it is very important to stay in touch with the research going on around you. However, as you hear and read other people's work, you need to get into the habit of thinking like a producer, not just a consumer, of research. That is, remember that their work, even if outside your immediate interests, may later prove useful. Recent work by Larry Kahn and myself illustrates this point. We were interested in the reasons for international differences in the gender pay gap (Blau and Kahn 1996b). In particular, we addressed the following paradox. While the relative qualifications of American women are high compared to women in other countries and the United States has had a longer and often stronger commitment to antidiscrimination laws than most industrialized nations, the United States has traditionally been among the countries with the largest gender gaps. At the time we were working on this problem, considerable attention in labor economics was focused on the marked trend toward rising wage inequality in the United States and other industrialized nations. Some recent papers investigating the sources of rising wage inequality in the United States emphasized the importance of rising returns to skills (e.g., Juhn, Murphy, and Pierce 1993; Katz and Murphy 1992) and a study by Juhn, Murphy, and Pierce (1991) had examined the impact of rising inequality on trends over time in black-white wage differentials in the United States.

This emphasis on trends in inequality made us wonder if differences in the level of wage inequality between the United States and other industrialized countries, specifically the substantially higher levels of wage inequality in the United States than elsewhere, might help to explain our paradox. This entailed a different way of looking at the sources of gender differentials. Research on gender pay gaps has traditionally focused on the role of what might be termed gender-specific factors, particularly differences in qualifications and in the treatment of otherwise equally qualified male and female workers (i.e., labor market discrimination). This research suggests that among the reasons women earn less than men is that they have less labor market experience and tend to be located in different occupations and industries. An insight of our study was to focus on the role of wage structure — the array of prices set for various labor market skills — in influencing the gender gap.

The traditional gender-specific factors imply a potentially important role for wage structure in influencing the pay gap. For example, suppose that in two countries, women have lower levels of labor market experience than men but that the gender difference in experience is the same in the two countries. If the return to experience is higher in one country, then that nation will have a larger gender pay gap. Or, as another example, suppose that the extent of occupational segregation by sex is the same in two countries but that the wage premium associated with employment in male jobs is higher in one country. Then, again, that country will have a higher pay gap.

What was perhaps surprising even to us was the enormous importance of overall wage structure in explaining the lower ranking of U.S. women. Our results suggested that the U.S. gap would be similar to that in countries like Sweden and Australia (the countries with the smallest differentials) if the United States had their level of wage inequality. Skill prices can be affected by relative supplies, by technology, by the composition of demand, or by the wage-setting institutions of each country. Specifically, centralized wage-setting institutions that tend to reduce interfirm and interindustry wage variation and are often associated with conscious policies to raise the relative pay of low-wage workers (regardless of gender) may indirectly reduce the gender pay gap. In subsequent work we explicitly examined the extent to which international differences in wage inequality are due to institutional factors and found considerable evidence that the highly decentralized wage-setting institutions in the United States contribute to the higher level of inequality here (Blau and Kahn 1996a).

In another paper in this volume, Paul Krugman emphasizes the importance of simplifying and honing your ideas. This is no less true for an empirical economist than for a theorist. Just as economic theory is a useful abstraction of reality and cannot and should not be a description of its every facet, the best empirical work proposes some story of what the results tell us, even if every piece of data does not conform. The challenge facing the empirical economist in presenting results is to give the reader as coherent a view of the story and its implications as possible, while still doing justice to any important divergences from the pattern. The researcher's view of the results may be challenged, and the careful empirical researcher will present findings in sufficient detail for readers to perform their own preliminary evaluation of the conclusions. Moreover, intellectual honesty as well as the continued progress of the field demand an honest assessment of the incompatibilities as well as the consistencies. However, it is also necessary to be selective in what is reported and emphasized. Not to do so is to leave the reader awash in a sea of numbers without a compass.

At the same time, one's understanding of an issue may deepen over time and across a number of projects. It would be nice to start off with a well-defined research agenda and a view of how a number of individual studies will fit together. More often, however, I find myself cast in the role of the detective, following leads thrown out by one set of results that suggest what would more fully answer my initial question or what important additional questions to pursue. In this way one project may lead to another. As I noted above, my study with Kahn of international differences in the gender gap raised the question we pursued in later work, of the sources of the underlying international differences in wage structure and in particular the role of institutional versus market factors in producing them. It also raised an interesting question regarding trends in the gender gap in the United States.

Our analysis implied that in the face of rising wage inequality, American women were essentially swimming upstream in a labor market growing increasingly unfavorable for workers with below-average skills. In the face of rising rewards to labor market skills, women's relative skills and labor market treatment have to improve merely for the pay gap to remain constant; still larger gains are necessary for it to be reduced. Yet the gender pay gap has actually been falling in the United States. How could we explain this apparent contradiction? We examined this in other work (Blau and Kahn 1997) and found that women were able to narrow the gender gap by improving their relative qualifications, particularly their relative experience and occupational distribution. They also benefited from a substantial decline in the "unexplained" portion of the gender gap that may reflect improvements in unmeasured characteristics or reductions in discrimination. Some of our work also suggests that, given gender differences in occupational and industrial distributions, women may have benefited from a shift in the composition of demand favoring them relative to men overall, and particularly among low-skilled workers. This in turn implies that skill prices may not change at exactly the same pace across groups of workers identified by employers as imperfect substitutes.

As you seek to deepen your understanding of an issue and refine your ideas, especially if your interest is likely to flow across a number of projects, it can be useful to explain your thinking at a number of levels. Describing your research in a talk to a general audience or to an undergraduate class helps you focus on the most important elements and clarify the essentials of your analysis — that is, see the forest for the trees. The audience benefits as well, since they get to learn about ongoing work in the field, and it will be work that you find exciting. Moreover, the questions and comments of those less immersed in the discipline may give you new perspectives on your problem.

Of course the first step in developing and refining your work is to share it with professional colleagues, seeking their comments and criticisms informally and at seminars, professional meetings, and so on. Communicating your work, especially at a relatively early stage, may not be easy. My instinct, for example, is to refine my work in private until it is at a finished stage. And since I am a bit of a perfectionist, I am not sure when that stage is reached. So, I have to put pressure on myself not to hold on to my work too long without getting feedback. Others may have the opposite problem of sharing their work widely before they have ironed out enough of the bugs. As in so many areas, the trick is in finding the right balance.

The recommendation to seek comments on your work brings up the issue of how to deal with the comments you receive. In the final analysis it is you who must determine if the advice is good or not. Many ideas that eventually prove their worth are disparaged initially. On the other hand, if you never think your work can be improved by taking the suggestions of others, you might question your judgment. Then there is the emotional issue of dealing with criticism and rejection. As a professional economist, you cannot advance professionally without risking criticism and rejection; that is, without presenting your research, submitting grant proposals and papers to journals, and so on. You are bound to find yourself the recipient of severe criticism, deserved or undeserved, at times harshly expressed. If you aim high, some disappointments are inevitable.

No critic needs to be nasty or hurtful. Almost any legitimate point can be made without recourse to scorn. But that doesn't prevent it from occurring. Moreover, to the sensitive, even tactfully expressed criticism can be painful. If you feel the criticism is unjust, it only adds an additional layer of frustration. And of course, a rejection is a rejection, regardless of how tactfully expressed. It may help to know that virtually all the economists you view as successful have come in for their share of rejections. My skin has thickened a bit over time, but I continue to encounter responses from time to time that wound or disappoint me. The really important thing is not how setbacks and disappointments make you feel, but how you persevere despite them.

In discussing feedback from colleagues another issue that comes to mind is coauthorship. I have throughout my career benefited from productive collaborations with a variety of people. In the best of these efforts, it is undoubtedly the case that the whole is greater than the sum of its parts. My husband and I have closely matched interests and have always enjoyed working together. We collaborated on a number of papers early in our careers; then our interests took us in different directions for quite awhile. In recent years, we have teamed up again in a number of projects, some of which I've described above. Moreover, we have always been available to each other for collegial advice and feedback.

So collaboration can be very beneficial. However, I would sound one note of caution on this issue. Many professional evaluations made about us, ranging from tenure to seminar invitations, must perforce be made about us as individuals. A long-standing collaboration may make it difficult for people to get a fix on each person's contribution. It is naive to ignore this consideration. Balanced against this concern, however, is the loss of good collaborations solely due to external considerations. A compromise is to make sure that no matter how much you enjoy working with a particular individual and no matter how productive the partnership, you establish an independent record either in single-authored work or in collaborations with others.

Optimal Overcommitment and the Time Management Problem

Time management is essential to professional success, and it is incredibly difficult. Taking the case of the academic, with which I am most familiar, you are bombarded with conflicting demands and requests, all legitimate. Any one of our activities — teaching, university and professional service, or research — could easily be a full-time job, especially if you are conscientious. The demands on your time, particularly in the service component, only increase with your professional stature. Ideally, one should be able to allocate time rationally, allotting a reasonable amount to do a satisfactory job on each activity and leaving ample time for research. In practice, I don't find choices to be so easy, and I suspect that I am not alone.

In some respects, time management can be more difficult for women than for men. Some women still retain disproportionate responsibility for home tasks. Even those who, like myself, are fortunate enough to have a partner who equally shares family responsibilities are at a disadvantage compared to the many men whose spouse shoulders most of these responsibilities. However, it is also true that problems of overcommitment potentially affect us all, since the fundamental problem is that time is limited and the uses of it potentially unlimited. Moreover, I see more and more of my male colleagues playing larger roles at home, so they increasingly have to balance these demands as well.

One problem is that nonresearch demands — teaching responsibilities and service activities — tend to place more immediate and urgent demands on your time than a vague desire to finish a research project. One strategy here is to make your research face deadlines, for example, by submitting abstracts to present papers at professional meetings, agreeing to present a departmental workshop, and so on. Collaborative work, which establishes commitments to co-authors, can serve a similar function. Necessity is the mother of invention, and by keeping the pressure on you will discover ways to carve out the time you need to do your research. Over the years, these strategies will tend to become habitual and will be second nature. As the demands on my time grow, I increasingly treasure the blocks of time I can set aside to do my own work.

Nonetheless, the issue of the number of commitments you should take on, in your research and in other areas, remains. I generally feel overcommitted and have noted that many other successful professionals do as well. There are a variety of reasons: the difficulty of judging how long a task will take, unexpected demands cropping up, reluctance to pass up a good opportunity, even when your plate is already full to overflowing. But an additional, perhaps subconscious, factor may be to raise your productivity. By taking on a great many research and writing obligations you essentially have yourself on what blue-collar workers call a "speedup;" only it is a self-imposed speed-up designed to squeeze the maximum amount of output out of yourself.

Thus, overcommitment has its uses. However, there is still a level of overcommitment that you exceed at your peril. Keeping your commitments within manageable bounds is important for a number of reasons. First and most obviously, it is necessary to preserve some degree of sanity in your life and to have at least a shot at an acceptable level of stress. Second, too many commitments can actually reduce your long-run productivity. Your research or teaching may suffer from the frequent disruptions of travel (to present papers, give talks, etc.) or the need to finish promised papers. More fundamentally, you would not want your research program to be dictated entirely by opportunities that come along. Third, there can be consequences for your family. If you have children, they will let you know explicitly or implicitly when you've crossed some limit in terms of absences from home or unavailability. Finally, and perhaps most importantly, if you take on too much, you may not be able to deliver—that is, you may produce an inferior product or default entirely. This will damage your reputation in the long run. Thus, time management requires saying no sometimes, even to extremely attractive opportunities; this becomes increasingly the case as your career advances and the invitations and opportunities multiply.

As the foregoing discussion suggests, a number of factors make it difficult to decide which opportunities to accept and which to decline. This problem is made all the more difficult because we lack information on the quantity and quality of future invitations. Basically, this means that, much like the acceptance wage in search theory, you need to have in mind some acceptance value of the quality of an invitation in professional terms. You may also want to take into account whether the person who is asking has some kind of claim on you, for example, is a close professional colleague or a former student, and how important your participation is from their point of view. This acceptance value may vary both over time and cyclically. As your career advances, the quality of the invitations will rise and, if you are not to overcommit, you will need to raise your acceptance value. Cyclically, you may take on an editorship or an extremely important committee assignment, or be up against a number of paper deadlines, or have recently relocated. Under such circumstances you may not be able to accept offers you would have jumped at under other circumstances.

It is surprisingly difficult to say no to a request or invitation, but learning how can be an absolute necessity to your professional survival. This, by the way, also applies to department or university service above some reasonable level. Women and minorities find themselves in high demand here. At an earlier stage of my career, a sense of responsibility to represent the interests of women on various committees led me to accept an inordinate share of these responsibilities. I have come to conclude that I cannot compensate for the dearth of senior women single-handedly, and I now try to keep my committee load and other service more manageable.

Declining good opportunities is not without its costs. The act of saying no is itself difficult. Often we must disappoint friends or professional colleagues. However, for what it is worth, I have found that, when I am on the inviting end, as disappointed as I may be to receive a turndown from someone I had hoped to include in a conference, on a panel, or as a speaker, the crucial thing for me is a timely response. This allows me to move on to the next person. So, if you are going to say no, don't compound the problem by procrastinating because it is an unpleasant task. Another cost of saying no is that the opportunity may be lost for good and indeed some future opportunities as well. Even a sincere statement that it is an exceptionally busy time but you would really like an opportunity in the future may not result in a later invitation. It is hard for people to tell if your expression of interest is sincere or simply polite. Some people may write you off — not out of pique, but because they conclude it is not worth their time to try you again. However, let me note that when I do the inviting, I try not to be put off by a past turndown, especially if it's someone who treated me reasonably — that is, was not incredibly difficult to reach and got back to me in a reasonable period of time. There may be reasons other than discouragement: the opportunity simply may not present itself again.

These costs mean that as the invitee you must face the fact that, for whatever reason, if you say no now, you may not get another chance at the specific opportunity or even at an equivalent one (these things tend to be lumpy) for some time. This means that there are invitations that you almost cannot refuse whatever their costs in sleepless nights and foregone weekends. Nonetheless even in such cases, I have occasionally said no when there was just too much on my plate (though I have probably erred by saying yes too often rather than the reverse).

Work and Family

Traditionally, women felt that they had to choose between marriage and family on the one hand, and a career on the other. It is now possible, although not always easy, to do both. As I mentioned above, I am married to a fellow economist, Larry Kahn. We have two teenage children, and both of us have very active careers. As challenging as this situation is, I would not have it any other way. Not everyone wants children or should have them, but they have added an immeasurable dimension to my life. Keeping my career afloat, especially when the children were small, was certainly demanding, but my work brings me enormous gratification, and I have always been too professionally ambitious to sit on the sidelines and let the parade pass me by.

The difficulties of combining work and family have received considerable attention, and, while I don't wish to downplay them, I would like to say that it is doable and, in addition, brings many rewards. Balancing conflicting demands is not something you figure out how to do once and for all; rather, you need to constantly assess and restore the balance when something throws it out of whack. The other essential ingredient in my case has been sharing the responsibility with my husband. I am not a superwoman and could not be one.

We have from the start both been deeply committed to fully sharing family responsibilities, and that has made all the difference.

Concluding Remarks

When I first contemplated sharing my thoughts on my life as an economist and on how I work, I found it quite daunting. How could I explain what I do, and why should knowing about it have value to anyone else? I have done my best to capture relevant aspects of my experience and some lessons distilled from them. I fear, though, that I have not adequately conveyed the excitement of being an active researcher, of constantly addressing new and difficult problems, and of pushing yourself to your limits. I find this all incredibly challenging and rewarding, but it is not always fun or easy. There are highs when things are going well and everything seems to fall into place and lows when you feel stumped or your work is not as well received as you'd hoped. So I come back to perseverance as an important key to a successful and rewarding career: pursuing your work rather single-mindedly in the face of any obstacles or distractions that come up, keeping at a problem even though it doesn't yield easily, persisting in the face of occasional disappointments. It is also important to stay fresh and engaged. You must constantly challenge yourself and continue to learn—from the work of others; from the example of those you admire; and from your own experiences and mistakes. It may be easier to rest on your laurels, but it is a lot less gratifying.

NOTES

1. This formed the basis of Blau 1977.
2. Bergmann 1974 was then circulating as a working paper.

REFERENCES

Becker, Gary S. 1971. *The Economics of Discrimination,* 2d ed. Chicago: University of Chicago Press.

Bergmann, Barbara R. 1974. "Occupational Segregation, Wages, and Profits When Employers Discriminate by Race or Sex." *Eastern Economic Journal* 1 (April–July): 103–10.

Blau, Francine D. 1977. *Equal Pay in the Office.* Lexington, MA: Lexington Books.

Blau, Francine D., and Lawrence M. Kahn. 1996a. "International Differences in Male Wage Inequality: Institutions versus Market Forces." *Journal of Political Economy* 104 (August): 791–837.

———. 1996b. "Wage Structure and Gender Earnings Differentials: An International Comparison." *Economica* 63 (May Supplement): S29–S62.

———. 1997. "Swimming Upstream: Trends in the Gender Wage Differential in the 1980s." *Journal of Labor Economics* 15 (January): 1–42.

Freeman, Richard B. 1989. *Labor Markets in Action: Essays in Empirical Economics.* Cambridge, MA: Harvard University Press.

Juhn, Chinhui, Kevin M. Murphy, and Brooks Pierce. 1991. "Accounting for the Slowdown in Black-White Wage Convergence." In *Workers and Their Wages,* ed. M. Kosters. Washington, DC: American Enterprise Institute Press.

———. 1993. "Wage Inequality and the Rise in Returns to Skill." *Journal of Political Economy* 101 (June): 410–42.

Katz, Lawrence F., and Kevin M. Murphy. 1992. "Changes in Relative Wages, 1963–87: Supply and Demand Factors." *Quarterly Journal of Economics* 107 (February): 35–78.

DAVID COLANDER

Confessions of an Economic Gadfly

How do I work? Hard and long. Why do I do it? I don't know, but then there are many things I do for reasons unknown. Actually, I am not totally the directionless, clueless person the above answer suggests. I have a number of conjectures about why I work hard and long. One is that I'm an inquisitive person who, like my three-year-old, keeps asking "Why?" until I come up with *an answer that satisfies me*. Combine that inquisitiveness with a dogged persistence that abhors fudges in answers unless they are called what they are — fudges — and you have the makings of a gadfly like myself.

The Yeah Criterion

In explaining what I mean by "an answer that satisfies me" I could discuss the nature of satisfaction, the Duhem Quine Thesis, proofs, refutations, and lines of demarcation, but that would be misleading since what I mean by "satisfy" is visceral, not intellectual. A satisfactory explanation for me involves an inner sense — an intuition — that tells me, "Yeah, that's right; that's the way it works." I will call it the "Yeah criterion." For an intuitive economist the Yeah criterion is central.[1]

In no way am I saying that the Yeah criterion is a criterion of truth. I recognize that what makes sense to me is structured by my training, my biases, and my vision of the world. As I learn more,

I would like to thank Harry Landreth and Tom Mayor for helpful comments on earlier drafts of this essay.

my common sense changes, and what is a satisfying explanation changes — sometimes the unsatisfying becomes satisfying, and sometimes the unsatisfying becomes more unsatisfying. For that reason the Yeah criterion is not a stand-alone criterion; for it to work requires an understanding of the literature and the thinking of both past and present experts. As I read the literature, I often discover that some problems that have bothered me have bothered researchers before me. This is why the history of thought and literature studies have been so central to my study of economics. In earlier writers I can often find pointed discussions of the problems I am having with my intuition, and explanations of why they did what they did.

Intuition, Ego, and the Yeah Criterion

For the Yeah criterion to work, one needs an enormous ego, and an ability not to be influenced by the crowd. Most nonegotistical people will reason, often implicitly, that if an explanation is good enough for the enormously bright individuals who have considered an issue previously, it is good enough for them. I try to keep such reasonable thoughts from my mind and avoid letting other people's acceptance of an argument either positively or negatively influence my own considerations.

For example, the standard cost curve analysis in the textbook does not meet the Yeah criterion for me, and I have been working off and on for the past fifteen years to understand why it doesn't in a way that I can explain to others. My intuition tells me that Jacob Viner's famous mistake — telling the draftsman to do the impossible — was not a mistake but was instead a misunderstanding about the existence of discontinuities as one moved from the long to the short period.[2] Viner wanted a smooth transition between the two, while his intuition was dealing with discrete jumps. If I am correct, Viner's recantation was misplaced, and a reconsideration of what structural aspects of the basic model of the firm will make his goof no goof at all. That reconsideration will give us a better understanding of numerous microeconomic issues.

The standard AS/AD analysis is another analysis that did not meet my Yeah criterion, and my continued attacking of the standard AS/AD analysis (most recently, Colander 1995) has led many economists to consider me nonmainstream. But, if accepted (a big if), my reinterpretation of AS/AD analysis will play a role in changing the profession's thinking about what the central aspects of the Keynesian revolution are.

I have no great sense that acceptance of my ideas is imminent; changing established beliefs, especially when they are deeply built in and little thought about, is not easy; it requires a strong reliance on, and belief in, one's understanding. I expect most gadflies rely heavily on their egos and their Yeah criteria.

The MIT and Chicago Approaches to Economics

I think the majority of people in the world approach understanding by using something similar to my "Yeah" approach. Most contemporary economists, at least in their stated methodology, don't, which is why I am considered a gadfly. Actually, I should clarify the above statement since the intuitive approach is often associated with the Chicago school, and, while that Chicago approach is in decline, it is still around, especially at the introductory level of economics. In fact, I suspect that many people are attracted to economics because of its ability to give one "Yeah" highs. (This is especially true of those who learn "Chicago economics" early on, as I did.)

I quite agree that Chicago economics is wonderful at producing superficial Yeah highs. In fact, if you really get into the Chicago model, you have the Yeah sense for everything you look at. A well-trained Chicago economist can explain everything with a simple economic model.

But like many highs, the highs from the simple economic model wear off and doubts emerge. The problem is the Chicago model explains too much. There are other factors that are determining what happens, which should fit into the explanation, but don't. When this realization hit me, as it did in my junior year in college, I was ruined as a Chicago economist. I had lost the faith.

I believe something similar happened to the economics profession over the last seventy-five years. The nonmathematical intuitive approach lost favor as it became associated with laissez-faire policy recommendations that were claimed to come from economic theory. The claim that laissez-faire policy conclusions followed from economic theory did not fit an informed person's Yeah criterion. But since many intuitive economists said they did, economic researchers went about showing formally that the intuitive economists were claiming far too much for their intuition and for laissez-faire.[3]

As this formal work showed the major failings of earlier economists' intuition, formal work acquired a higher and higher stature. Intuitive understanding based on informal models was looked down upon. For lack of a better term I call this formalism "the MIT approach." It understands the economy through simple, but formal, models. In the 1990s this MIT approach has replaced Chicago intuition except in a few market niches. (With the death of George Stigler, and with Milton Friedman moving to the Hoover Institute, the MIT approach has even largely replaced the Chicago approach at Chicago.)

Thus, in the 1990s the MIT approach is mainstream economics, and any intuitive understanding of economic issues that carries over from the early economic courses (one of the niches where the Chicago version still is strong) is frowned upon and discouraged. Most economists have it brainwashed out of their minds. Those few who do not succumb to the brainwashing, and who continue to approach economics using the Yeah criterion, are selected out of the profession by the institutions that determine who advances and who doesn't. The Yeah criterion doesn't cut it with most journal editors or tenure committees.

The MIT approach is, in my view, sterile and highly limiting for most economists. By eliminating, or at least significantly suppressing, the Yeah criterion, it eliminates the passion in doing economics and instead directs economists' goals toward financial gain and institutional success. Economics becomes a job, not a vocation.

The above discussion will get me in hot water with both Chicago and MIT economists. Chicago economists will argue that their approach has no ideological slant, and MIT economists will argue that the MIT training does not diminish intuition — it simply raises intuition to a higher level. I won't argue with either side here, other than to say that an approach must be judged not by what its best practitioners say it is, but by its fruits — what the standard person trained in that tradition comes away with. Judging approaches by their consequences, I have no trouble with my criticisms of either school, nor do I think a neutral observer will. In fact, Robert Solow recently said as much — that the problem with economists today is that they don't use their intuition enough (Solow 1994). I agree. What Solow will object to is my argument that the MIT approach to training has eliminated the intuition.

Let me give an example of what the MIT approach does. A while back I went to dinner with some economics professors. I was describing the reasoning behind the market anti–inflation plan that Abba Lerner and I had been working on. An MIT-trained economist asked me if I had a formal model of it, and when I said no, he said that he couldn't discuss it. For him, the Yeah criterion was irrelevant; understanding had to go through a prism of a formal model. In the MIT approach the standard student comes away with a belief that if an issue doesn't have a formal model, it cannot be discussed or thought about.

When I have pushed MIT economists on the role of intuition, they agree that economists should be able to deal with issues on an informal intuitive level, and those who cannot are bad economists. They point to economists such as Paul Krugman and George Akerlof, who combine both. I agree, Paul and George are superb economists. They can rise above the models because they have superb intuitions and a vision different from many other economic researchers. But they both play the game by MIT rules. What's modelable guides their research and their intuition. They have made important contributions, but imagine what they could do if their intuitions were freed from the shackles.

Contrasting my approach with that given by Paul Krugman in his essay in this book is a useful way of seeing the difference between what I'm advocating and what I would call the best of the MIT approach. I'm the extreme opposite of Paul. Modelability, for me, is a technical issue to be dealt with only after one has chosen what to study by the Yeah criterion. It's a way of demonstrating, checking, and refining what one already "knows." I deal with ideas on an intuitive level, not on a formal-model level. Formal modeling, for me, is useful to answer fine points, not to create and understand theory.

Paul follows the MIT approach; he understands things such as the importance of nonlinearities and increasing returns and then puts them to the model criteria. If it doesn't make the model criteria, it doesn't meet his understanding criteria. That's why many intuitive economists don't see Paul's work as innovative, and they see him as claiming far more originality for his work than it deserves. In the

MIT approach, he is correct; in the intuitive approach his critics are correct. I follow the intuitive approach and put existing models to the intuitive-understanding criteria. If a model doesn't make intuitive sense, it must be wrong, and I focus my work on explaining why.

Simple formal models that MIT economists find so enlightening often grate on my intuition. True, they may be an improvement on the existing simple, formal model, but often they simply add one new twist formally — a twist that informal, intuitive economists have long understood. Moreover, often the intuitive economist will have recognized that the relevance of this particular twist can only be understood by adding seven or eight additional twists concurrently. The MIT approach doesn't see an issue in an alternative way unless it is in a formal model, whereas I see any simple formal model as far too limiting to the twists I intuitively believe are necessary.

Put simply, I do not believe that most of the economic events I am analyzing can be explained by a simple, formal model without the addition of enormous institutional detail that simple, formal models cannot accommodate. Krugman argues the MIT line that we should "simplify, simplify." I follow Einstein — "Models should be as simple as possible, *but not more so.*" My vision of the economy is one of complexity, and any explanation that fits my Yeah criterion must incorporate that complexity, or at least tell me why the complexity isn't going to affect the analysis. When I try to conceive of a general mathematical statement of the economic problem, I come up with an extraordinarily complicated set of interrelated dynamic equations that lead to chaotic, super-non-linear dynamic models.

The MIT vision sees it as possible to reduce that chaos — without formally modeling the institutions — to simple, formal models with linear dynamics and deterministic results. They have to do so to arrive at a tractable model. Tractability runs roughshod over intuition and creates a set of models that, for me, do not meet the Yeah criterion. The only way I can see an economy such as ours as working is with institutions limiting changes and creating some stability out of chaos. Somehow in the educational process of children enormous limitations on individual's choices are placed on them by institutions and social pressures. Society shapes us to fit into a workable marketplace. Whenever I see analyses — such as the standard analyses of production or of distribution — that don't include that shaping process and the institutions that play such an important role in shaping us, I cringe. I cringe a lot when reading economics.

The Possibility of Trade between High-Level Theorists and Intuitive Economists

The problem with simple, formal models is that they constrain one's intuition. They embody implicit assumptions that one doesn't even know exist. The mathematics one uses in those models is a language, and languages are limiting. There are two ways to confront this problem. One way is to delve deeper and deeper into the math — dealing with the complex issues in a highly abstract way so that the few implicit assumptions that remain are clear. Some of the complex game-theoretic work fits this approach, as does some of the recent work on chaos and nonlinear dynamics. At that level one can integrate one's intuition with formal modeling and the results can be impressive. The models that such economists develop are far from the simple policy-oriented MIT models that Krugman exalts; these are models that have no policy implications because they generally have no analytic solution — at least not yet — or are so abstract that they have no obvious relation to reality.

Relating such abstract, formal models with real-world observations is extraordinarily difficult, for most people impossible. Thus, while I try to follow the work of modern researchers such as Buzz Brock and look to it for inspiration, I make no pretense of dealing at that level myself. I go to the other extreme and deal informally with loose ideas that better fit observed reality, but that oftentimes hide logical relationships. Such specialization opens up the possibility of trade, and, ideally, economics would have two types of economic researchers making trades — formal theorists dealing with highly complex and abstract analysis almost devoid of institutions, and intuitive, institutionally based theorists dealing with real-world institutions and informal abstract analysis. The MIT approach of simple formal models would make sense if there were not increasing returns to scale in research, but it seems obvious that there are increasing returns, so not to take advantage of them and not to encourage specialization is, in my view, a highly inefficient approach to understanding. If you are going to be formally abstract, then go all the way and don't let the real-world issues contaminate the purity of your analysis. If you are going to be concerned with the real world, don't formalize more than the least precise real-world element. To do so is to violate the law of significant digits.

To make sure that I am being clear, and to get me in as much trouble as possible, let me state my position more bluntly. I would say that the MIT approach has played an important role in bringing economics to its current sterility. I say this regretfully because I also believe that MIT economics has played a significantly positive role and that it was necessary to get the blatant ideological aspects of earlier intuitive economics out of the models.

My Road to Becoming a Gadfly

Having arrived at the view of simple, formal models described above, I found myself in a difficult position in my graduate work. I did fine in the mathematics they taught us, but I was not an ultramathematician and did not want to be one. I had been attracted to economics by the intuitive understanding it gave me of events, and its ability to supply me with Yeah highs. But I had rejected the Chicago creed that the market was inherently good and beyond question.

Faced with my disillusionment with both the Chicago approach and the MIT approach I was in a bind — a bind that I resolved initially by not considering it. Instead, I focused on more immediate concerns, such as getting my dissertation done and getting a job. That meant following the MIT approach, which, interpreted down to a third-year graduate student level, meant that the best, quickest, way to a dissertation was to take a simple, formal model and permutate it.

Optimal taxation was hot at the time, and Ned Phelps and Bill Vickrey, two of the most interesting professors of economics at Columbia, were interested in it. So it seemed like a good idea to write a dissertation on optimal taxation, especially since they would allow me to write three essays that I could easily translate into articles. The math in my essays would look impressive and the topic was hot. It was the perfect combination for a thesis. It wasn't a very good thesis, but I soon had two essays done and was working on my third. That was in 1974; I was on my way to becoming a mainstream economist.

The decision to become a gadfly was made, as are most decisions, in a sequentially rational way. The first step along the path occurred in 1974, when one of those defining events of one's life happened. While I had suppressed my intuitive approach to economics, I had not totally annihilated it, and one day I was sitting around thinking about inflation, trying to understand why we were having so much inflation and what could be done about it, when I conceived of an economy in which there were property rights in prices.[4] In such an economy individuals wanting to change their nominal price would pay someone else to change their nominal price in the opposite direction. Only relative price changes would be allowed in such an economy; inflation would be impossible. It was an intriguing idea to me since it allowed the society to control the price level, but it left all relative prices free to fluctuate.

The idea led to numerous questions: What price would these rights to change price sell for? How would that price vary with change in aggregate demand? I played around with the idea for a while, and one afternoon sat down and wrote it up in a piece I called "The Free-Market Solution to Inflation." I sent copies around to a few people, including Bill Vickrey. I soon got a letter back from Bill (with a copy to my chair) telling me the idea was brilliant. Now it isn't often that one gets such a letter from one's adviser who himself is an innovative economist, and it led me to make a fateful decision: to dump my thesis on optimal taxation (which was almost finished) and to expand this short paper on the free-market solution into a thesis.

Actually, the decision wasn't quite so gutsy as it sounds; I explained the situation to Vickrey and asked him if he felt I could finish a thesis on the topic in a year, the time I needed to have it done if I was to stay at Vassar, where I was then teaching. He said I could. I then went to Phelps and told him that Vickrey felt I could expand the paper into a thesis in a year, and asked if he felt it was a reasonable plan. He also said yes. So essentially, I had tentative approval from both my advisers before I began.

And a good thing, too, because a year later, when I handed in my finished thesis, it was not very good. The title was "Microeconomic Stabilization Policy for an Economy with Simultaneous Inflation and Unemployment." It was provocative and imaginative; it was also vague, incoherent in parts, and incomplete in others. Still, they let me through, perhaps because they had made almost no criticism when I handed in successive drafts. Whether this was because they hadn't had the time to read the drafts carefully, or because they didn't know how to comment on such a vague and incoherent thesis, I don't know.

The only real hurdle I faced was my oral defense, and luckily for me, Sidney Morgenbesser, a well-known philosopher who cared little about formal economic models, was one of the outside examiners. At the beginning of the defense he suggested that the rules be changed — that the thesis looked like something Vickrey had worked out and that we should have Vickrey, not me, defend it. This provoked laughter and pleasant discussion, leaving little room for piercing questions.

I suspect that that thesis decision set me on my gadfly path, because while the thesis wasn't much, it contained the seeds of the ideas for most of my later work. Many of those seeds are still germinating, which gives you an idea of how incomplete the thesis was.

The chance to plant the seeds of new ways of looking at problems is something that few modern economists have, and I am eternally grateful to Bill Vickrey and the almost-directionless Columbia Ph.D. program for allowing me that chance.

Of course, seeds of ideas aren't going to get one a job, so I still had the job problem to deal with. I should have been scared to death, but in my immaturity, and with my almost total lack of knowledge about the system, I wasn't. After all, Vickrey had told me my paper was brilliant, and when I asked if he thought I could get it published in a top journal, he had responded, "Yes — no problem." I started to get worried when I got my first rejection (from the *AER*); it wasn't even polite. It said, essentially, that the paper was garbage, poorly written, incomprehensible, and wrong. After a couple more rejections, I began to suspect that I was in trouble. Maybe that fateful step into following, and trying to develop, my intuition was a step into a deep abyss.

I began to consider other options; I was selected as a Brookings policy fellow and went on leave at Vassar to work at the GAO on cost analysis, one of the many areas my thesis had touched on. A study I did there argued essentially that it was technically impossible to distinguish a fee from a tax, and that when handing out limited entitlements, one had to base the fees on scarcity costs, not on costs as they were currently being interpreted in the law.

I further argued that when scarce entitlements were involved, costs could only be defined in relation to demand — since the value of the scarce resource was determined by demand. Demand elasticities had to be taken into account in allocating joint costs. While my arguments made good economic sense, they were not what most politicians wanted to hear, and I quickly discovered that I did not have the temperament to play the political-economy game in government. So much for that option.

I suspect that many gadflies arrive at a similar stage in their careers and leave the profession. I certainly considered leaving it, and at that point I seriously considered going to work for a management consultant firm. The pay was much better, and the likelihood of success much higher. I might well have done that, too, had it not been for Sidney Weintraub and Abba Lerner.

With a Lot of Help from Friends

While a Brookings policy fellow I intermittently continued my work on my free-market solution to inflation, but it wasn't going anywhere fast; I gathered another couple of nasty rejections, which told me what I now knew very well—that the paper didn't have the right form—that it discussed an idea without a formal model! I now knew that a paper without a model was not allowed in any mainstream journal. It was at that point that I began considering nonmainstream outlets.

One place I looked was to the post-Keynesians. Sidney Weintraub, together with Henry Wallich, had a TIP (tax-based income policy) proposal that was something like my free-market solution to inflation. The difference was that theirs was a tax-based policy, and mine a market-based policy. Theirs was designed as a policy that would work; mine was designed as a theoretical policy with no concern about how it would work out in practice. Sidney was also editor of the *Journal of Post-Keynesian Economics,* and as a last resort I sent my paper there. He did not reject it outright, but he did reject it as too abstract and too theoretical. He suggested I write a new paper that emphasized TIP more, and then touched on my idea of a market plan. I jumped at the chance and got a paper accepted. My academic life was not a total failure.

I met Sidney later and liked him personally, but we didn't agree on many issues in economics. There were major differences in our thinking about anti–inflation policy; he was concerned about practical matters, and my concern was about the way nominal-price-setting institutions could be integrated into a general equilibrium system: thus his analysis of TIP was partial equilibrium; mine was general equilibrium. He also focused on wages, and he took it as given that a wage/price markup had been, and would remain, constant. My proposal focused on value added, and I argued that one couldn't take any wage/price markup as constant when imposing a policy affecting wages. Despite our differences Sidney was generally supportive. I think it is important to note that gadflies exist in the profession only because of the nurturing of existing economists such as Sidney. I will be forever grateful to him.

The second fortuitous event was a seminar that Brookings held on TIP, which occurred because Art Okun was there and was interested in TIP. Unfortunately, I was not asked to prepare anything since Art saw my work as off in left field. He was concerned with politics and getting something implemented. He felt, I suspect rightly since his political instincts were impeccable, that my discussion of a new market in some abstract concept would have killed the practical hopes for the TIP plan. His focus was on policy. I was disappointed.

Nonetheless, that Brookings seminar in April was another turning point in my career. The reason was that Abba Lerner came, I think almost uninvited, and discussed what he called WIP (wage incomes policy). This proposal was very similar to mine in that it would control inflation by creating property rights. A major difference was that his proposal was a modification of the wage-based TIPs, and hence it focused on wages, not prices. A second difference was that he was interested primarily in practical issues (to the degree that Abba could be concerned about practical issues), while I was interested in the underlying theory and what it implied for macroeconomic theorizing.

After the seminar, Ned Phelps introduced me to Abba and told him I had a proposal somewhat similar to his. Abba nodded. Actually, I believe, I had sent Abba a copy of my early proposal, but I doubt he had read it, or if he had, that he had thought much about it. A couple of days later Abba was on the program at the Eastern Economic Association meetings and I decided to attend; we spoke briefly and I outlined the differences between my proposal and his. He was pleasant, but otherwise noncommittal.

The next time I saw Abba was at the AEA meetings in Chicago. TIP was politically hot then, and there was a session with Abba, Sidney, and Henry Wallich, who was on the Fed board. The room, which held three hundred or so, was full; I sat there listening, depressed that my work was being ignored. At the end of the session I got recognized by the chair and asked Abba three questions that I felt showed the weaknesses of his analysis and the strengths of mine. One seldom gets answers at such events, and I didn't, but at least I had had my say, and I felt better for it.

I was presenting a paper on the general topic at the last session of the meetings. There were two people in the audience — friends of the presenters. But then, right after the beginning of the session, in walked Abba. He sat down and listened to the presentations and afterward came up and said that he had been thinking about some of the questions I asked, and that he thought that I might be right. He said that we should talk. I was delighted, and asked when. He responded, "Now," and so he and I spent the next three days holed up in a Chicago hotel room, arguing technical points about our anti–inflation plans and talking about economics in general.

At the end of the three days I had convinced him that my value-added price control approach was more general than his wage control approach, and that I had thought of a number of issues and nuances of the idea that he had not. His openness and total commitment to understanding was both unexpected and delightful. We could talk about highly abstract ideas that didn't have formal models. He suggested we should do a book together, spelling out the idea we had discussed. I asked when; he said, "This December," so that December I flew from Europe, where I was a research fellow at Oxford, to Tallahassee to work on the book. There, I rose at 6:00 every morning, and we worked until 9:00 P.M. I'd write a draft; Abba would rework it, and we'd continue working like that throughout the day. Although Abba was in his seventies then, he still lived and breathed economics. At the end of December, a draft of an article and of the book was complete.

Abba and I got along fantastically; our views of economics were almost identical. We differed primarily in two ways: First, Abba was an unabashed utilitarian, and I was not. Second, while he was much more interested in the idea as a practical policy than I was, he was amazingly naive about politics. I was far more politically aware than he: he felt good ideas rose because they were good; I, at that point, was far more jaundiced and felt that everything happens because it is in the relevant people's interest, and good ideas are often not in the relevant people's interest.

We were, however, quite different in temperament. Abba was the perfectionist who would work over every word and phrase; I was interested in the grand conception — the specifics were simply a boring job that had to be done. This difference in temperament made the collaboration even more fruitful, and it was a delight working with him. (His wife, Daliah, made it even more of a delight; she put up with us and made the technicalities of life disappear.)

In writing jointly with someone, one of the two must have final say, and given our different positions, it was clear that Abba would have final say. This presented no problem on most issues, since we agreed, but there was one area of disagreement where our conception of what we called MAP (the Market Anti-inflation Plan) differed, even after long discussion. Abba saw our market anti-inflation plan as simply a way to control the price level, and that when imposed, the price of changing price would quickly go to zero, since all people would be doing would be setting relative prices. I argued for a quite different conception in which the nominal and real sectors were intertwined; depending on aggregate demand pressure, there would be a different equilibrium level of output with each different equilibrium price of raising price. Abba saw a knife-edge equilibrium, except for frictions; I saw a multitude of equilibria and the likelihood that, given existing institutions, the aggregate equilibrium the economy reached was an excess-supply equilibrium.

This was a major theoretical difference. My interpretation required a radical rethinking of macro theory since it meant that the nominal price-setting institutions influenced real economic variables in a systematic way. His interpretation saw MAP as fitting in nicely with existing macro theory. It was simply a way to control the price level.

In our joint work we followed Abba's conception; in my individual work I spelled out my conception, and we continually discussed the differences when we were together. The last serious discussion we had about it was in England in 1980 where we were attending a conference on TIP. That evening we sat around arguing, and I related the idea back to Abba's seminal 1934 article on degrees of monopoly. If was as if a lightbulb went off in his head, and he finally tentatively agreed with me. We agreed to discuss it more when he returned from Israel, which was the next leg of his journey. Unfortunately he had a stroke in Israel that impaired his language ability, and we never had that conversation. Happily, he remained physically well after his stroke, but we never again could work together. We remained close friends until his death in 1982.

The importance of Abba to my career as an economist is inestimable. It is entirely possible that I would have left the profession had not Abba picked me up, encouraged me, and made it possible for me to publish. The reception accorded to our joint work was fundamentally different than the reception my solo work got; it was considered; people actually talked about the idea, even though it didn't flow from a formal model. The reason was that Abba was known as the generator of odd schemes and was also seen as an icon from the past. But Abba was also known for being quite impractical and far out, so the idea was not taken seriously. But at least it was discussed, and it made a nice follow-up to discussions of TIPs—it was the market equivalent to TIPs, just as marketable permits for pollution are the market equivalent to pollution taxes.

Abba lived and breathed economics and would take me around with him to the inner-circle cocktail parties where the insiders of the profession meet and informally talk economics. It is here where the old-timers meet the newcomers. Abba would introduce me to people and say very nice things about me. Sometimes that introduction would cause people to remember my name and treat me a bit differently. I became known as Abba's protégé, and many thought that I had been his student. Put simply, Abba made it possible for me to exist in the economics profession.

But while Abba had access to the inner circle, Abba was not an inner-circle economist; instead, he was a tangential iconoclast who in his old age was adopted by the profession much more than when he was young.

In many ways Abba was a bit of an embarrassment to the inner circle of the profession in that he continued to come up with politically hopeless schemes to improve the efficiency of the economy. It was rumored that Abba was on the short list for the Nobel Prize—I suspect our work on MAP played a role in his not getting the prize, since MAP was far too controversial, and he would likely have used the Nobel speech as a podium for telling people about it and claiming it was the solution to society's ills. That is not what I suspect the inner circle would have wanted from a Nobel Prize winner. Thus, Abba's high regard for me was both a blessing and a curse since, if Abba liked me, I, too, must be a tangential iconoclast. It was a curse I could live with.

My association with Abba catapulted me from struggling outsider to a small-time, known, but somewhat strange, gadfly economist. Being so known within some circles meant that I could get published reasonably easily within a restricted range of journals. It also led to my being offered an endowed distinguished chair at Middlebury College, which I accepted. I have enjoyed teaching there immensely.

Abba and I worked together for only four years; Abba had his stroke and I was on my own again. But life after Abba was quite different than life before Abba. The chair gave me some influence and respect, as well as a small budget to run conferences. At these conferences I tried to bring economists of different persuasions together and to look at issues from a slightly different perspective. They focused on ideas, not models. Those conferences, and the volumes I edited based on them, gave me a chance to meet, and carry on, the acquaintances I had made while with Abba, and to develop an independent reputation as a nonpartisan heterodox economist.

The move to Middlebury also helped change my research agenda — from one focusing on abstract theory to one focusing on teaching and methodology. The reasons for this change were twofold. First, when I came to Middlebury, I tried to teach an upper-level course on the micro foundations of macro; I had three students sign up, two of whom were mathematically unprepared. Moreover, the passion of the one who was mathematically prepared was for music, not math. (She has since become a professional harpsichordist.) It was clear to me that if I were going to keep an active research agenda and be a good teacher, these two areas of my life must be combined. So I began concentrating more on what I call "the translation problem" — reducing the high-level theory to teachable models that convey the essence of the high-level theory.

As I studied this issue I became convinced that, as a profession, we were doing a horrendous job in that translation, and that the models we taught to undergraduates were not the models we believed, and that the empirical work we were doing and teaching students was not the way we convinced ourselves of the validity of propositions. The recognition of this conflict led to my work on the profession, which has been far better received by the profession than my theoretical work.

As I was doing this work on models I discovered that I had a knack for textbooks. Textbooks gave me a wider forum for my ideas and were profitable. I have come to believe that what goes into textbooks probably plays a more important role in the future direction of the profession than just about anything else economists do. Textbooks' tone and the vision they convey play an important role in selecting who chooses to continue studying economics, and what vision they carry with them. It is in textbooks that the foundation of the future of economic research is laid.

With each successful book and article more offers to write come in, and I am now at the stage of my career where I am having to learn to say no to invitations to write and speak. I am learning to do this in an attempt to maintain my sanity and my creativity. The reason I say the latter is that there is a perverse connection between the requests one gets to write and how well known one's views on a subject are. The better known one's views, the more requests to express them one gets. So I am now trying to follow the philosophy of turning down most requests to write on the profession, where my views are relatively well known among economists, and am concentrating on areas where my views aren't well known, and where I will likely get rejected. My latest work on the macro foundations of micro falls within this classification. That work, however, meets my Yeah criterion, so I will predict that within ten years some variation of it will be all the rage in macro. When I've had my say there, I will then turn my attention to the cost problem and to showing the profession that Jacob Viner's intuition was right after all.

NOTES

1. Tom Mayor pointed out to me upon reading this essay that the Yeah criterion is similar to Fritz Machlup's "ahaness." I suspect that it appears under other names for other intuitively oriented economists and scientists.

2. For those who do not know of Viner's mistake, it was telling the draftsman to draw the short-run marginal cost curves through the minimum point of the short-run average costs curves and to simultaneously draw them through the point where the short-run cost curve is tangent to the long-run average cost curve. Scholar that he is, Viner left the mistake for all to see, along with his admission that it was a mistake, when his famous article that set up the standard cost analysis was reprinted. See Viner 1931.

3. J. B. Clarke's relating of marginal product and justice is an example of the type of problem that existed. Obviously not all nonmathematical intuitive economists have believed that markets solve all problems. For example, in the early 1900s institutionalism was strong. But, by the 1920s the more doctrinaire laissez-faire economists were an important part of the inner circle of the profession.

4. I often try to conceptualize fundamentally different systems as a way of gaining insight into our current system; thus I have worked through in my mind multiple goods-monies economies, economies in which all consumption is joint and all production is individual, and economies in which production, not consumption, is the goal.

REFERENCES

Colander, David. 1995. "The Stories We Tell: A Reconsideration of AS/AD Analysis." *Journal of Economic Perspectives* 9 (summer): 169–88.

Solow, Robert. 1994. "Review of Thomas Mayer's *Truth and Precision in Economics.*" *Journal of Economic Methodology* (n.d.).

Viner, Jacob. 1931. "Cost Curves and Supply Curves: *Zeitschrift Fur Nationaloekonomie.*" Reprinted in American Economic Association, *Readings in Price Theory* (Homewood, IL: Irwin, 1952), 3:23–46.

WILLIAM DARITY, JR.

Why I Work

Beginnings

For a while I have been skeptical about a recent tendency among academics and various public intellectuals to utilize autobiography as a device to illustrate grand social themes. I have been especially skeptical when no serious attempt is made to establish the boundaries of the generalizability and uniqueness of one's own self-reflected life history. Social inquiry puts on the coat of anecdote and becomes absorbed in unraveling the details and implications of episodes in the writer's life that he or she has identified as relevant to the controversy at hand.

Nevertheless, although I am still two decades away from sixty-five, the age when an economist legitimately can look back on a career, here I am joining in this self-exploration that may yield additional episodes for the personal case studies file. But whether the experiences that I will present selectively, for both conscious and unconscious reasons, have any utility for social analysis, I leave to the reader to decide. As should become clear below, social analysis by personal anecdote has not been the way that I have engaged in research in the past, and I do not expect it to become the way I do research in the future.

The particular outcome of human interaction that has dominated my intellectual curiosity for as long as I can remember is the problem of economic inequality and the related problem of poverty. As an undergraduate at Brown University in the early 1970s, I first started taking economics courses because I wanted to understand why a few people were rich and so many were poor, why some people had a wide range of life options and others were faced with limited opportunities.

This curiosity stemmed from my childhood, when my father, who worked for the World Health Organization in the Middle East at the time, took me with him to Palestinian refugee camps. I also saw desperate beggars in the streets of both Cairo and Alexandria. I knew from traveling with my parents that, in general, the people of the African continent had a very different material existence from the people of the European continent.

I also was aware at a very early age that back home in the United States the worlds of opportunity for most black people and most white people were sharply different. These circumstances were unjust, and I have dedicated most of my intellectual life to understanding how these unjust global arrangements came about, what forces sustain them, and what, if anything, might be done to alter them. These are the questions that drive the passion that shapes my craft.

It was obvious to me that my own life chances were wider than many other people simply because of a parental luck of the draw. While none of my grandparents, rural black Southerners on both sides, attended college — indeed, both of my father's parents never had the chance to attend school beyond sixth grade, although both of them managed to become completely literate — both of my parents ultimately became academics, my father in public health and my mother in education.

Theirs was the breakthrough generation that placed my upbringing solidly in the middle class; I never knew want for food, clothing, shelter, or access to learning. Recognizing that my opportunities were unusual and that my parents' social-class transition was an exception rather than a normal pattern, I developed a deep and abiding skepticism for theories — like the most unvarnished form of human-capital theory in economics — that explain inequality by locating a deficiency in the individual or the group experiencing inferior status.

I certainly believe some individuals by dint of good fortune or extraordinary effort can rise "above" their origins. But as I said at the outset, I do not believe in social science by anecdote. These individuals are rarities; they are anomalies. It is valuable to understand their experiences, but it is even more important to recognize that the world — not merely Hindu India — generally is bound by principles of caste. Social status typically is replicated across generations, perhaps with growing rather than diminishing rigidity, as we approach the close of the twentieth century.

Working

While inequality and poverty may be the central themes of my research, the glue that binds all the strands of my work, those strands are quite disparate and far-ranging. This is because my style is to pursue whatever issue or problem excites me at a given moment. These are issues or problems that I view as important, whether or not they are in vogue in my profession at large. My soul is the soul of a generalist rather than a specialist, although there necessarily are many arenas in economics about which I know very little. I have followed my soul, which has been fun, but I do have a nerve-wracking tendency perpetually to overextend myself.

When I first was on the job market in 1978 while completing my dissertation at MIT, a faculty member at Duke, struck by my diversity of interests and my desire to pursue them all, urged me to follow the path of least resistance — to narrow my interests, and to specialize. Duke did not offer me a position at the time. The faculty at the University of Texas at Austin was more receptive to my catholicity of interests and wayward, unorthodox tendencies. I never have been comfortable or persuaded by the elixir that is mainstream/orthodox/ neoclassical economics. At this late stage in my career I remain convinced that the dominant theory cannot provide a satisfactory explanation for the persistence of discrimination, for the recurrence of aggregate unemployment, and for sustained international and intergroup economic inequality.

I suppose that I also was geared by my MIT training to have a portfolio of technical skills in applied mathematics and econometrics sufficiently state-of-the-art to make me acceptable to all wings of Texas's department. Of course, that same package of skills by now is far from state-of-the-art.

One of the great lessons I learned at Texas was to listen to and to collaborate with your friends. Friends who share in the research endeavor have been vital throughout my career. There has been reciprocity in the formulation of ideas. Sometimes I have invited others to join me on a project; sometimes they have invited me to join them. The professional collaborations wax and wane, but the friendships and intellectual exchanges continue to this day.

One of the most important things I discovered early in my years at Texas was how little I really knew despite my MIT training. My understanding of economics lacked context. To do a Ph.D. at MIT in the late 1970s required reading very little, if anything, published before 1960 or 1965. Because of the technical emphasis and an orientation focused on whatever was current (or "hot"), you could do a Ph.D. without reading anything written by Adam Smith, David Ricardo, Joseph Schumpeter, Karl Marx, or, for that matter, Maynard Keynes.

Unfortunately, this pattern of training for budding economists was not unique to MIT. It is pervasive in the United States. Recent claims that, substantively, endogenous-growth theory with its emphases on human capital, research and development, and increasing returns is the "new" growth theory demonstrates the inattention given to doctrinal history by our profession. The new growth theory is, in its essentials, a formalization of Adam Smith's model in *The Wealth of Nations*.

After recognizing the limitations of my own training I decided to invest the first two years *after* having finished my Ph.D. doing a close reading of these important texts in economics that I had never examined closely. A more rational course of action may have been to learn more mathematics and/or theoretical econometrics at the time. But from the standpoint of my own intellectual breadth and my subsequent ability to situate accurately developments and debates in economics, no other course of action could have been more valuable.

This personal history may suggest to some readers that I am hostile toward the use of mathematics in economics. Nothing could be farther from the truth. What I especially value in my MIT training is my ability to recognize the discipline that mathematical formalization brings to analysis. Certain results simply cannot be seen or established by rhetorical methods.

On the other hand, I view mathematics as an instrument for economists. The amount and type of mathematics that an economist needs to know will vary with the problem at hand. I definitely do not view the indiscriminate acquisition of more and more mathematical know-how as equivalent to becoming a better economist. Nor do I believe that arguments presented rhetorically are inherently weak or that economists who are more skillful at mathematics are inherently more inventive or interesting than those who are less skillful at mathematics.

In recent years, since I have been on the faculty at UNC, I have been deeply involved with the humanities. I spent a year as a fellow at the National Humanities Center in 1989 working on several manuscripts on Abram Harris, the first black academic economist in the United States. I have been an active participant at seminars at the Institute of Arts and Humanities at UNC. I also serve as director of a Mellon-funded summer program, the Minority Undergraduate Research Assistant Program (MURAP) that is intended to encourage black, Hispanic, and Native American undergraduates to pursue the Ph.D. in the humanities or social sciences. I actually have a dream of developing courses or seminars that compare the view of slavery in fictional literature and economics and the view of the future in fictional literature (science fiction in particular) and economics.

In all three contexts my encounters with scholars in the humanities has made it abundantly clear to me that very powerful, rich, and rigorous analyses can be performed without any resort to mathematics. Of course, language artistry can be used to mask a lack of substance just as readily as mathematical formalization can be used to restate the obvious. What matters is the substance of the work; the mode of presentation is secondary.

More Friends, More Work
During the spring of 1980, I took a leave of absence from the University of Texas and went to Washington, DC, to serve as the Urban League's economist and as a visiting faculty member in economics at the University of Maryland at College Park. I discovered my preference for the academy was justified, and that I was not particularly susceptible to Potomac Fever.

While I was in DC I worked closely with an older scholar, Jewell Mazique, who was the first person to take an advanced degree in African Studies at Howard University. Her son, Jeff, and I had been roommates when we were undergraduates at Brown, but it wasn't until my leave that I had the chance to really benefit from her scholarly guidance.

It was Jewell Mazique who prompted me to explore the proposition that the class structure in the United States (and elsewhere) is inadequately understood as a simple bipolar relationship between capital and labor. This led me to work systematically to develop the theory of the managerial class in a series of papers stretching from a

1982 contribution to a Resources for the Future conference (written with Ronald Johnson and Ed Thompson), to a related 1983 contribution to *Society,* to a 1995 contribution to *Daedalus.*

When I was a Ph.D. student at MIT, I was troubled by the knock given to neo-Ricardian economics by Samuelson and Modigliani's clever discovery of the dual equilibrium for the Pasinetti system, a steady state where labor ends up owning the national capital stock via its savings behavior. That prospect only seemed likely by force of a social revolution. So eventually I was able to demonstrate that there also is a potential antidual result, where, in the limit, the entire capital stock of a growing economy is owned by the capitalists. The dissertation also contained an essay with a continuous time formalization of Ester Boserup's model of agricultural growth under population pressure and an essay that presented a general equilibrium trade model of the Atlantic slave trade.

My supervisor, Lance Taylor, made it possible for me to complete the dissertation in one year, so that I actually finished my Ph.D. in three years. I would drop work off in the morning in his slot, and he would have comments back to me by the same afternoon. I wish that my behavior with my own graduate students were as good, but my tendency toward overextension leads me to take considerably longer in giving them systematic feedback. Not only do I count Lance as a valued adviser but also I count him as a close friend.

Indeed, in all the areas where I believe I have made contributions in economics, the interaction with friends who are simultaneously colleagues has been important. And it has not mattered a great deal whether or not we are physically located in the same place or same institution.

The antidual result appears in a paper of mine published in the *American Economic Review* in 1981. The Boserup model appeared in 1980. It contains an algebra error that was spotted by Frederick Pryor and Stephen Maurer from Swarthmore College that resulted in a paper of their own that extended the development of the model. It has taken a long while, but I finally have come back to Boserup in the mid-1990s in collaborative research with a terrific former graduate student, William Winfrey.

The slave trade model was published in *Research in Economic History* in 1982, the first of a series of papers that have resurrected Eric Williams's hypothesis about the role of the Atlantic slave trade and plantation slavery in British-cum-European industrialization.

The hypothesis seemed to have been buried by Stanley Engerman's critique in the *Business History Review* in the early 1970s, and while many historians who have not kept up with the literature still think it is buried, Engerman himself has moved somewhat discreetly to a greatly modified position in light of the work of Joseph Inikori, Ronald Bailey, Barbara Solow, and myself.

In conjunction with Sam Myers, Jr., I have maintained an extended research inquiry into the empirical determinants of black-white earnings disparity and black-white family structure differences, and, most recently, into the nature of the black underclass.

Myers also has been involved in a related project that seeks to develop an economic theory of race and racism and an endogenous theory of discrimination. James Stewart at Penn State pushed the limits of orthodox theory in developing an economic theory of racism in his 1995 Presidential Address to the National Economic Association. Our endeavor seeks to pursue his lead as well as explore nonmainstream avenues toward such a theory.

Rhonda Williams, Patrick Mason, and I started full steam down this road when we concluded in the mid-1980s that the theory of discrimination needed to be redesigned on the basis of classical/Marxist competition rather than neoclassical competition. The genesis of this analysis began in conversations Rhonda and I had during the brief period when we were both at the University of Texas. Begrudgingly, we accepted the proposition that persistent discrimination is not reconcilable with conditions of neoclassical competition.

But rather than conclude that discrimination progressively must vanish, as much of the economics profession has, we concluded that the problem was with the orthodox theory of competition. We then discerned that persistent discrimination can be reconciled with classical/Marxist competition. The evolution of these debates, including elements of our own thinking, is presented in detail in a two-volume set of papers that I have edited for Edward Elgar, *Economics and Discrimination.*

My interest in inequality between countries and regions led me to follow Lance into North-South modeling. My UNC colleague Patrick Conway collaborated with me on one of these papers, published in 1991 in the *Southern Economic Journal,* where the North has increasing returns as a manufactured-goods specialist and the South has decreasing returns as a primary-products specialist. My goal has been construction of models that identify the conditions that maintain persistent inequality in incomes and/or wages between North and South. More recently I have been encouraged by Caren Grown and Nilufer Cagatay to examine the role of gender inequality in economic development, particularly from a macro standpoint.

The body of research on North-South models prompted by work by Lance Taylor and Ronald Findlay long predates the recent literature on international convergence or divergence. As a group those of us who have been North-South modelers generally have started with the presumption that international divergence was the norm that had to be explained. Our work also has centered on the assumption that there are long-standing fundamental structural asymmetrics in the world economy, rather than the initial symmetry characteristic of the new growth literature.

One of the most important theoretical contributions in my work, I believe, is the demonstration that Keynes's concept of involuntary unemployment need not be associated with the failure of a market or markets to clear. While I think the central insight came to me the day I had had my molars extracted in Austin, the evolution of the argument has evolved to touch upon the inadequacies of the natural-rate hypothesis, hysteresis, and the neutrality of money.

Warren Young was introduced to me by Geoff Harcourt as "the Miss Marple of economics." Warren had done the sleuthing that had established that Hicks's famous SILL model—the original IS-LM diagram—really was a contrivance born of blending papers by Harrod and by Meade, *not* a product of Hicks's deep involvement in Walrasian general-equilibrium analysis, as the mythology had it. We resolved to do a full paper on the development of IS-LM (now in the 1995 issue of *History of Political Economy*) as well as some other projects, including a major study on the role of expectations in economics. We have been somewhat delinquent on this most recent project, but we hope to have it out in the near future.

Art Goldsmith was a colleague at UNC until he moved to Washington and Lee. He had an important idea that he shared with me, the idea that exposure to unemployment should have an effect on the time path of unemployment in the economy because of the adverse psychological effects experienced by large numbers of persons subjected to joblessness. He asked me if I would like to work with him on a research program intended to tease out all the implications we could think of along these lines. Of course, I said yes because this struck me as incredibly interesting. We are continuing to generate research in this area, blending research findings from social psychology and economics.

Presently, in conjunction with econometrician David Guilkey and graduate student Jason Dietrich, I also maintain a research program that involves the use of multiple decennial censuses to partition the U.S. population into fifty racial/ethnic groups. We address whether there is evidence of a differential incidence of discrimination in economic outcomes across these more refined social groupings. I also am now extending the analysis of intergroup disparity to a cross-national comparative inquiry.

Finally, I believe that I was the originator of the notion that the LDC debt crisis of the early 1980s was predominantly the product of "loan pushing" by the commercial banks. The idea was advanced in a discussion paper prepared while I was a visitor at the Board of Governors of the Federal Reserve. In fact, in conjunction with Bobbie Horn, I published an ill-fated book (Ballinger, the publisher, was dismantled shortly after the book came out) called *The Loan Pushers* that told the whole story as we saw it. The book — and the argument — has gained much greater notoriety and attention in India than in the United States.

Frankly, I have not had much luck with books. James Galbraith and I labored hard to put out a macroeconomics textbook that we believe covered, fairly, all the competing traditions. The book still was pitched as a "niche" book by Houghton Mifflin and not promoted at all after substantial staff turnover. At least, I knew the rule of thumb about books before I began to write them: in economics, do not bother with trying to publish a book until *after* you have tenure. Ours is a profession that values refereed articles.

Race and Work

I would be remiss if I did not talk about the role of involvement in professional organizations and the evolution of my career to this point. I belong to several, but I have been most active as a conference participant and presenter in the Southern Economic Association, the Allied Social Science Association (including the American Economic Association and the National Economic Association), the History of Economics Society, and the Eastern Economic Association meeting.

These meetings are a vehicle for sharing work, exchanging work, and delivering and receiving criticism. While the quality of sessions is uneven, this is the space where you can interact with friends/colleagues you do not normally have the opportunity to see. I recall Art Goldsmith and I sketched out several papers on two different occasions in the same bar in the Fairmont Hotel in New Orleans. I expect we will do it again soon.

While I especially have enjoyed my participation in the Southern, I do want to say a few special words about the National Economic Association, the organization of black economists. My first involvement with the NEA was indirect. In 1974 I received the Class of 1896 award for the best paper written by a senior in economics at Brown University. I submitted the paper, entitled "Economic Theory and Racial Economic Inequality," to the NEA's journal, the *Review of Black Political Economy.* It was accepted and published in 1975, my very first publication.

The *Review* also was connected at the time to the Black Economic Research Center (BERC), an organization headed by Robert Browne. BERC was one of the few institutions created by the muted response to James Forman's 1969 call for reparations when he interrupted the Sunday service at the Riverside Church in New York City.

I do not recall the precise moment when I first learned about the NEA, the *Review,* or BERC. All of that simply was in the air at MIT because there was an unusually large cohort of intellectually and politically active black Ph.D. students there at the time. The group included Sam Myers, Jr., Julianne Malveaux, Glenn Loury, Ron Mincy, Ron Ferguson, Virgulino "Vic" Duarte, Darius Mans, Maurice Boissiere, Linda Datcher, and Sylvia Roberts. We were not all in the same class, but we were all there together. Rhonda Williams and Susan Collins were to follow us. Oddly, I did not meet Phyllis Wallace, the black economist who was on the faculty of the Sloan School, until I left MIT.

The group possessed a general connection to the NEA, so it was natural that I join; I suspect that such a general connection does not exist for new black Ph.D.s coming on the market today. But when I attended my first ASSA convention seeking employment in December 1977 in New York City, I went as a member of the NEA also. That's when I first made contact with the wider NEA membership.

I have been involved regularly with NEA activities since then. I suspect that I was somewhat notorious for being inclined toward fairly radical views and for my reservations about orthodox economics. I suspect that I never will be invited to be on *Black Enterprise* magazine's Board of Black Economists because I remain wholly unconvinced that black business development will mean general economic improvement throughout the black community. I have long argued that the black middle class is in a near intractable, contradictory position, and I have been willing to argue explicitly that the rise of capitalism was intimately linked to slavery and the slave trade.

I find myself in a profession where a significant number of nonblack economists start with the prior belief that blacks, on average, are intellectually inferior. This means that the black economist must engage in a continuous act of double validation. The NEA always provided warmth and camaraderie where ill-formed or newly formed ideas could be tested more comfortably than elsewhere. When an idea fell flat, it did not mean that you were cast back toward the mean of the putative black frequency distribution. After all, here was one professional group of economists whose members did not start with a belief that there was a separate or distinct black frequency distribution of ability. Here was a group with whom I felt compatible both intellectually and socially. The NEA has been important to my professional development and my sanity.

I had the honor of serving as president-elect and president of the NEA in the mid-1980s. Other organizations have elected me to serve as an officer subsequently—the Eastern, the Southern, the AEA—and I have been honored to serve. But the NEA was the first. It is hard to say what the full scope of my contributions have been to the NEA. They certainly do not outweigh the benefits I have enjoyed from participation.

The first presidential address for the NEA was given by David Swinton. He started a new tradition for the organization. When I became president, I gave an address on Abram Harris. I believe that I inaugurated the lecture series in honor of the late St. Lucian economist and Nobel laureate Arthur Lewis during my presidency. I invited Lance Taylor to give the first address. Lewis and his wife, Gladys, attended the first lecture.

I also have served as chair of the Board of Editors of the *Review of Black Political Economy* for several years. But during my tenure all the hard work has been done by the editors—first, Margaret Simms, next James Stewart, and now Danny Boston. And I hope the NEA will find a way to make the connection with the new black Ph.D.s in the way that the connection was made for me in the late

1970s as a young man leaving MIT to embark upon an academic career.

Last Thoughts for the Moment

I am not certain that the path I have traveled provides a recipe for others to be "successful" as economists. Therefore, unlike some of the other essayists in this volume I have refrained from treating my path as a guidebook for others. In many ways, the route I have taken is the antithesis of what the best advice would dictate for professional success in this field.

I have opted to be more of a generalist than a specialist. I have an affinity for nonmainstream traditions in economics, rather than neoclassicism. I believe in the selective use of mathematical formalization, rather than its universal application. I am a black economist who has maintained a commitment to directing a large portion of my research agenda toward issues of concern to African-Americans, rather than staying away from research on race. Admittedly, I have followed the dictum "publish or perish" fairly closely, occasionally placing my work in highly visible journals. And, thus far, I have not perished.

The foregoing is a synopsis of the path I traveled and the way I traveled it. But more important are the reasons that motivated the journey, the reasons why I have done the work that I have done. Their origins lie in the person that I was becoming in my childhood and youth, and the central questions that disturbed and beguiled me. They still disturb and beguile me. And that is why I hope to continue to do the work that I will do.

AVINASH DIXIT

My System of Work (Not!)

Among the signals of approaching senility, few can be clearer than being asked to write an article on one's methods of work. The profession's implied judgment is that one's time is better spent giving helpful tips to younger researchers than doing new work oneself. However, of all the lessons I have learned during a quarter century of research, the one I have found most valuable is always to work as if one were still twenty-three. From such a young perspective, I find it difficult to give advice to anyone. The reason I agreed to write this piece will appear later. I hope readers will take it for what it is — scattered and brash remarks of someone who pretends to have a perpetually juvenile mind, and not the distilled wisdom of a middle-aged has-been.

Writing such a piece poses a basic problem at any age. There are no surefire rules for doing good research, and no routes that clearly lead to failure. Ask any six economists and you will get six dozen recipes for success. Each of them will flatly contradict one or more of the others. And all of them may be right — for some readers and at some times. So you should take all such suggestions with skepticism. Give a good try to any that appeal to you, but don't fear to disregard all the rest.

There is also the problem of judging the target audience. What works for academic research is not best suited for policy or consulting

This essay was previously published in *American Economist* 38, no. 1 (spring 1994): 10–16.

research, and the right strategy for advancing the frontier of research is not the same as that for later work of consolidation or synthesis. I will assume that the readers of these essays are actual or potential economists with high ambition; they aim to excel in whatever area of research they choose and are looking for good habits to speed their journey. In short, I will take it that the readers hope for success at the top levels of the research community.

These general difficulties are compounded by my own limitations. First, I am a theorist, albeit of a relatively applied kind. That is to say, I build mathematical models to address specific issues and contexts of economic interest, rather than abstract systems of general and overarching significance. And I try to get specific results from the models (What cause has what effect?) rather than prove theorems (Does equilibrium exist, and is it unique?). What works for me is governed by what I am trying to accomplish; the same approaches and techniques may not suit the more abstract theorists or the empirical economists.

My second limitation is even more severe. I have always worked on the next problem that grabbed my interest and tackled it using whatever approaches and techniques seemed suitable, never giving a thought to how it might fit into an overall worldview or methodology. It is hard for me to evaluate such an unsystematic and unphilosophical approach, and even harder to give any advice based on it. But I shall try.

My Own Experience of Research

Readers of these essays are surely not too interested in the drab and dreary lives of economists for their own sake; they are in search of research methods they can emulate. But one's advice is colored by one's experiences, and I owe the reader a brief statement of the reasons for my biases.

Most of us spend hours discussing at which restaurant to have dinner and make decisions like what career to pursue and whom to marry instinctively in an instant. So it was with my entry into economics. I got my first degree in mathematics and had just started a master's in operations research, when I was converted to economics by a chance conversation with Frank Fisher. He should get all the credit, or the blame.

I started on my research career in 1968, at a time of turmoil in the academic world of Europe and the United States. The prevailing atmosphere was decidedly left-wing and antiestablishment, and research was almost required to be "relevant." Most theorists were affected by this atmosphere, and I was no exception. Important topics included problems of less developed countries, urban problems, and environmental problems.[1] I dabbled in all of these.

Looking back on those years, one sees that much of the "relevant" research in economics left little lasting mark. Problems of less developed countries and urban areas proved so political that good economic advice would have achieved nothing even if we had been able to give it. No, the topics that proved to have lasting value in economics were quite different, for example the theory of rational expectations, the role of information and incentives, and later in this period, game theory. In the early 1970s much of this work seemed abstract and irrelevant and would have been called "politically incorrect" had that phrase existed in those days.

My own work also met the same fate. My "relevant" work is mostly and justly forgotten.[2] What has come to be regarded as a success—for example the theory of product diversity in monopolistic competition, the theory of entry deterrence in oligopoly, a reformulation of the theory of international trade, and some recent work on irreversible investment—was not motivated by any sense of relevance or any high-minded desire to do good. It is almost embarrassing to think back on how I came to work on some of these topics.

The book on international trade grew out of a lunchtime conversation with Victor Norman. He knew a fair bit about the subject, I knew almost nothing, but both of us knew a lot of duality theory and had a sense it might be useful in simplifying some of trade theory. We decided to learn by doing and spent so long at it that we had to write a book. As we went along, more than half of the time we found that someone else had been there before. But it was much more fun to do it ourselves.

The model of entry deterrence in oligopoly came from an uneasy feeling that the accepted theories—Bain-Sylos, and even Spence—were not doing it right. At the time subgame perfectness had just made its appearance in the game theory literature, but I was in rural England, far removed from the centers of game theory like Stanford, and had never heard of the concept. So I had to work it out from scratch, and that took a surprisingly long time. The breakthrough came when I had by mistake gone to the airport far too early and had to kill a couple of hours. Once the right idea came, everything worked out really fast. Since then I have often deliberately got to airports too early, but alas, with no similar success.

Much of this work was received favorably by some existing specialists in the fields but got puzzled and negative reactions from others: "Optimum product diversity? Surely the market finds the optimum. Monopolistic competition? That's a dead end." "Duality? What's wrong with the way we have always done things?" For years Ron Jones dismissively referred to the group working on oligopoly in international trade as "Imperfect competitors." By now I expect a "long and variable lag" between the time I work on something and the time enough others find interest or use in it. But I have learned the importance of trying to shorten the lag by conveying my ideas simply and clearly.

In this I am but one minor member of an extremely distinguished group. For example, William Sharpe struggled to get his now-famous CAPM paper published and recalls the reaction even after its appearance in print: "I knew . . . [t]he phone would start ringing any moment. After one year, total silence. Nobody cared. It took quite a while."[3]

As you can see, my approach to research is too opportunistic to have a constant direction. But taking stock of it for the purpose of writing this piece, I could see a recurrent if not dominant theme. Scale economies and sunk costs keep appearing in my papers with great regularity. Imperfect competition is the norm, and market equilibria are not socially optimal (but government interventions have more subtle effects than naive intuition would suggest and may actually make matters worse). And therein lies an irony. The left-wing critics of the late 1960s and 1970s, who influenced many youngsters when I started out, reserved their strongest criticism for the perfectly competitive equilibrium of the neoclassical system. Of course they did little by the way of offering a viable alternative. It has been the unexciting incremental work, to which I have contributed a little, that has built into a major shift in our understanding of how the economic system operates when the assumptions of neoclassical economics fail.

That is enough autobiography, and more than enough self-justification. For the rest of the article, I shall elaborate and paraphrase my experience into statements of what I have found to be good work habits. I will find it convenient to express these as items of advice, but let me repeat my earlier caution to the readers—be skeptical, pick what you think might suit you, and discard the rest.

On Choice of Topics

My most important advice here is stark and politically very incorrect: Don't give too much weight to the social importance of the issue; instead, do what captures your intellectual interest and creative imagination. This is not to deny the importance of paying attention to the real world. Nor is it to say that abstract theory is necessarily more valuable than applied work. Nothing could be farther from the truth. But I do believe that mere relevance of an issue will not guarantee good research unless you have a genuine drive to work on it. If not, leave it to someone else. Good work on an apparently unimportant problem will have more long-run value than mediocre work on one of greater intrinsic importance. And one's judgment of importance can always be wrong; concepts of relevance can change over time.

Of course if you find genuine passion for an issue of real social importance, count yourself twice blessed.

How can you know if you do have the real drive to do research on a particular topic? Perhaps the surest sign is that the work is fun. Richard Feynman, in a wonderful collection of anecdotes from his life ("not an autobiography," he insisted), gives a classic example of this.[4] Some students in the cafeteria were tossing around a dinner plate like a Frisbee. It was wobbling, and the red Cornell medallion on the plate seemed to be revolving faster than the wobble. Feynman set out to calculate the relation between the two rates and found a remarkably simple two-to-one ratio. He showed his work to a senior colleague, Hans Bethe.

> He said, "Feynman, that's pretty interesting, but what's the importance of it? Why are you doing it?"
>
> "There's no importance whatsoever. I'm just doing it for the fun of it." . . . And before I knew it . . . I was "playing"—working, really. . . . It was effortless.
>
> There was no importance to what I was doing, but ultimately there was. The diagrams and the whole business that I got the Nobel Prize for came from that piddling around with the wobbling plate.

Feynman uses a very revealing word: "playing." If your work is as enjoyable to you as play, that is a good sign that the topic suits you.

Looking over what I have just said, I realize that I am advocating something very radical: not only a nonsystem, but also a nonsystem for nonwork. But what did you expect from someone of twenty-three?

Every bright student who passes his/her general examinations sets out to revolutionize the subject. But revolutions are not best made by setting out to make them. In Thomas Kuhn's terminology, scientific revolutions are the consequences of attempts to resolve anomalies that are observed in the course of normal science. And the best way to notice anomalies is to do normal research. Kuhn has explained the process brilliantly.[5]

> Only investigations firmly rooted in the contemporary scientific tradition are likely to break that tradition and give rise to a new one. That is why I speak of an "essential tension" implicit in scientific research.
>
> At least for the scientific community as a whole, work within a well-defined and deeply ingrained tradition seems more productive of tradition-shattering novelties than work in which no similarly convergent standards are involved. How can this be so? I think it is because no other sort of work is nearly so well suited to isolate for continuing and concentrated attention those loci of trouble or causes of crises upon whose recognition the most fundamental advances in basic science depend. . . . Though the ability to recognize trouble when confronted by it is surely a requisite for scientific advance, trouble must not be too easily recognized. The scientist requires a thoroughgoing commitment to the tradition with which, if he is fully successful, he will break.

Discover your best "distance." Some people are good sprinters in research. They can very quickly spot and make a neat point; they do this frequently, and in many different areas and issues. Hal Varian and Barry Nalebuff are two of the best sprinters I know. In the same metaphor, others are middle-distance runners. In fact most economists are at some point in this broad category. A few, for example Robert Lucas and James Mirrlees, are marathoners; they run only a small number of races, but those are epics, and they get the most (and fully deserved) awe and respect. In contrast, the profession seems to undervalue sprinters. But each kind of work has its own value, and the different types are complements in the overall scheme of things. Progress of the subject as a whole is a relay race, where different stretches are of different lengths and are optimally run by different people. Find out where your comparative advantage lies.

Many ideas, and techniques for theorizing, will come to you by accident. But don't wait for such accidents to happen; facilitate them. Always be on the lookout for examples, questions, and so on that relate to what you are doing, or something you worked on once but set aside. A newspaper article or a current-affairs program or a chance remark by a colleague can get you started. A totally unrelated theoretical article may use a technique that proves useful for your problem and gets you restarted on something that had stalled. Seemingly far-fetched analogies turn out to have some deep basis. Therefore you should keep all of your work in your semiactive memory all of the time — the work in progress as well as that not making progress.

Learn to manage your time. When asked to contribute to a collective volume or present a paper at a conference, unless the assigned topic happens to coincide *exactly* with your interests, follow the Nancy Reagan strategy: "Just say no." You will invariably find the demands of such assignments crowding out the time that you could have spent on ideas of much greater intellectual interest to you. (In fact I took on the task of writing this article just to get that out.) Stick to what you would best like to do; if you are successful, some years later people will be holding conferences on your topic. (Of course by then you will be interested in something else.) In the meantime, you will have much more fun working on something that you really like. And even the material rewards of a successful frontier research article easily exceed the honoraria of ten conference articles of topical interest.

There are people who can turn a conference assignment into real research. Or to be accurate, there is one such person — Paul Krugman. Unless you have that very rare skill, get your priorities straight.

On Habits of Work
Management of your time is again of paramount importance. This is especially true when on occasion you are forced (or just irresistibly tempted) to violate the Nancy Reagan strategy and take on a conference-type assignment. Then I recommend the Nike strategy: "Just do it." Don't procrastinate to the deadline. If you do, you will waste a great deal of time all the while, thinking about the assignment and its impending deadline. You will also expend a lot of mental energy feeling weighed down by the task. Much better to get it out of the way as quickly and effortlessly as possible and get back to the real stuff.[6]

On the other hand, when doing frontier research of real intellectual importance and challenge, do not be afraid to spend a lot of time thinking vaguely, or even "daydreaming" around the subject. This time is not wasted. All the associations you ponder, and all the calculations you try for a few lines and abandon, will prove a useful input to the process that ultimately leads to the answer.

Having posed the question and worked on it for a while, give the subconscious a chance. Perhaps the best advice on this comes from the mathematician J. E. Littlewood, in his lovely article, "The Mathematician's Art of Work."[7] He distinguishes four phases in creative work: preparation, incubation, illumination, and verification. "In preparation, [t]he essential problem has to be stripped of accidentals and brought clearly into view, all relevant knowledge surveyed; possible analogues pondered. It should be kept constantly before the mind during intervals of other work. . . . Incubation is the work of the subconscious. . . . Illumination, which can happen in a fraction of a second, . . . almost always occurs when the mind is in a state of relaxation, and engaged lightly with ordinary matters." Littlewood recommends "the relaxed activity of shaving" as a fruitful time for illumination; I shudder to think how much *more* David Kreps, Paul Krugman, and Lars Svensson would have accomplished if they had known this.

In our profession it is customary to stress the importance of economic intuition and deride abstract or formal thinking. I have found this to be right on balance, but not to the point of dogma. People and problems vary in the kind of thinking that suits them best. For example, it appears that John von Neumann had a very abstract kind of mind. He once advised a coworker: "Oh no, no, you are not seeing it. Your kind of visualizing mind is not right for seeing this. Think of it abstractly. What is happening [on a photograph of an explosion] is that the first differential coefficient vanishes identically, and that is why what becomes visible is the trace of the second differential coefficient."[8] How many of us, hearing such an explanation from a colleague or a student, would have admonished them to "be more intuitive?"

Keep a "portfolio" of problems to work on. If you are not making progress on one, switch to another. You will not only diversify your risks, but also increase your chances of success on each, because your mind will stay fresher and you will feel less depressed about the lack of progress on one problem. But don't switch too rapidly; if a problem is at all challenging, less than a month's concentrated thinking about it may not be good enough.

Joint research is becoming more common in economics, and that is a good thing. A good research collaborator is worth any number of casually interested readers of your papers. The close but sympathetic criticism at an early stage that comes from a fellow worker helps you avoid many blind alleys or wrong tacks from which you might otherwise never recover. As Francis Crick put it, "The advantage of intellectual collaboration is that it helps jolt one out of false assumptions."[9] You and your ideal coauthor will have enough overlap to give both a common frame of reference and language for thinking, but enough difference to generate real synergy and complementarity rather than mere duplication.

Reserve your best and most alert period of the day for real research and use your tired, dull, or slack stretches for correspondence, meetings, administrative chores, and the like. Alas, this is often not possible. Keep in mind, too, the possibility that your best period changes with the seasons, age, etc. I have heard Paul Samuelson claim that for most people a switch occurs at around thirty-five years of age: morning becomes a better time for research instead of late at night. (Here I mean physical age; of course your mental age should stay constant at twenty-three.) My own experience confirms this.

Continue revising your papers to improve them, but not forever. The Austrian capital theory that you learned as a dry textbook model has practical application. Papers should be improved only to the point where the rate of improvement equals the rate of interest. The latter rate will vary over your life-cycle, but striving for absolute perfection is wrong for most people at most times. From a private perspective, it will delay the spread and impact of your work too much and risk preemption. From a social perspective, public release of something that is less than perfect has value; it may be someone else's comparative advantage to contribute the next step of improvement.

Read other people's papers either seriously, or not at all. When you read them seriously, read them as you read papers when you were a graduate student, checking all the details and questioning everything. This is a good way to get new research ideas of your own. I owe my own understanding of the importance of this principle to Richard Feynman. He describes how he came to discover the law of beta decay.[10]

At that particular time I was not really quite up to things. Everybody seemed to be smart, and I didn't feel I was keeping up. . . . At one point there was a meeting in Rochester . . . and Lee was giving his paper on the violation of parity. . . . I was staying with my sister in Syracuse. I brought the paper home and said to her, "I can't understand these things Lee and Yang are saying. It's all so complicated." "No," she said, "what you mean is not that you can't understand it, but that you didn't invent it. You didn't figure it out your own way, from hearing the clue. What you should do is imagine you're a student again, and take this paper upstairs, read every line of it, and check the equations. Then you'll understand it very easily."

She was right. Not only did Feynman understand the paper, but he remembered something he had done a while ago, used that method to simplify Lee's solution, and forged ahead to develop the whole new theory.

Oddly enough, when I read this I was in a somewhat similar state of mind with regard to the literature on trade policy with asymmetric information, and the same recipe worked for me.[11]

On Writing

My first suggestion is: Keep it simple. The temptation to show one's technical wizardry is overwhelming, particularly for the fresh Ph.D. Resist it. It will only make your paper less easy to read and reduce its impact. If an idea can be conveyed in a simpler way, without spelling out every epsilon and delta, do so. Littlewood says of Jordan that if he wrote an article with only four symbols they would be called a, M'_3, ϵ_2, and $\Pi''_{1,2}$ instead of a, b, c, d; don't be like that.[12] If needed for completeness, put the more formal proof in an appendix. However, I find totally unacceptable the current and growing practice of many papers in economic theory, which merely state the results in the text without any explanation and relegate the proofs to an appendix.

I said earlier that pure economic intuition may or may not be the right way to *think* in research. Its importance increases when one *writes* research results, and even more when one *talks* about them, particularly if the intended audience is larger than that of specialists in a very narrow area. (Many fresh Ph.D.'s giving job talks do not realize the importance of a simple and intuitive exposition, and this costs them dearly.)

My second suggestion is: Keep it short. In this I agree with Piet Hein, the Danish scientist turned poet who wrote aphoristic verses called Grooks. He preferred writers

> who find their writing such a chore
> they only write what matters.

But this seems a lost cause. Over the last two decades the average length of economics papers has increased quite a lot. Advances in word-processing technology have greatly reduced the cost of producing words, but not the cost of producing ideas, with the result economists should expect — massive substitution.

My ideal is neatly captured in a question Frank Hahn posed to an author. As an editor of the *Review of Economic Studies,* Hahn asked the author to cut down his paper from forty pages to its essential core of three pages. When the author wrote a long and indignant letter, Hahn responded in two sentences: "Crick and Watson described the structure of DNA in three pages. Kindly explain why your idea deserves more space." An ideal that, alas, neither I nor Frank Hahn nor anyone else seems to come close to.

Listen to referees: Referees may be prejudiced, they may be hurried, but they are almost never stupid. If you are doing innovative work, be prepared to meet bias, and be prepared to meet careless dismissal. Give such reports due consideration — even they may contain useful tips for revision — but if you have basic confidence in what you are doing, press on. If you meet sheer incomprehension, however, take that as a sign that your writing has failed. Clarify, if necessary overhaul the whole notation of your formal model, and try new drafts on colleagues and students, until you communicate better. I come across many economists who constantly complain that "referees don't understand them." When I hear this, I think of Tom Lehrer's remark: "If a person can't communicate, the very least he can do is to shut up."

There are conflicting considerations on how hard to sell your work. On the one hand, if you don't sell your own work, the chances are that no one else will. Littlewood has the mot juste once again.[13] "He that bloweth not his own trumpet, his trumpet shall not be blown." On the other hand, excessive claims about the importance of your work will get you a bad reputation in the profession and will jeopardize the reception of your future work. I prefer to claim a little less for my work than I feel it deserves.

If you must exaggerate, do so in a skillful way. Joseph Schumpeter claimed that he set out to become the best horseman in Vienna, the best lover in Europe, and the best economist in the world, and had achieved two out of the three. This is brilliant exaggeration, reducing the risk of being found out—anyone who could personally assess Schumpeter's prowess in any one of the three things would give him the benefit of the doubt and assume that he had excelled in the *other* two.

A Concluding Word

I have saved for the end the most important lesson I have learned from my experience, and which I believe has very general validity. Maintain a youthful sense of freedom to choose problems and the directions of work on them. Imagine yourself at twenty-three, not yet labeled or confined to a particular "field," and not yet pressured to produce something quickly for the approaching tenure review. Try to preserve this mental frame in your research, even as your body, and the part of your mind dealing with other matters, continue to age and decay.

Unfortunately, in the United States most academics do not regain this freedom until they are thirty-five, by which time it is too late for many of them to be twenty-three. Their research brain is beyond rejuvenation, and it is time for them to leave the research frontier and join the conference circuit or the policy community. My reaction as a theorist echoes what Clemenceau said on hearing that the famous pianist Paderewski had become the president of the newly founded Polish Republic: "What a comedown!"

NOTES

1. And for reasons that escape me, quite abstruse arguments in capital theory that acquired inexplicable ideological significance. But that fashion died, as it richly deserved to.

2. I wrote one paper in urban economics—a model of the optimum size of a city trading off scale economies in production and congestion diseconomies in transport—that achieved some success. I like to think that even now, when theoretical urban economists meet for a beer at a conference, someone might remark: "Wonder what became of that guy Dixit. He wrote one paper that wasn't bad and was never heard from again. I guess some people just don't have staying power in research."

3. Quoted in Peter Bernstein, *Capital Ideas* (New York: Free Press, 1992), 199.

4. Richard Feynman, *"Surely You're Joking, Mr. Feynman!"* (New York: Norton, 1985), 157–58.

5. Thomas S. Kuhn, *The Essential Tension: Selected Studies in Scientific Tradition and Change* (Chicago: University of Chicago Press, 1977), 227, 234–35.

6. I have to confess that I have not optimized my own time as I advise you to, and that I have too often violated both the Nancy Reagan strategy and the Nike strategy. These are merely what in the light of hindsight I wish I had done consistently.

7. J. E. Littlewood, "The Mathematician's Art of Work," in *Littlewood's Miscellany,* ed. Bela Bollobas, (Cambridge: Cambridge University Press, 1986).

8. Norman Macrae, *John von Neumann* (New York: Pantheon Books, 1992), 211.

9. Francis Crick, *What Mad Pursuit: A Personal View of Scientific Discovery* (London: Penguin Books, 1990), 70.

10. Feynman, *"Surely You're Joking,"* 227–28.

11. But, as with the Nancy Reagan and Nike strategies above, I must confess that I have not followed my own advice on serious reading as consistently as I should have.

12. *Littlewood's Miscellany,* 60. Incidentally, on pp. 49–53 of the same book, Littlewood gives a beautiful example of how not to, and how to, write up a mathematical argument; I urge every young theorist to read it and absorb its lesson.

13. In *Littlewood's Miscellany,* 158.

BENJAMIN M. FRIEDMAN

Principles of Economics

Most kinds of intellectual endeavor hold out the prospect of a particular satisfaction, that associated with expanding the possibilities for thinking about ourselves and the world in which we live. Economics is no exception. To be sure, economics does have its particularities—an idiosyncratic mixture of a priori theorizing and data-based empiricism, a commitment to apply the scientific method despite the inability to carry out replicable or even controlled experiments, a closeness to certain contentious political issues, and so on—and as economists we are rightly aware of them. But in the end it is the similarity to other avenues of the intellectual enterprise that is more compelling, including not just the physical sciences but history, philosophy, and even literature and the arts. As a consequence, the core principles of what makes for good economics are probably pretty similar to the route to finding satisfaction in most other intellectual pursuits: Have an agenda, and know why it's important. Be awake; look around. Be ambitious but not overambitious. Have staying power. Decide who is the audience, and learn how to reach it. Keep things in perspective.

These principles may sound obvious, or empty, or both, but I doubt that when I first became an economist I understood them in the way I do now, and I certainly don't pretend that I have unfailingly adhered to them at every point since. Economics, again in common with so many other endeavors, is very much a matter of learning by

This essay was previously published in *American Economist* 39, no. 2 (fall 1995): 28–36.

doing. I think I have learned, along the way, about what the satisfactions of doing economics are and what general working principles are helpful for achieving them. My object here is therefore not so much to report what I have done, or even what I always now do, but to extract from both what I believe works best.

Have an Agenda, and Know Why It's Important

The agenda of economics is to understand an important aspect of the human experience: why we behave as we do in certain contexts, both individually and collectively; what consequences follow from the fact that we behave in this way; and in light of this behavior and its predictable consequences, what we might do, either individually or collectively, to improve our lot in this world. Saying this, especially to trained professionals, may seem either trivial or trite. But it is surely not trivial, and if it is trite it is also very often forgotten.

A distinction between empirical and axiomatic approaches to the questions at hand is familiar in many sciences, and economics is again no exception. In my own work I have always felt more comfortable following an empirical approach, by which I mean starting with some aspect of economic behavior that we actually observe and seeking an explanation. Why do aggregate production and income grow faster at some times than others, and sometimes not at all? Why do interest rates vary, and why do they covary among one another, as they do? How do businesses decide how much to borrow, and in what form? The axiomatic approach, starting with a few first principles and logically determining what consequences follow from specific additional assumptions, has been just as central to economic inquiry if not more so. But the greater risk, I usually think, is that of applying impeccable logic to proceed from assumption to conclusion when neither bears much actual connection to the behavior of the real people and institutions, and hence the real economies, that I regard as our subject's proper object of study.

Under either approach, however, it is essential to be able to say why the effort is worthwhile in the first place. The initial question I try to answer for myself whenever I embark on a fresh project — when I begin a new (at least for me) line of research, or pursue an intriguing loose end left by work I have been doing, or offer a new course for students — is "Why am I doing this?" What can I learn, and why might that be valuable? Is the behavior I want to examine important in its own right? Or is the knowledge to be gained important because it might shed light on some related question? In that case, why is this other question important? The main reason I find it more comfortable to begin work from an empirical direction is that that way I find it easier to answer these questions — and they can often be hard questions — about what I am doing and why.

By contrast, setting out to do research without thinking through why it is potentially worth doing is like trying archery in the dark. There is some small probability that any randomly directed arrow will reach the target, and with enough bowmen taking enough blind shots, inevitably some will. Similarly, some few economists who are entirely unaware of the broader context that might make others value their findings will probably hit the bull's-eye anyway. But the likelihood of doing so is far greater if a keen sensitivity to just that broader context shapes not only the selection of the question to be attacked but also the means of investigating it. Some empirical findings, and some theorems, become important because they give answers to questions people genuinely want answered; others don't because they don't.

The immediate implication of this seemingly obvious point is that, with limited time to spend, not everything that is doable is worth doing. Specifically, not every extension to a theorem is worth proving, nor is every empirical observation worth explaining. Even more to the point, especially for purposes of younger researchers, the mere fact that so-and-so has published a paper on some subject or other does not by itself make that subject worth further investigation. (It may not have merited so-and-so's original paper either, but that's a different matter.) Reading the journals is an excellent way to learn research methods; it's a poor way to choose research topics.

What does lead to good research questions? Here too, I have usually found the attractions of the empirical approach compelling. If the object of economics in the first place is to understand certain aspects of behavior by individuals and institutions, or its consequences for whole economies, then the most straightforward way to find simulating topics is to observe that behavior. For behavior in the aggregate, that mostly means listening to the questions concerned people are asking. For individual behavior, just watch. For behavior by institutions, find a way to watch.

When I was a graduate student, I took on a series of either part-time or limited-term assignments for various components of the Federal Reserve System. One was to study the conceptual structure underlying the Board staff's presentation of information to the Federal Open Market Committee. (The key question was how to structure the conditionality of future economic outcomes on the committee's own monetary policy decisions.) Another was to serve on a committee, made up of representatives from the Board and some of the regional banks, to recommend how best to introduce money growth targets into the Open Market Committee's policy decisions. (In those days — as is the case again today — the Federal Reserve didn't use money growth targets.) The first job I took after finishing my formal education was working at a New York investment banking firm. I wasn't in the economics department (the firm didn't have one at the time) but rather divided my time between the part of the business that worked with corporate clients on their bond issues and the part that sold the securities to institutional investors. Much of my subsequent research — on the theory of economic policy, on targets and instruments of monetary policy, on corporate-borrowing decisions, on portfolio behavior and the determination of interest rates, on the role of credit markets in influencing macroeconomic activity — grew out of these early firsthand exposures to actual economic behavior. For just the same reason, in more recent years I have valued highly the opportunity to work with some financial institutions on the kind of sustained basis over time that has let me watch, and ask questions about, how they conduct their business. (By contrast, I rarely accept one-shot assignments.)

Regardless of whether research is empirical or axiomatic, however, the question of importance remains essential. The value to me of those early opportunities to see some interesting institutions at close hand was not just in suggesting research questions but in showing me who wanted to know the answers to what questions, and why. The object — the source of satisfaction from the enterprise as a whole — is not to maximize the number of published papers to one's credit but to shed as much useful light on the subject as possible. If the first question I ask myself is why I think a potential topic is important, the second is who will be interested, or better yet surprised — or even better still, discomfited — by the potential findings. In much of my work on monetary policy, for example, the objective has been to show that key aspects of behavior in the economy in which we happen to live make mechanistic rules for central-bank conduct unhelpful. I thought that work was worth doing (and I still think so) not just because the subject is inherently important but also because so many people prefer to think the opposite. The ultimate question for any researcher is always how people will see that particular slice of the subject differently because he or she has worked on it.

Be Awake: Look Around

If the objective is to shape one's own research agenda in light of the actual behavior we observe and seek to explain, it helps to pay attention. New phenomena — the corporate debt explosion of the 1980s, for example, or the OPEC oil price increase in the 1970s — are especially interesting, either because they represent a new form of behavior or because they provide a new window for analyzing aspects of economic behavior that are already familiar but only from other lights. But it is striking how much there is to learn from simply watching people and institutions do what they have always done, or from listening to people describe what they do.

One reason this kind of observation of the ordinary is so important is that economic thinking (that is, the thinking of professional economists) is so often blinkered by the assumptions we impose and, moreover, that those assumptions are themselves so arbitrary. Aspects of everyday behavior that do not fit conveniently within the framework determined by whatever assumptions are fashionable at the moment remain, for all practical purposes, invisible. An example on which I worked for a while, alas in the days before doing so was fully respectable, is credit rationing. It is embarrassing today to recall the air of derisive ridicule with which distinguished economists not long ago dismissed even the possibility that lenders might adopt any strategy other than raising the interest rates they charged so as to bring loan demand into equality with loan supply. The fact that almost everybody who knew at close hand about loan markets thought bankers did sometimes ration credit, and said so, was simply no match for the fact that there was no formal maximizing model capable of rationalizing such behavior. But as soon as someone thought to bring to bear in a formal way such notions as asymmetric information, adverse selection, and moral hazard, then of course credit rationing might occur, and a subject once better ignored in polite professional company became open game for accepted scientific investigation.

The point is not that simplifying assumptions (in this case, perfect information) are not useful — indeed, they are necessary to carry out any serious analysis — but that the conventionally accepted simplifying assumptions of the day are often highly arbitrary and hence subject to change, and therefore that there is no shame in choosing new ones when observed behavior doesn't fit snugly within the usuals. Just as for a long time the prevailing theoretically correct thinking rejected even the possibility of credit rationing, for a time (mercifully brief) the prevailing theoretically correct opinion took on faith that because people's expectations were rational, preannounced monetary-policy actions simply couldn't affect output or employment. In this case it wasn't long before numerous economists pointed out that the models that gave rise to this conclusion rested not only on a quite specific (and, on reflection, perhaps unsuitable) notion of "rationality" but also on a host of other questionable assumptions like frictionless adjustment of prices and wages. Even so, for some years every conference on macroeconomics was forced to listen to the repeated assertion that economists would have to proceed as if this model were a good characterization of the world because "it's the only well worked out model we've got." Here again, the presumption was that behavior simply could not exist because there was (as yet) no maximizing model to account for it.

For purposes of doing theoretical economics, the antidote to such wrong-headedness is to look for new assumptions. As in the credit-rationing example, maybe information isn't perfect. As in the monetary-policy example, maybe markets don't adjust frictionlessly. The range of conventional assumptions subject to challenge is enormous. Maybe personal utilities aren't independent. Maybe aggregation does matter. Maybe the dependence of this on that isn't linear. (Much interesting literature in recent years has usefully explored conditions that give rise to multiple equilibria, but of course that possibility follows immediately when the relevant behavioral relationships are nonlinear.)

For purposes of empirical work, the message is that an observed phenomenon is no less interesting to study just because nobody has yet written down a maximizing model to explain it. Indeed, in that case empirical findings may be the best clue to what assumptions need changing in order to deliver just such a model. As I have listened over time to the questions that my friends in public-policy institutions and in private business firms ask, I am often struck by how little we —

economists — have to say about what they want to know. (Sometimes I am struck by how much we know, but here my point is different.) In part, these lacunae persist because it is genuinely hard to learn about some kinds of behavior and their consequences. But in some cases we have just not asked the right questions.

A whole other reason for paying attention to what is happening, and to what people are saying, is that the behavior we study changes. Not behavior in the sense of the ultimate underlying "metamodel," of course; but what economists actually study is not the metamodel but behavior in one usually tiny piece of it that takes the rest as given. For just this reason, institutions — legal arrangements, business practices, social mores, and so on — matter importantly for many aspects of economic behavior. And when those institutions change, economic relationships that depend on them, in ways either obvious or subtle, change as well. There is a tautological sense in which it must be true that inflation is "always and everywhere a monetary phenomenon," but that is not the sense in which many people in the United States understood this notion a couple of decades ago, before observed inflation and the conventional M's began to go their separate ways. Simply to assume that answers to important questions derived from past experience remain right answers is to miss much of what is interesting and important about our subject.

Finally, yet another reason why it helps to look around is that the questions people ask change too. To be sure, issues like the real costs of disinflation, or the value of creating a market for price-indexed securities, or the gain in efficiency from indexing the tax code, are always valid subjects for economic research. But it is hardly surprising that more people want to pay attention to the findings of research on those questions when prices are rising rapidly than when prices are more nearly stable. For the same reason, whether government budget deficits in a fully employed economy crowd out private capital formation, or under what circumstances a deficit would have to be monetized, was not much of an issue in the United States before the 1980s. This did not mean that there was no point in addressing such questions before then. But the context that determines whether any specific piece of research speaks to a matter of broad concern, and hence has the potential ability to have significant impact on widespread thinking, clearly changed. People who don't look around don't notice.

Be Ambitious, But Not Too Ambitious

Rabbi Tarphon, a noted sage of the first century, declared, "You are not required to finish the task, but neither are you free to neglect it altogether." Tarphon's injunction has always seemed to me a useful beacon for researchers, especially in economics. The part about not neglecting the task is obvious enough, but I think the idea that finishing it is not required is useful, indeed important, for maintaining a sense of purpose.

A curious outsider, taking a fresh look at economics, is less likely to be struck by how much we know than how much we don't. Few established empirical findings are genuinely stable across time and space. Most theoretical results depend on a vast array of simplifying assumptions. Many of these assumptions — atomistic competitors, independent utilities, linear functional relationships, identical "representative" agents, and so on — have over time become sufficiently conventional in the eyes of practicing researchers that they seem to require no justification (indeed, they are often taken for granted without even an explicit mention); but to the thoughtful outsider they may seem not just strange but factually wrong (as, of course, they are). Especially for someone newly beginning a research career, the resulting temptation can be to reject the entire working apparatus of modern economics as epistemologically flawed, and set out to erect a whole new edifice in its place.

That strategy is a recipe for failure. Discontent with the artificiality of whatever set of arbitrary assumptions is in fashion at the moment is a healthy motivation for making progress. Seeking to abandon useful workaday assumptions wholesale is a bar to making any progress whatever. There is tension but not conflict in wanting to change many aspects of how economists think yet actually investigating only one such change at a time. There is conflict but not fundamental inconsistency in attacking one unappealing assumption in one line of research while going ahead to use that same assumption, unappealing though it may be, in another line of research where the focus is different. The history of our subject shows that progress comes incrementally, in the middle ground between finishing the task and neglecting it altogether. Economics is a task that no one is required to finish, not even in one lifetime much less in one paper. The practical consequences of trying to finish this particular task are often indistinguishable from those of simply neglecting it.

A different form of overambition in economic research is the

Icarus problem: trying to fly too close to the universal sun, in the sense of supposing that a particular piece of research comes closer to the ultimate metamodel than it (or anything else that is really feasible) can. The metamodel by definition takes all factors into account. It doesn't change with circumstances not controlled for, because it controls for all relevant circumstances. By contrast, fruitful economic research focuses on only a few key variables at a time, leaving the rest aside. This is not a flaw to be endlessly lamented but a fact to be usefully remembered.

In particular, this means that the universality that we might like to pretend for our findings, because we appropriately aspire to it, just isn't there. Our results are local results. As environments and institutions change, so will even our favorite empirical relationships, and even our favorite theorems depend on more assumptions than we usually enumerate. This does not make our work valueless, just limited. By now many of the empirical relationships describing credit market behavior (and especially the borrowing behavior of firms) that I labored to investigate some years ago no longer correspond to current data. I may be sorry about that, but I do not have to regard the basic lessons of that work as worthless. The models I used were at best only small pieces of the metamodel, and as factors that I omitted from my analysis changed, so did the observed behavior.

A closely related temptation, also to be avoided, is the monocular syndrome — that is, the tendency of economists to assert monocausal explanations for complex phenomena. For many if not most problems, the most effective research strategy is not only to work on explaining one aspect of economic behavior at a time but also to focus on only one part of the explanation at a time. Not infrequently, a useful exercise is even to see how far it is possible to go in explaining the behavior in question on the basis of the one causal factor under investigation at the moment. All this makes for good economics. But it is important not to take such exercises too seriously and so conclude that some important aspect of economic behavior really does have only one causal force behind it.

For reasons that are closely related to both the Icarus problem and the monocular syndrome, I have always been reluctant to extrapolate what we know from one context to others where essential aspects of the environment are different. A useful example is the study of hyperinflation (about which I too once wrote a paper). Hyperinflations are certainly interesting phenomena in their own

right, not least because of their sometimes powerful political consequences. But can we apply the lessons drawn from examining the
demand for money during hyperinflations, when one influence on
portfolio choice is enlarged to a magnitude such that it actually does
dwarf all others, to draw inferences about money demand under
more ordinary circumstances? Can the experience of ending hyperinflations usefully inform our estimate of the likely costs of a transition from moderate but persistent inflation to price stability? I am
usually inclined to be skeptical of such extrapolations. Instead, if I
want to learn about a question, I try to study it in its own context.
(For just the same reason, I almost always disappoint foreign journalists who ask me what advice I would give their own governments. I'm
not being either politically careful or overly polite; I just don't think I
know.)

Yet a different form of overambition in economic research is to
require too much of a model, and in particular to strive for false
depth. Here the example that comes most readily to mind is the
treatment of the demand for money. Some years ago it became fashionable to argue that it is illegitimate to draw inferences about monetary policy from any model that lacks an internal explanation for why
people hold money. (For reasons that I never understood, in much of
this literature it was further regarded as bad form to acknowledge
that the reason for holding money might have something to do with
its usefulness in effecting transactions.) Why people hold money is
surely a useful and important question for economic research to
address. But it is also surely useful to do different research on the
basis of assuming that people in fact do hold money and proceeding
on from there. Insisting that both efforts must cohabit within the
same model is a bit like wanting the driver's manual to contain a
chapter on the origins of the convention that cars go on green and
stop on red, or on why different countries opt for the right or the left
side of the road. Division of labor does have its uses.

Have Staying Power

One of the hardest things to decide in pursuing any agenda, including
an intellectual one, is how long to stay the course. Nobody wants to
give up too easily, just because people are initially resistant to a
seemingly worthwhile idea, or because a few pieces of partial evidence point the other way. At the same time, nobody wants to hold

onto an idea long after overwhelming evidence has contradicted it. Resolving this tension is rarely easy.

On balance, though, I'm usually inclined to stay the course more persistently than not. One reason is that much of economics suffers deeply from the short-sample problem. It is not just that we can't conduct replicated experiments to address most economic questions, or that the one history we have does not represent a controlled experiment. The added difficulty is that for purposes of many of the questions we want to ask, that history is short. It is short in part because environments and institutions matter, and they change. We may have data on the volume of bank loans extending back into the nineteenth century, but the loan market today differs from the markets of earlier eras in so many ways — loan securitization, hedging capabilities, and competition from the commercial paper market as well as from abroad come immediately to mind — that data from decades ago is of limited value for many research purposes. Our history is short also because observations are not independent across either time or space. Regardless of whether we divide the data yearly, quarterly, or monthly, how many genuinely independent observations does the postwar rise and then decline of inflation contain? How many independent observations does the growth experience of twenty-four OECD countries contain? While this line of thinking is certainly not ground for despairing of ever learning from empirical analysis, it does make me pause before too quickly changing my mind because I have seen one new set of regressions.

The continually shifting tide of fashion in acceptable assumptions provides yet another reason for resisting pressure to abandon an idea that usefully seems to explain the behavior we observe. As the example of credit rationing shows, what respectable opinion deems impossible can become part of what "everybody knows" with astonishing suddenness. I sometimes wonder whether I should have continued doing research on credit rationing, since I have always believed it is an important aspect of bank behavior. I know I would not have worked out the crucial maximizing model based on asymmetric information and adverse selection — my personal toolkit is not well designed for that particular task — but I am at least curious about what evidence and insights a sustained program of empirical research on just this aspect of financial behavior might have produced.

But saying that one should stay the course despite opposition and even some contrary evidence is not to say never to change one's mind. The object, after all, is to learn. Sometimes observed behavior actually does present pretty dramatic statements one way or the other. For example, I used to be receptive to the idea that saving is positively interest elastic, and I therefore was sympathetic to the general class of policy proposals for stimulating private saving to which a positive elasticity gives rise. After the decline in U.S. saving rates in the 1980s, in the face of truly extraordinary increases in real after-tax returns, I have changed my view. (I think the same decline in saving, in the face of record government deficits at full employment, was likewise pretty devastating to the notion of Ricardian equivalence; but on that one I was a disbeliever much earlier on.)

I have also learned over time that the United States is much more of an open economy than I used to think. The biggest mistake I made in thinking about the policy issues of the last decade and a half was to underestimate how much the U.S. government's budget deficit would affect the country's net export balance (and thereby change the direction of capital flows), and correspondingly overestimate how much it would affect our domestic investment. The standard closed-economy model that shapes my most basic economic intuitions just wasn't adequate. I've also learned over time that price inflation is a much more serious problem than I used to believe — even though I still don't think our profession (me included) has much understanding of why.

So, changing one's mind is important too. But on balance, when the issue is in doubt, I'm inclined to stay the course and wait for others to change theirs. Most of the pictures on the walls in my study are portraits. The largest by far is of Winston Churchill, a man of determinedly held views if there ever was one. From the late 1920s on, Churchill was not just out of office but without real influence, his views rejected and ultimately ridiculed by the conventional wisdom of the time. He did not hold public office again until the fact of the opening of the war made it obvious that he had been right all along, and he became prime minister just nine months later. He was then sixty-five years old.

Decide Who Is the Audience, and Learn How to Reach It

I occasionally hear it said of some economist or other that he would be happiest just writing papers and putting them in his desk drawer, deriving ample satisfaction from the repeated act of analytical creation without ever showing its fruits to other people. I have never met such an economist. In a very few instances I have heard an economist I knew described in this way, but in each case I knew the person well enough to realize that what was said about him wasn't true.

Most economists, perhaps all of us, want not only to do interesting thinking but to communicate it to others. More than that, most of us want to persuade other people to accept our thinking. The principal means of communication are talking and writing. Of the two, writing is what lasts.

In our era writing by academics in general, and by economists in particular, has become the butt of stock jokes. I think that's unfair. To be sure, much writing by economists is simply bad. But much is quite good, and many economists write extremely well. Making younger economists think that they have somehow inherited a generic professional disability, a kind of congenital handicap against which they will have to contend for the entirety of their careers, does no one a service. The point is simply that writing well is an important part of communicating effectively, and an especially important part of persuading effectively, and that this is true for economists in the same way it is true for people who seek to communicate and persuade in countless other professions. As with anything else, the main secret to success is working hard at it. In the case of writing, this mostly means going back to it again and again and again — to find just the right word, to restructure a sentence or a paragraph, to insert a new thought, and sometimes even to change around the whole logical flow. My colleague John Kenneth Galbraith once referred to "the appearance of effortless ease that creeps into my [Ken's] prose on about the eighth draft." He was indirectly offering me advice, and I've tried to take it seriously.

Some dimensions of the matter, however, probably are harder for economists. The one I think is especially important is that many economists want — appropriately — to communicate with several different audiences who happen to use different languages. We want, in the first instance, to speak among ourselves. But academic economists also need to speak to their students, and business economists need to speak to others in their firm or to their customers. Many economists also want to speak to policymakers from time to time. Some occasionally want to address a more general public.

The problem of different languages is real. My first exposure to the Federal Reserve System was a summer job in the research department of the Federal Reserve Bank of New York. By then I had studied economics for four years in college and two more in graduate school. Although most of the people I talked with at the bank that summer were professional economists, I quickly realized that I just didn't understand what they were saying. (I don't mean that I didn't understand why the theory underlying what they said was valid; I literally did not understand many of the conversations taking place.) As I eventually discovered, they were in fact talking about things I had learned about. But they used a different vocabulary than I knew, and they left much of the context implicit.

Vocabulary and context are crucial to communicating effectively, and it makes little sense to address an audience in anything other than its own vocabulary or without providing the right context. I think much of the usual popular derision of academic writing stems from the reaction of one audience, either practitioners or perhaps even interested laymen, to material written for research professionals who constitute a wholly different audience. The vocabulary is strange, and even the words that should be familiar lack the context to give them genuine meaning.

American populism has always exhibited an anti–intellectual strain, and so the congressman who wants to score points by making fun of the silly professors can easily draw laughs by reading selected passages from the professional journals in just about any academic discipline. While few layman are inclined to think they should be able to understand astrophysics or Byzantine theology, many non-economists do think they should be able to understand matters of economics. More importantly, citizens in a democratic republic have not only a right but, indeed, an obligation to understand major issues of economic policy. While I am often struck by how little economists know about the questions that interested laymen or public-policy officials or business executives ask, in many cases I think we do know much that is useful. But it remains to communicate to them what we know. I think it is to our credit that so many economists want to address these nonprofessional audiences. But we can do so effectively only if we use a vocabulary that they can understand and if we provide the context that makes what we say meaningful.

Here too, what makes this kind of communication succeed is largely putting effort into it. If I think congressmen, or bankers, or businessmen may be interested in the findings of the research I have been doing, I have to accept the fact that simply sending around reprints of my latest journal articles won't do. I have to decide whether I want to convey my ideas to those audiences or not. And if I do, then I know I have to write an account of those ideas directed at the audience I want to reach.

Some of my academic colleagues who read my *Day of Reckoning* book, as well as some friends in the financial community, told me they would have found the book easier to follow — not to mention a lot shorter — if I had included some tables and time series plots to exhibit the most important trends and relationships in the data. They were right. (One person, whom I didn't know, sent me a letter saying he assumed I must have been writing from a set of tables, and asking if I could provide him with a copy.) But I didn't write that particular book for them. I deliberately chose a purely literary presentation — no tables, no data plots, no diagrams, and certainly no equations — because I wanted people to read it who would simply have put it down if they had paged through it and spotted any of these devices. I knew that once people actually decided to read the book, some well-chosen tables and plots would have made it easier for many if not most. But I decided that for this particular effort at communication, the audience I wanted to reach included large numbers of people who, if they saw tables and data plots, would probably never read it at all.

Writing a book this way — producing a purely literary presentation of a subject we economists usually discuss among ourselves using both shorthand and shortcuts — was, of course, time consuming. It took away from research I otherwise could have done. (That book was not research; I like to think of it as high-class journalism.) But I took the time because I thought that that particular effort at communicating, and persuading, was important. I felt about it, in some ways, a sense of moral obligation.

Keep Things in Perspective
One of our presidents once remarked that a major personal challenge for people charged with public responsibility, especially at high levels, is to take their decisions appropriately seriously yet not take themselves too seriously. I think scholars face the same tension. We devote our lives to research and teaching on issues that we deem important. We take these issues and our work on them very seri-

ously, and we are right to do so. But we do ourselves — and others too — a disservice if we fall into the trap of also taking ourselves too seriously.

Steering clear of this particular temptation is no doubt a matter of many dimensions, but in my own experience two especially stand out. First, some of the friendships I have valued most over the years have been (and still are) with economists whose views directly contradict my own. We disagree with each other in our papers, we debate each other at conferences, and we argue with each other when we get together just to enjoy each other's company. I admire these friends, and I have learned from them. But more important, in the end, they are my friends and I value them simply for that. Another eminent sage, Isi ben Judah, asked "Why do scholars die prematurely?" His answer? "Because they abuse one another." Taking ourselves less seriously than we take the ideas on which we work may or may not enable us to live longer, but I think it does help to keep our work from obstructing personal relationships that can be deeply satisfying.

The other sense in which trying not to take ourselves too seriously has been important to me reflects a lesson I learned in a vivid way years ago when I worked in investment banking. I frequently worked on assignments with Robert Baldwin, a quite senior partner who soon afterward became head of the firm. I remember especially clearly the experience, on several occasions, of sitting in his office with a team of other partners and staff members, trying to schedule an important meeting with one major client or other. Somebody would suggest a date, everybody in the room would agree, and then Bob would check his calendar and declare that that was impossible because it was the day of his son's school play (or hockey game, or whatever was the particular event that time). Everybody else would exchange knowing glances, as if to say, "This guy is nuts, but we have to humor him," and eventually somebody would go on to suggest a new date. In the meanwhile, my own (silent) reaction was more along the lines of "This guy is the only one here who understands what's important."

Balancing our personal and our professional involvements is a tension that we all face. As is usually the case with such tensions, having a clear sense of priorities helps. I've always had mine pretty clear. My wife and sons come first.

But all this brings me back to where I began: Having an agenda is crucial. So is knowing why it's important.

CLAUDIA GOLDIN

The Economist as Detective

I have always wanted to be a detective and have finally succeeded. As a small child I was determined to become an archaeologist and learn the secrets of the mummies at the Museum of Natural History. But when I read Paul de Kruif's *The Microbe Hunters* (1927) in junior high school, I realized that my true calling was not in archaeology but in bacteriology. Microscopic mummies were more challenging and held secrets of greater consequence. I was no fickle child, however. The archaeologist urge remained for six years; the bacteriologist aspiration stayed with me for another five. Until my college years they were the only careers I considered. I had the good fortune to attend the Bronx High School of Science, where I studied the subject that had, long before, brought fame to Koch, Pasteur, Lister, and others. But it wasn't fame I craved; it was the thrill of discovery. Truths were hidden under the microscope, and I was going to find them.

Whatever truths were hidden under the microscope would remain unknown to me after my first year at Cornell University. I entered college to study microbiology but soon discovered that there were other subjects — the humanities, history, social sciences — about which I knew little. Knowledge was deeper and broader than I had been led to believe at Bronx Science. So little time, so many truths. The microscope was abandoned, and I moved on to libraries and dusty archives, where I have remained ever since.

I advise my students today to take courses from the best minds at their universities, independent of subject matter. I followed that dictum when I was an undergraduate. Among the best departments at Cornell were government and history. But *my* mind did not function best in those fields. The truths were murkier; the detective could rarely frame the case, let alone solve it. In my sophomore year I encountered Alfred (Fred) Kahn, whose utter delight in using economics to uncover hidden truths did for economics what Paul de Kruif's stories had done for microbiology. I didn't know what I would do with economics, and that took many years to resolve. But I was assured that I would eventually resume being a detective aided by both theory and evidence.

After earning my B.A. in economics at Cornell, I entered graduate work at the University of Chicago. I was ill prepared for study in a top-ranked department, having taken almost as many credits in government and history as I had in economics. I hadn't realized that detectives needed math and statistics; guidance for graduate school was nonexistent in my undergraduate days. I went to Chicago because I wanted to continue my study of industrial organization and regulation, begun at Cornell with Fred Kahn.

It was almost pure luck to have chosen Chicago, and I still don't know what led me to believe that it would have been a good place to study and live. It wasn't a good place to live; it was lousy. But it was the very best place to begin graduate work in 1967. The greatest minds were in Chicago—Friedman, Stigler, Becker, Harberger, Fogel, Telser, McCloskey, Griliches, Coase, Gregg Lewis, Harry Johnson, among others—and they taught with religious zeal. All of economics became exhilarating; I became a true disciple.

I did exams in both industrial organization and labor economics. But their methodology and questions seemed too narrow, and I ultimately returned to the study of history, government, and the social sciences in general. With the framework of economics the real detective work could begin.

I must underscore several admissions before continuing. First is that I was easily led, although not misled, by others—great minds, powerful personalities, all men. Fred Kahn was a guiding light in my undergraduate days. Gary Becker took his place in my second year in graduate school. And Robert Fogel was the mentor who directed my dissertation and much of my early career. Detectives question authority. That would come later. Second is that I had no clear vision of my future. I was, and continue to be, gleeful to research and learn about a wide range of subjects. That may seem overly solipsistic, perhaps a bit naive. But I now realize that much of my work concerns the origins of current policy issues (e.g., economic inequality, education, role of women in the labor force, impact of social insurance, immigration restriction). The subconscious plays a major role in one's research agenda. As one of my teachers, Ronald Coase, noted: "I came to realize where I had been going only after I arrived. The emergence of my ideas at each stage was not part of some grand scheme" (1994). Third is that I find it hard to describe what I do as work because it gives me the same joy as did my two previous and fanciful careers, existing entirely in the mind of a child. I am the same person, delighting in the discovery of something I believe to be a fact through detective work.

Finally is that I look back on my years as an economist with no sense that there have been watersheds related to appointments, promotions, fellowships, honors, acceptances. I do, however, remember the precise moment that I found the slave bills of sale at the Mormon Genealogical Society; documents at the National Archives containing information on whether firms hired married women; and surveys covering the labor market histories of women during World War II, oddly enough squirreled away in the building in which I worked. I remember the "eurekas" I quietly exclaimed when my model or framework took life and began to "talk back" to me.

How I became an economist says much about how I work as an economist. There has often been no agenda or program, no particular theory that must be followed, no one econometric technique to be used, and no agency or foundation to pay for a bottom line. Yet the subconscious produces nagging questions. Mine concern the evolving human condition and the material conditions of life, the long-run issues of economic development. It doesn't seem to matter what I work on, I return to these issues. I also am dedicated to seeking the "truth" through fact-finding detective work. It is frequently a highly descriptive truth (e.g., what percentage of women were in the labor force in 1890? what proportion of their lifetimes did they work full-time?) but is also an analytical one (e.g., what fraction of the increase in female labor force participation between 1940 and 1950 was due to World War II?).

My first project as an economic historian was my dissertation. It began as a term paper on the role of slavery in the urban and industrial development of the antebellum South. Robert Fogel strongly encouraged me to expand it into my dissertation, although it was only later that I would discover his broader interests in the subject of slavery. In those days I thought of myself as an industrial-organization, or labor, or even urban economist. Although I had taken much history as an undergraduate, I was reluctant to write in a field about which I knew so little. At the same time, however, I was excited by the prospect of working on broader questions.

Anyone who has argued with Robert Fogel knows that battles are not easily won. I didn't try and, for that, I'm grateful. Had I won, and the odds were against it, I would actually have lost. (Another case in which my lack of questioning authority paid off.) I was persuaded to write in economic history and to call myself an economic historian (although for long after I was convinced I did not know the subject well enough to teach it).

After graduate school I continued to work on the economic history of the South: the Civil War, emancipation, the postbellum era, and the role of slavery in the labor force participation of black women. It was a heady period in the field of economic history (see Goldin 1995) — a great time to be doing economic history and to be studying the economics of the American South and the history of African-Americans. But although the topics were of interest and I argued with force for one side or another, it is clear, looking back, that I was sniffing around for something of deeper personal interest. I had stumbled upon it when thinking about black married women after emancipation, but I was not to know that for a few more years. I meandered for a while, becoming involved in another area gaining strength in the late 1970s — quantitative social history and the economics of the family.

The economics of the family was then in vogue in both economics and history. My work focused on family decisions in the late nineteenth and early twentieth centuries about who worked and went to school, when children left home, where the family resided, and so on. The work sustained me for some time, but around 1980 I realized that something was missing. I was slighting the family member who would undergo the most profound change over the long run — the wife and mother. I neglected her because the sources had. Women were in the data when young and single and often when widowed. But their stories were faintly heard after they married, for they were often not producing goods and services in sectors that were, or would be, part of GNP.

I recall the precise moment when I switched my attention to the evolution of the female labor force. I had few ideas about the location of evidence; fewer still on what the evolution was. But I knew it would be a story of importance, relevant to the current period, and a project for which my detective work would pay off. I also knew that I was the one to do it.

Women's role in the American labor force appeared to be unfolding before me, and I had personally experienced many of the changes I would be studying. Yet I would come to realize that change was not as precipitous nor as recent as most thought. No matter how much change there appeared to be, vestiges of the past remained. And the voices of the history told similar stories. Each generation would lay claim to being the first to experience truly meaningful change in the economic role of women. If change were continuous, how could so many generations, such as my own, consider theirs to have lived through the pivotal era? Questions led to answers; answers led to more questions. I became consumed by the history of women in the labor force.

Whatever you research, choose a subject (in theory or reality) about which you feel passionately. You will go to sleep with it and you will wake up with it. You'd better love it, or you will hate yourself. I cannot emphasize this more. I know that there will be times when you will work on subjects because they are au courant, because they fill a niche, and because they will appear to guarantee publication. But your brain will never last long if you only "play the game." You must simply crave the answers to the questions you pose.

The central question I posed was, Why did the female labor force expand at certain times and for certain cohorts? What had caused married women to increase their market participation rate from around 5 to 70 percent across this century? I first had to track the expansion in every possible way. I began by assembling as much data as I could find in easily accessible sources. In the absence of spreadsheet programs, I recall a nightmare of matrices. I pushed the project forward in time (almost to the present) and backward (to the 1790s) and tackled various topics in turn, producing series or estimates on the labor force by age, marital status, race, and ethnicity. I also produced series on earnings, work experience, "wage discrimination," among others. When I began the project, I thought I could find all the data I needed in published census documents. I soon discovered that even recent data were not as I wanted, and, strangely enough, data from the more distant past were often better than those nearer to the present.

I quickly realized that because labor force participation tells one nothing about who participates and for how long, such data were insufficient for my project. To understand how the expansion of the female labor force affected the work experience of women I had to know something about the distribution of work. I had to know whether a 20-percent labor force participation rate meant that 20 percent of all women participated for the entire year or whether all women participated for just 20 percent of the year. I needed work histories, either longitudinal or retrospective, for the period prior to 1960. But longitudinal surveys, such as the National Longitudinal Survey, begin in the late 1960s. Too late for my work.

I soon discovered, as well, that today's labor force construct was not used prior to 1940. Rather, individuals were asked about their "gainful employment." If a woman worked twenty-five weeks out of the year, would she answer that she didn't have an occupation? If she worked twenty-seven weeks, would she then have put down an occupation? I became more aware of the fact that the bounds of market work omitted many women who labored in their homes as family-business workers, boardinghouse keepers, family-farm laborers, and piece-rate workers. There was also the nagging question of whether the social norms of the day meant that married women gave census takers the socially accepted answer rather than the factually correct one.

Before I could answer the original question about the expansion of the female labor force, I needed to describe it more meaningfully and factually. And for that I needed retrospective work histories predating modern collections, data on how much time women spent in the labor force over the year, and information on the "hidden market work" of married women, among other facts. I needed to know the truth about the female labor force from 1790 to the present. What would a great detective do?

I am an incurable optimist, some may say naive. I was convinced that I would find enough clues to piece together the history of the female labor force. My detective work began with some obvious sources ("round up the usual suspects") — the published documents of federal and state agencies. They were insufficient, and off I went to the National Archives, Washington, D.C., in search of surveys I believe existed.

The National Archives today is a tightly controlled place. No one is allowed into the stacks except the official "searchers"; nothing can be taken into the reading room except a laptop and a pencil (not even a pad of paper). But when I went to the National Archives in 1981 and requested information about the Women's Bureau records, I discovered that the "finding aid" for the documents was vastly incomplete. The "searcher" invited me into the stacks — "minimize transport costs by taking the researcher to the documents" was his motto, apparently. What I uncovered would not have been possible without his kindness, intelligence, and trust. I would have had to request hundreds of boxes without knowing their contents. Not knowing their call numbers would have further complicated the task. But I was fortunate to have been at the right place at the right time. I was able to sit in the stacks for hours, riffling through the boxes, taking copious notes on my own pad of paper. I eventually figured out what was in most of the boxes and wrote my own "finding aid" for the Women's Bureau Record Group (an aid that they couldn't officially use because it wasn't done "in house"). I had found a gold mine of original surveys.[1]

After that visit to the National Archives I knew I had found something special, but I wasn't certain exactly what I had found. The surveys were not designed with my questions in mind. Many were executed to make a particular political point about the role of women in the two world wars or during the depression. Some concerned immigrant women. Others were about clerical workers, those in particular industries, and those in certain cities. Without examining them in detail I didn't know whether the surveys were complete enough or contained sufficient observations to be useful.

One of the surveys concerned office workers and covered a host of industries across many cities in 1939. The information was contained on individual cards for both men and women and included data on education, earnings, and work experience, among other variables. Several years later I discovered that the firms employing these office workers were also surveyed (these surveys eluded my initial and hurried search). Managers were asked mundane questions about how many office workers they hired, what type of machinery they used (the survey was intended to reveal the impact of "new" office technology), and what worker benefits were. The second page of the survey contained the more remarkable questions — whether the firm "discriminated on the basis of race," if "there were any jobs for which you would not hire a woman (a man)," whether "married women were not hired and single women were fired when they married," and if "married men were paid more than single men." Without any antidiscrimination legislation, managers answered the questions candidly.

The Women's Bureau boxes yielded five data sets for my project. One allowed me to produce work histories for women before 1940 (Goldin 1989), another exposed much about the extent of and reasons for "marriage bars" in the 1920s and 1930s (Goldin 1991a), and one enabled estimates of "wage discrimination" in 1939. I had, indeed, located much of what I had gone to the National Archives to find. But what was I to do about the nineteenth century, when the sources were far less abundant and less quantitative?

Once again, I first tapped the obvious—the census of manufactures. That revealed the extent of employment in just one sector. How was I going to find evidence of "hidden market work" of married women during a period when family businesses were significant to the economy? I discovered that all major and many minor cities had extensive city and business directories dating back to the late eighteenth century. (One can think of these as phone books before the telephone.) I used them to find out husbands' occupations just before they died (there were many untimely deaths during yellow-fever epidemics) and what their widows were doing just a year later. If an innkeeper's widow was also an innkeeper, a reasonable presumption is that she did the same the previous year, when her husband was alive.[2]

I have many stories of successful detective work, but none that makes me gloat as much as finding the surveys on World War II. Much of my research for the project was completed by 1987, and I had a full and rich story to tell about the evolution of the female labor force. But I was still lacking evidence on the role of World War II. What did happen to Rosie and her compatriots? I wasn't certain, but I knew that I couldn't delay my book on American women to find the answer. There will always be someone who will find new evidence, a better econometric technique, or a more appropriate framework. I spent the academic year of 1987–88 writing my book (Goldin 1990). But I wasn't pleased that I came up short in finding a retrospective data set covering the 1940s, and so I continued to pursue further data leads even though the book was written.

I was aware that the economist Gladys Palmer had worked at the University of Pennsylvania (my employer at the time) on surveys concerning unemployment and labor force mobility beginning in the 1930s. My colleagues in the sociology department believed that many of the original surveys were in boxes in the McNeil Building, where I worked. When we finally located the boxes, I discovered the treasure for which I had been searching. The boxes contained thousands of surveys of working women (and men) in 1951 and their complete work histories back to 1940. The data had been, literally, right under my nose. Combined with other information that serendipitously showed up, I was able to piece together a more complete history of the female labor force during and just after World War II, although I wasn't able to include the findings in my book (see Goldin 1991b).

How did I collect all of these data? Much of it was collected the old-fashioned way — by hand and by me. Until recently I didn't trust data collection to a team of research assistants. I always insisted on doing much of it myself (I call it "dirty work" because it is — dusty). But as the data collection activities became larger and as I encountered surveys that were more systematic, I learned to trust my research assistants. I still do a large chunk of the coding myself before I train the assistants. I learn while collecting data. The forms tell stories and I listen.

I am currently involved in a data collection from the 1915 Iowa state census, the first and only U.S. census to inquire about education, earnings, religion, ethnicity, and property values. Only by entering hundreds of observations myself did I discover important details about education on the eve of the great expansion of U.S. high schools. The latent demand for high schools is revealed in the excessive number of years youths were spending in common schools in rural areas. I might not have discovered this important point had I not read the schedules myself. You must get to know your data.

The same advice can be given for data that are already in machine-readable form. I'm not suggesting that you obtain the original census documents and stare at them, although it might be a humbling experience. I am suggesting that you scan your data for outliers and that you look at some of their other properties before you subject them to more heavy-duty statistical procedures.

Although I eventually wrote *Understanding the Gender Gap: An Economic History of American Women* (1990), I wasn't certain, until the year of its writing, that a book would emerge. A book requires that the author find a "voice," and my voice kept changing. Analytically, I began by working within the accepted framework of female labor supply, pioneered by Jacob Mincer and Gary Becker. The framework, however, had to be bent to fit the historical reality. We economists still don't know how to incorporate changing norms, and I was researching a subject in which norms played a major role. As I wrote the book I began to "question authority" much more. The book still bears the strong imprint of a neoclassical economist, but it is also a considerably more nuanced piece of work than I had originally intended.

I'm asked frequently when I'll write a more popular version of *Understanding*. I wish I had the time to do it. I should. But I'm happiest being a detective. To write a popular version of a book I've already written would be like writing a textbook. There isn't much discovery involved. Rather, there is packaging and communicating. I should want a larger audience, and perhaps I will someday.

What did I do after writing *Understanding*? I ambled around researching subjects about which I was curious (and some that I had simply promised for essay collections) and searched for the new project about which I would feel passionately. I was lucky and found both subject and coauthor, although not necessarily in that order. My most recent project is a joint venture with Lawrence F. Katz, about whom I feel even more passionately than I do about the subject matter.

After working on historical aspects of unemployment, seasonality, savings, immigration restriction, and earnings inequality, I decided to study the history of education in the twentieth century. When I was a graduate student at Chicago, Gary Becker told us that even though the returns to education were high, they must have been higher still before 1940 when educational attainment was rising rapidly. But not until 1940 did the U.S. census of population request information on either education or earnings. Evidence for the pre-1940 period was almost entirely lacking. I was finally in the position to attack this important issue, and I heard the clarion call for the economist detective.

Educational change in the United States occurred during three transformations defined by the schooling levels common (or grade), secondary, and higher. The transformation that occurred in secondary education, from 1910 to 1940, was considerably more rapid than in the other two levels. I set out to track the expansion at the state level and to uncover the forces that set the extraordinary change in motion. I also set out to study the impacts of these changes on the economy in the immediate period and for the rest of the twentieth century.

The project was begun just three years ago when I was on leave at the Brookings Institution. By scouring various educational data sources at the federal and state levels, I pieced together the state-level data on the expansion of secondary schools. I soon discovered that the expansion by state from 1910 to 1940 was far more rapid than the national data suggested. The leading states geographically formed an "educational belt," running from parts of New England to the central portion of the Plains states to the Mountain states and on to the Pacific. These were rich, relatively homogeneous, primarily nonmanufacturing, and nonsouthern states. The proportion of their youths graduating from high schools in 1925 was almost double what it was in the rest of the nation.

I then studied the impacts of these large and sudden shifts in the supply of educated labor on the wage structure. There was, as Becker and others had conjectured, a collapse in the premium to ordinary white-collar office workers by the early 1920s. Relative to production workers, the clerk, stenographer, typist, secretary, and bookkeeper saw their wages fall as the supply of high school graduates expanded. Various high-technology industries were introduced in that period, including electrical machinery, aircraft, nonferrous metals, chemicals, and paints. I turned my attention to whether these industries were hiring disproportionate numbers of high school graduates as blue-collar workers. The answer was that they were. Education endowed workers with valuable cognitive skills, and firms in particular industries prized these abilities. The industries that were more willing to pay for the higher-priced blue-collar workers were more capital intensive, newer, and higher-tech.

The education project, even more than that on the evolution of the female labor force, is connected to the policy issues of our day, such as rising inequality. We wonder today whether certain types of technological advances are expanding the wage distribution and whether educational increases can ameliorate widening inequality. Studying the history of education, technology, and the wage structure has shown that major technological changes of the past also increased the relative demand for skills but that educational advances prevented the wage structure from widening (Goldin and Katz 1996).

What is it like to be a woman and work in a field still dominated by men? When I was an undergraduate at Cornell there must have been a mere handful of women in my economics classes. But I don't recall. When I went to graduate school there were three other women in my first-year class (one left in the first year to go to Columbia) out of about fifty-five in total. But I don't remember anything peculiar about that either. I have been the first female economist to be offered or to achieve tenure at the University of Pennsylvania, Harvard University, and Princeton University. But I don't find that odd or distinctive. Why? In part because I know history. I'm simply much too young to be a pioneer. Many women, more brilliant and accomplished than I, came before me. I did nothing to open doors for women other than to provide an example and be a teacher. I also don't feel that I have been disparately treated by my teachers in graduate school or by most of my colleagues (there are exceptions). I am occasionally bothered that I wasn't encouraged by anyone to continue my studies in microbiology and that no one (not even my family) questioned my giving up a goal that had once seemed so important. Would anyone have done so had I been male? Perhaps.

I haven't said much about how an entire project gets accomplished. I begin, as I have already said, with a large subject or question, about which I feel passionately. I then narrow the topic and form several subquestions and subprojects. Three elements of research must then be tackled: *(a)* ideas, *(b)* theory, and *(c)* data and empirical methods. I work best by tackling all three at once. At my desk will be several books on the subject, often history books, sometimes sociology, occasionally fiction, rarely economics. I will also have the accessible data close at hand. I read and read until my mind begins to wander into economic theory and then I sketch simple models.[3] At the same time, another part of me is searching for more data. How do I know what is relevant before I have formulated hypotheses? I have some suspicions, and I'll be partly correct. I'll fill in the rest later. The ideas suggest theory that suggests the data; the data may lead to revisions of the ideas and the theory; and so on. Each part informs the other. Round and round I go until I believe I've come up with something that is a truth about a subject or question of importance.

As I work I pretend I'm my worst enemy and attack every idea, piece of theory, and empirical method. Battles rage and often I lose. But I really win, of course. Out there lie sharp critics. I might as well lose in the absence of an audience and without humiliation, to retreat into my office to revise the paper.

Presenting your ideas out loud (to a seminar, a friend, your dog) subjects them to a scrutiny that is different from the act of writing them down. I'm not certain why that is the case. It may be that writing allows one to disguise and obscure errors of logic, but that saying the words out loud (even to a dog) makes one painfully aware of the inconsistencies. Students are important for just that reason. They respond with basic, elementary questions, often the ones that your colleagues won't ask. Even when they don't respond, they at least take the place of the dog (by the way, I love dogs). Teaching and research have always gone hand and hand in my life. I can't do one without the other. I'd like more time to write, but I would never want to be without students, both undergraduate and graduate. Some of my grandest ideas are expressed in my undergraduate course. I don't know if I'll ever go to press with them, but they get my juices flowing with interest for the smaller subjects that nest within.

Certain pieces of economic research are so flawlessly executed and so elegantly written that we are lured into believing that their authors are simply better researchers and writers than we are. That may be true. But the person whose work we so admire has also worked very hard at both the substance and the writing. Too many youthful writers believe that the perfect article is effortlessly conveyed from head to hands to printer. When their first draft is imperfect (and that is guaranteed), they give up and merely submit it to a journal or as a working paper. Nothing could be more stupid. Critics abound like vultures on the Serengeti. My teacher and friend Deirdre McCloskey taught me that no one whose writings we admire wrote as admirable a first draft. Write, rewrite, and then rewrite again. I'll never write like McCloskey, and neither will you, but we will both write much better if we follow that advice.

I learned much about our craft when I was the coeditor of the *Journal of Economic History,* a post I held from 1984 to 1988 and for two of those years with McCloskey. We do not instruct our students well in the art of crafting papers, possibly because there are so many idiosyncratic elements. Editing or refereeing manuscripts teaches us what distinguishes a well-crafted paper from an ordinary one. We should take on these chores not only because they are public services but also because they are the only means of learning how to write. Reading your own papers or those that are published cannot teach you the craft of writing. Unless you have put your paper away for several weeks, possibly months, you will read it with too friendly an eye and ear, for the same reason that parents are never adequate critics of their own children. And the papers that get published are a selected group that have been through countless revisions. Learn how to write from the errors of others. They provide a limitless supply.

Summary

1. Most importantly, find a topic of substance about which you feel passionately.

2. Then be the best detective you can be. Don't just "round up the usual suspects"; don't simply look under the existing lamppost. Locate new suspects. Turn on lights where they have never shone before. Follow Holmes's dictum, "There is nothing like firsthand evidence," as well as his admonition, "Any truth is better than indefinite doubt."

3. Go back and forth among theory, empirics, and stories until you iterate on the very best truth you can tell. Sherlock Holmes was known to remark, "It is a capital mistake to theorize in advance of the facts." And Joe Friday always sought "the facts, ma'am, just the facts." They may have been great detectives, but they would have made lousy economists.

4. And, because nothing of value is easy or simple, you must plod, plod, plod; question, question, question; write, rewrite, and rewrite again. Be your own worst enemy, so that no one else is. Put the work away and read it with new eyes, not those of its creator.

5. Find your own voice.

6. And I hope that you will discover the importance of history and of long-term trends in the knowledge you create.

NOTES

1. The stacks of the National Archives were later closed after it was discovered that valuable documents were being routinely stolen.

2. Goldin 1986 reports the findings from the project using the city and business directories.

3. See Hal Varian's fine advice in this volume on modeling.

REFERENCES

Coase, Ronald H. "My Evolution as an Economist." Unpublished version of a lecture in the Lives of the Laureates series, Trinity University, San Antonio, Texas, April 12, 1994. Cited in William Landes's essay in this volume.

Goldin, Claudia. 1986. "The Changing Status of Women in the Economy of the Early Republic: Quantitative Evidence." *Journal of Interdisciplinary History* 16 (winter): 374–404. Reproduced in Nancy Cott, ed., *History of Women in the U.S.* (New York: K. G. Saur 1992).

———. 1989. "Life Cycle Labor Force Participation of Married Women: Historical Evidence and Implications." *Journal of Labor Economics* 7 (January): 20–47.

———. 1990. *Understanding the Gender Gap: An Economic History of American Women* (New York: Oxford University Press).

———. 1991a. "Marriage Bars: Discrimination against Married Women Workers, 1920 to 1950." In *Favorites of Fortune: Technology, Growth, and Economic Development since the Industrial Revolution,* ed. H. Rosovsky, D. Landes, and P. Higgonet (Cambridge, MA: Harvard University Press).

———. 1991b. "The Role of World War II in the Rise of Women's Employment." *American Economic Review* 81 (September): 741–56. Also NBER Reprint No. 1619.

———. 1995. "Cliometrics and the Nobel." *Journal of Economic Perspectives* 9 (spring): 191–208.

Goldin, Claudia, and Lawrence F. Katz. 1996. "Technology, Skill, and the Wage Structure: Insights from the Past." *American Economic Review* 86 (May): 252–57.

DAVID M. GORDON

Politics and Precision: Pursuing Economics outside the Mainstream

Life as a left economist has its quite specialized rewards and frustrations. But I doubt that as a left economist I practice the daily rituals of doing economics all that differently from most of my more mainstream peers. We use the same word-processing programs and many of the same econometrics packages. We rely on many of the same data sources. Many of us men scratch our heads in the same balding spots when we're cogitating. I may listen to different music when I work — an unpredictable combination of chamber music and rock 'n' roll — but I doubt that this has much to do with my intellectual and political orientation.

Does working to the left of the mainstream in economics matter at all? In my own case I would guess that two particular features of life as a heterodox economist have most strongly influenced the way I've practiced economics.

- First, progressive political involvements and concerns have persistently and insistently shaped the questions I've asked and the problems I've explored through economic analysis — endowing the term *political* economy with real bite.

- Second, the continuing risks of marginalization and dismissal as a nonmainstream economist have pushed me more and more toward formal quantitative analysis in nearly every project I undertake, regardless of the methodological complexities that emphasis has required.

Through these two influences, the continuing and considerable tensions between political passion and analytic craft have shaped much of my work like the poles of a powerful electromagnetic field.[1]

Politics Framing Science

I belong to a family of well-known economists—father, the late Robert Aaron Gordon, former president of the American Economic Association; mother, the late Margaret S. Gordon, expert on trade, employment and migration, the economics of aging, social insurance, and higher education; and brother, Robert J. Gordon, currently a leading mainstream macroeconomist. One family, two parents, two sons, all economists. (Those who are already appalled may be slightly reassured to learn that neither my wife nor my brother's wife practices economics.) When our parents were both still alive, *Business Week* once labeled us "The Flying Wallendas of Economics."

As a result, those who know something of my family history often assume that I was genetically programmed to enter economics or at least that I began prepping for my Ph.D. qualifying exams sometime before the age of puberty.

Quite to the contrary, I resisted becoming an economist until the last possible moment. I did not major in economics as an undergraduate. When I graduated from college, I had little idea what kind of career I planned to pursue—although I was fairly certain I didn't want to become an academic. (Growing up in an academic family, one begins at an early age intuitively to perceive some of the petty politics and hypocrisy that shroud life in the modern university.) As an eager and increasingly active participant in some of the political struggles of the mid-1960s (civil rights work in the South, organizing against the Vietnam War), I was clearer how I wanted to change the United States—radically—than how I proposed to support myself while I tried.

Circumstances intervened (the details of the story are mostly beside the point), and despite my better instincts I began graduate school in economics a year after I graduated from college, and I have worked professionally as an economist ever since. As a result, my baptism in politics *preceded* my baptism in economics. I knew what I wanted to pursue politically before I even began to consider what kinds of issues I might explore analytically.

And from that time forward, now covering a span of almost thirty years, the strongest among many influences on my research program have been my concern and involvement with ordinary people and their lives as workers and citizens; my strong commitment to the objectives of promoting greater equality, decency, and democracy; and my perception that radical political transformations would be necessary in order to advance those objectives.

Intuitions

This pattern revealed itself from the beginning. Having worked on a civil rights project in the southern United States, I began to recognize that we of northern origin had plenty of our own problems of racism and poverty and that it made more sense for me to try to tackle those problems "back home," where I could claim some familiarity with the history and mores, than in a region with dramatically different roots and trajectories. So the summer before graduate school, in order to begin getting a feel for life in the field, I worked on a project evaluating some model Great Society programs targeting the "hard-core unemployed" in Oakland, California.

The premise of the programs, typical of the day (and hardly different from much more recent public initiatives), was that these potential workers were unemployed or underemployed because they had vast and multiple skill deficits. The programs, sophisticated for their time, sought to address these disadvantages with a wide range of training, from work on literacy skills to tips on taking job interviews. I mostly hung out with the program participants, trying to get a sense of who they were, what they wanted, and why they thought they were experiencing employment problems.

After weeks of such conversations, it seemed reasonably obvious (to me at least) that the primary problem for the participants was not securing employment as such but finding jobs that paid enough and offered enough security to make the jobs worth keeping. It became quite clear that the participants were uninterested in the kinds of jobs most employers had to offer them. Among themselves they mocked the premises of the programs — that it was *their* fault they were underemployed. Their own experiences convinced them, intuitively and sometimes remarkably coherently, that problems lay elsewhere, with the structure of work and the legacies of discrimination.

After a year in graduate school, I landed a research assistantship helping evaluate some similar programs in Boston. As I and my coworkers sat in the program offices reading participants' files and talking with the participants about their experiences, the same impressions asserted themselves. Human-capital theory, recently ascendant in neoclassical labor economics, insisted that the skill characteristics of *individuals* largely governed their labor market outcomes. Our own experiences with the objects of such wisdom were persuading us that the characteristics of *jobs* mattered more, that seeking to change the character of available jobs should command a much higher priority than seeking to change the character of their potential occupants. (In more formal language, this fueled a mounting suspicion that earnings and working conditions on the demand side of the labor market were highly inelastic with respect to the supply of individual characteristics on the supply side of the market.)

From that starting point, this kind of involvement with ordinary people, based on respect for the authenticity and legitimacy of their perceptions and experiences, led fairly directly to the first formulations of what became "dual labor market" and "labor segmentation" theory. Working initially in collaboration with Peter Doeringer, Penny Feldman, Michael Piore, and Michael Reich, and then later with Richard Edwards and Reich, I tried to contribute to a heterodox view within labor economics not primarily or originally because I detected flaws in the logic of human-capital theory—which I later perceived—or because I didn't like the protocapitalist symbolic implications of the term *human capital*—which I also came to suspect—but rather because that view of the world didn't seem to fit very well with (my impressions of) the ordinary lives of some of the people whom policies based on that theory were purporting to help.

These kinds of intuitions, born of continuing contact with ordinary people facing extraordinary problems, have remained as a kind of conscience shadowing my work ever since. Many years developing and testing outreach educational programs with local union leadership and rank-and-filers, beginning in the mid-1970s, gave me an acute sense of the rhythms and reality of capital-labor relations on the shop and office floor, deeply embedding a feel for the interplay at the workplace of power and constraint, of aspiration and humiliation, of evolving games and struggles that any labor economics ought to feature at the very center of its investigations. Widening involvement during the 1980s as an economics policy adviser to left and progressive political movements and candidates gave me an education, mostly frustrating, in how narrowly constraining the mainstream economic-policy consensus had become and how crucial it was to find ways of framing economic analysis pointing toward a wider menu of policy options — which included those potentially advancing relatively more equal, decent, and democratic futures.

Questions
Popular involvement has also helped shape many of the actual problems I've chosen to explore.

In the mid-1970s, for example, in our outreach educational work among unionists and rank-and-filers, colleagues and I at what is now called the Labor Institute were experimenting pedagogically with ways of encouraging workers to define the kinds of economic issues they wanted to study and the kinds of problems they wanted to tackle politically. Since these explorations came on the heels of the sharp recession of 1973–75 and in the throes of that strange new phenomenon called "stagflation," we expected that the workers in our classes would steer the conversations toward problems of job security and inflation.

Much to our surprise — we were, after all, still wet behind the ears — they were more interested in talking about problems they were constantly experiencing with their bosses on the job. They complained that their supervisors were always on their case, that bureaucratic harassment was a daily burden. They wanted relief, and they insisted that we discuss more powerful remedies than Rolaids.

A novice in these kinds of interactions with blue-collar workers, I was nonplussed. As an educator, I didn't have a base of experience upon which to draw. As a social scientist, I had no idea whether these were the common and enduring complaints of similarly situated workers at any time and place, or whether their urgency perhaps followed from a recent intensification of bureaucratic supervision on the job.

This led me to begin to look at basic data on what we have come to call in later work the "intensity of supervision." It turned out, upon initial investigation, that the ratio of nonproduction and supervisory workers to production and nonsupervisory workers had been rising dramatically in the United States. And it turned out, further, that what I've come to call the "bureaucratic burden" was dramatically weightier in the United States than in other advanced economies.

I continue to this day to explore the contours and determinants of the intensity of supervision. I teach about it with my graduate students in labor economics. And it's become an important theme in a number of my collaborations. I didn't come upon the interest originally by staring at the ceiling, waiting for a lightbulb to pop; my curiosity was piqued simply because the workers with whom we were working insisted that we take heed. I've since learned that the percentage of nonfarm employment in administrative and managerial occupations is three times higher in the United States than in Germany and Japan. I doubt that I would ever have bothered to uncover and explore those patterns if I hadn't been sitting in union halls in the mid-1970s, chewing on stale jelly doughnuts, learning to share in serious conversations with workers about what they most wanted to change about their daily lives.

Similar kinds of examples abound; I mention here only two more:

- Many early investigations of labor segmentation often asked whether workers in the secondary labor market earned *any* — not just lower — returns to education when compared with other workers. We were asking those questions in large part because of our experiences with people working in those kinds of secondary jobs. As we were pursuing that work, I often joked with my graduate students in labor economics that fervent believers in human-capital theory, impressed with returns to education at *every* level, were often recounting their own autobiographies of a successful passage through our educational institutions. If one ever bothered to talk with people who had followed dramatically different life paths, I coyly suggested, one might begin to imagine that education didn't provide a ticket to heaven for everyone.

- I spent some time during the 1970s exploring the interactions between power and spatial organization, critiquing the sufficiency of technicist explanations of the modern patterns of urban location and regional development. One of the principal impulses for my skeptical questions came from an unlikely source: In 1972 I was a member of one of the first groups from the United States to be allowed to tour the People's Republic of China. This trip came at the height and passion of the Cultural Revolution. Among their many provocations, proponents of the Cultural Revolution dared to challenge the geographically concentrated pattern of resource and industrial development in China, arguing that a much more diffuse and decentralized geographic pattern could be pursued. I am no apologist for the excesses of the Cultural Revolution, but their political challenges — issued under the rubrics of democracy and equality — to modes of spatial organization that many had long thought were largely determined by technology echoed resonantly for me. I came home and immediately began to hit the U.S. history books, wondering about the role of power and politics in our own quite different trajectories of urban and regional development.

Strategies
Perhaps most fundamentally, some of my work has followed directly from overt and explicit reflections about the obstacles facing democratic and egalitarian movements in the United States.

This kind of linkage became evident from the beginning. As a fledgling left political economist in the late 1960s and early 1970s, when I and many of my peers began to join the socialist project of transforming capitalism, we seemed to be climbing slippery slopes. If it were true, as seemed plausible at the time, that post–World War II capitalism was rolling along the tracks of perpetual prosperity, that perhaps even the business cycle was "obsolete" — as many self-confident Keynesians were imagining at the time — then it followed that ordinary consumers would be reluctant to abandon the capitalist cornucopia for any other kind of system. Yes, indeed, we could potentially argue that workers and citizens were "alienated" under capitalism, that their lives would be more fulfilling in a more democratic and egalitarian regime, but would they be frowning all the way to the bank? If capitalism was so palpably efficient, how far could our politics advance by arguing for only one side of the efficiency/ fulfillment trade-off?

We felt stuck on the horns of a political dilemma. And the horns were sharp enough to prompt many of us to begin rethinking the basic presuppositions framing that dilemma. Was capitalism so clearly and inevitably the most "efficient" of all possible economic systems? Is it not possible that productivity would be higher in a system based on workplace democracy and reduced hierarchy?

These possibilities now seem virtually self-evident after a couple of decades of both mainstream and radical research tracing the connections between greater worker participation and control, on the one side, and higher productivity on the other. But more than twenty-five years ago the questions were difficult even to formulate, much less to explore, because the axioms of capitalist efficiency were so unyielding.

I still remember one moment in those early explorations with acute pain. Though a graduate student at Harvard, I lived in New York City while I was working on my dissertation because my new wife had an appealing job there and I had moved to join her. So I was wrestling with these kinds of basic questions on my own, even though I knew that many of my peers back in Cambridge were also puzzling over similar kinds of conundra. At one point during that first year I returned to make a presentation at an informal seminar organized by the Cambridge chapter of the newly organized Union for Radical Political Economics. I tried to lay out what I thought might be some of the theoretical foundations for a possible argument that profit-maximizing capitalists would "choose" a production system that was less efficient than other potential, relatively more egalitarian and democratic systems — in order to enhance their power and ultimately their long-run profits. I encountered withering skepticism — with every analytic hypothesis challenged and every theoretical ellipsis exposed. And these were my friends and comrades! It was that difficult to get our grips on such complicated systemic issues. If I had been presenting to a mainstream labor economics workshop, I probably wouldn't have been able to finish the first paragraph.

But still many of us persisted, haltingly, often retracing steps, to our first published discussions on these problems — such as Marglin's on "what do bosses do," Braverman's on the "degradation" of work, our own early discussions of some of the "divide-and-conquer" origins of labor segmentation. By now these lines of inquiry are well established within a variety of literatures. But it seems clear to me from hindsight that many of us would never have attempted to climb some of those early theoretical slopes had the *political* motivation not been so compelling.

The political context shifted in the mid-1970s, of course, but this kind of linkage between strategic considerations and conceptual explorations became even clearer. Now, rather suddenly, the capitalist express had switched on to a sidetrack. Stagnation was spreading. Some of us even began to suspect that a crisis of the magnitude of the

1930s or the 1880s was possible. So what should be our political response?

The inherited political strategy on the left, stemming from discussions of "breakdown" theory in the 1920s, involved a curious kind of political fatalism. First, so the reasoning went, capitalism would collapse. Once it collapsed, people would begin to recognize that it didn't work very well. And then, but only then, people would be "ripe" for discussions of socialism. Until the days of the final collapse, apparently, one would simply sit on one's hands, waiting.

One problem, of course, was that capitalism had proved itself remarkably resilient historically; it was the "golden age" itself that had sprung like a Phoenix from the ashes of the 1930s, not the long-awaited socialist paradise. Another problem was that capitalists were not standing by idly in the mid-1970s, waiting to see what would happen. They were beginning to reflect on some of the systemic features of spreading stagflation and to map out alternative strategies for resolving what many viewed, indeed, as an emergent crisis.

The questions seemed to hang like ripe peaches from the limb. If the long boom of the 1950s and 1960s was waning, if socialist transformations did not necessarily follow from crisis, if the powerful were already conferring to plot their strategies for recovery and restructuring . . . What should we do besides sit on our hands? Was there a level of struggle over the paths of institutional restructuring that might not yet point toward socialist objectives but might be consistent with their ultimate realization? If so, what were those institutions and how did their architecture interact with ebbing prosperity and spreading stagnation?

These questions pointed rather directly toward the work I began and then shared with many others on stages of capitalist development and "social structures of accumulation" (SSAs). When I first conjectured theoretically and methodologically in those directions in the mid-1970s, with great imprecision and halting elaborations, I was spurred primarily not by deep immersion in the contours of institutional configuration and restructuring over two centuries of capitalist development—although those kinds of investigations immediately became necessary to wander through the doors these questions opened—but much more innocently by an urgent concern about the directions in which left political struggle might respond to a shifting political economic environment.

It's hard for me to speculate with hindsight about the different paths along which our work on "social structures of accumulation" *might* have developed . . . because political circumstances soon intervened. In 1978–79, more than two hundred progressive organizations in the United States, representing among many the labor, citizens, civil rights, women's, and senior movements, joined to organize a political coalition called the Progressive Alliance. Concerned about spreading stagnation and rising unemployment, it aimed to challenge increasingly centrist Democratic Party politics in order to promote more democratic and egalitarian policies.

I thought the initiative was extremely promising and was happy when asked to become one of four cochairs of a subcommission exploring alternative economic policies. We met a few times and conferred with a broader "issues commission" considering policies that the Progressive Alliance might promote. We drafted articulate and sensible position papers about inflation and unemployment whose proposals, if pursued, might have advanced the broader goals of the coalition.

But I had to admit, quite frankly, that I didn't think we on the economics subcommission knew what we were talking about. Fueled by my recent ruminations on stages of capitalism and institutional restructuring, I suspected that we were playing in a game whose rules were rapidly changing. I told the executive director of the coalition that, in my humble opinion, many of us weren't really ready to provide such an important political initiative with the kind of analysis and policy advice they needed — recommendations that built on a clear apprehension of changing times and emerging circumstances and could presume to fashion policy proposals that, rather than retreading old tires, would sensibly respond to new problems and new possibilities.

The executive director was sage and patient enough not to kick me out of his office as a timorous academic but at least to ask what it might take to develop some analyses and proposals about which one might feel more confident. I told him I didn't know but that I was willing to try to find out. So he and I agreed on a small travel-study grant with which I could put together a group of like-minded political economists and search for a more confident and useful understanding of what seemed like an emerging crisis.

Responding to that challenge, old friends Sam Bowles, Tom Weisskopf, and I first met in my dining room in New York in April 1980. We began our discussions with clean lined pads and mostly open minds. Our instincts led us to focus initially on the productivity slowdown and the dynamics of stagflation. But we soon branched out in nearly every direction.

And thus began more than a decade of collaboration among the three of us on productivity, profitability, and investment; on social structures of accumulation and the postwar corporate system in the United States; on the anatomy of failure of right-wing economics and the logic and possibilities for a democratic economic alternative. Although the Progressive Alliance disbanded soon after our own collaboration began,[2] we often toasted the moribund organization for having pushed us to begin figuring out what we understood about the emerging crisis of U.S. capitalism and what it implied for a democratic and egalitarian challenge to reigning orthodoxy.

Hold on. Politics framing science? Isn't this a violation of the canons of objective scientific inquiry? Haven't I just confessed a cardinal sin in the halls of academe? I can imagine that some readers may have heard the echoes of such questions as they read the preceding discussion. But there is a fundamental difference between politics "framing" science and politics "invading" science.

How does anyone come to the questions or intuitions that stimulate scientific inquiry? Personal idiosyncrasies, random events, scientific anomalies, *and* political imperatives often condition the paths we tread on the way toward scientific inquiry itself. What is crucial for the integrity of scientific investigation is not the process by which we pose our questions but the methods by which we investigate them and draw conclusions from those investigations. Robert Heilbroner has written recently about the importance of "vision" in shaping inquiry in economics and other social sciences. To deny the importance of our vision of what makes for interesting and important questions is to pretend that we exist in scientific isolation, divorced completely from our lives as individuals in society, subject to a welter of overdetermining influences on our ideas and priorities.

What is interesting for me in thinking about the influences on issues I've explored as an economist is not that politics has helped frame my science, because I would take that kind of influence for granted, but how my *particular* brand of politics has helped shape my *particular* kinds of investigations. The clearer we all become about these kinds of forces affecting the objects of our economic inquiry, I think, the clearer we can all become about the limits and potential implications of the work we do and the conclusions we reach. I'm not at all reticent or apologetic about the effect of my politics on my economics. Rather, I wish that other economists were equally open and reflective about the influence of their politics on their economics. Rather than keeping this all backstage, hidden from view, we should put it right up front, under the spotlights' glare, so that we and our audiences will understand better what we are about.

Marginality Demanding Precision
I've always enjoyed working with numbers. As a kid, I used to keep voluminous statistics about a mock baseball league I administered with my generation's precursor to today's computerized games. In college one of the course papers I enjoyed most was a detailed statistical investigation of the results of a local election on a fair-housing referendum. And when it came to a doctoral dissertation, I gravitated naturally to an econometric project using micro data samples to test some hypotheses derived from the emerging dual-labor-market literature.

As many of us began in the late 1960s and early 1970s to explore the theoretical and methodological foundations of an alternative "radical" or "left" economics, however, I was drawn away from formal quantitative work toward other modes of investigation. (Indeed, I never got around to publishing any of the econometric pieces of my dissertation because I was less and less sure what they implied and how they fit into a broader analytic enterprise.) It seemed less important empirically and formally to test tractable hypotheses than to try to develop a clearer understanding of where our work was heading, what it meant, and what kinds of implications it would possibly carry. Through most of the 1970s, therefore, it seemed to me that theoretical, methodological, and historical investigations deserved higher priority than econometric studies.

One obvious problem with this intellectual strategy, of course, is that it made our work increasingly vulnerable to dismissal by mainstream economists. How many times did I hear during the 1970s that my and our work seemed better suited to sociology and psychology than to economics? And those were the fields, indeed, where our work seemed to receive the more interested response. I read recently that in 1980 I was the individual economist most frequently cited in the two leading sociology journals; a comparable study of economics journals would surely have found that I didn't even make the charts.

For a variety of reasons, more or less around 1980, I began to return to more formal econometric work. I was beginning to feel more confident about theoretical foundations. Some of the historical work colleagues and I had been pursuing was beginning to give me some self-assurance that I knew what mattered and what didn't. I was getting more and more curious about the empirical plausibility of some of our ideas and felt it was time to put them to the econometric test. I wanted to try to provide a wider range of models of analytic modes of investigation for our graduate students as they approached dissertation time. And, quite frankly, I was growing irritated about the continuing — and even broadening — dismissal of our work by the mainstream. I wondered whether more formal econometric testing of some of our hypotheses might not garner more respect.

The payoff seemed immediate. At the American Economic Association meetings in 1980 I presented a first tentative effort to integrate some formal hypotheses about capital-labor relations into a time-series analysis of the productivity slowdown in the United States. The next day's feature *New York Times* story about the AEA meetings carried the headline, "Why Does Output Lag? Marxists Try an Answer." Mainstream discussants at the session seemed responsive. "The non-Marxians have no basis for being smug," one neoclassical discussant was quoted by the *Times* reporter.

A few years later, Bowles, Weisskopf, and I felt prepared to present a much more systematic analysis of the productivity slowdown building on our analysis of the postwar SSA and especially of the erosion of its "capital-labor accord." For our own purposes, as background and evidence for our book *Beyond the Waste Land,* we had already developed a core econometric model. But we hadn't yet formally tested our "social" model against what we called the "technical" models characteristic of neoclassical approaches. And we were determined to engage mainstream economists in debate about alternative perspectives on the productivity slowdown — and especially some of the policy implications of those alternatives.

Brookings Papers on Economic Activity seemed the ideal forum: it repeatedly published useful applied analyses of policy-related issues, it had already included some of the best standard studies of the productivity slowdown, it reached a broad audience, and its format, including both presentation to the Brookings Panel and published discussants' comments in the *BPEA,* seemed a model for encouraging dialogue. The problem, of course, is that one must be invited to present papers at the panel and thence to be published in the *BPEA*. And we were hardly in the pool of regular participants from whom the panel and the *Papers* drew.

So we began a tortuous process of inviting ourselves to be "invited" to present our paper. We had what seemed like endless discussions with one of the editors, responding to a number of reasonable concerns about our analysis and some hand-wringing about whether our results were "plausible." It sometimes seemed during those preliminary discussions that the editor was more worried about how he would appear to his colleagues if he invited us to enter the sanctum than about the actual content of our paper.

Ultimately, for whatever combination of reasons, we wore him down and we were able to present our paper, "Hearts and Minds: A Social Model of U.S. Productivity Growth" to the panel and to secure its publication in a 1983 issue of the *BPEA*. It seemed that the exercise had been worth the effort and even worth enduring all the hand-wringing. Many participants in the panel meetings gave us very favorable comments on our effort to model formally and operationalize econometrically a number of hypotheses about the social relations of production. Several seemed especially to appreciate our commitment to anticipating alternative mainstream counterhypotheses or objections and to test those against our own model. The editor who had invited us came over to us after the meetings and confessed with obvious relief that the discussion had seemed to him like a "lovefest."

Particularly after that apparently positive experience, I found myself drawn ever more insistently toward formal econometric tests in nearly all of my work. (There are of course exceptions. In one ongoing sideline activity, for example, I'm writing a book about the transition from feudalism to capitalism in Western Europe. I confess that I have not yet come up with any formal econometric exercises involving hypotheses for the period between 1000 and 1700 A.D.) I've presented an econometric critique of the conventional models apparently supporting the NAIRU hypothesis. With Bowles and Weisskopf, I've studied determinants of the rate of profit and the flow of investment. I've looked closely at some critical issues in some of the recent literature on long swings.

Most saliently for this discussion, I've devoted considerable attention to econometric formalization of some of our most unconventional hypotheses about institutions and social relations. I've been pursuing, for example, some econometric investigations of the transition from one SSA to another, involving studies of the transitional period over which econometric models appearing stably to characterize the behavioral relations of one institutional structure appear to acquire their force and maximum explanatory power.

Most ambitiously, I've been working for a number of years on construction of a medium-scale macroeconometric model that embodies a number of the "social" hypotheses that have developed through my and our joint work on SSAs in general and the postwar U.S. corporate system in particular. Many of my best friends have told me privately that they regard this enterprise as "David's folly," worrying that I would one day sink below the surface of the quicksand of operational and technical obstacles to substantial and effective macroeconometric modeling. But I've persisted for four main reasons. First, I've wanted to try to show that what many of us now call "structuralist" macroeconomics can be rendered coherently and applied econometrically as a legitimate, fully articulated alternative to various stripes of mainstream macro. Second, it's become a kind of challenge that my intellectual curiosity has found more and more intriguing as I've progressed, in spite of some of the difficulties. Third, I confess that I find some of the work involved simply and plainly a bundle of fun. And fourth, I continue to hope that the project as I've designed it — once it's completed — will provide the possibility of formal and commensurable comparisons between mainstream and structuralists models that will help clarify their most important differences and help persuade neoclassical economists to take at least some branches of left economics at least modestly seriously.

And so the formal econometric investigation of questions partly framed by my political involvements and interests continues. While my own independent interests have driven much of this work, I have continued to place a high priority on formal econometric analysis in part because I continue to hope that such formalizations would contribute to greater attention from and engagement with the mainstream.

But I confess, with substantial doses of hindsight, that I now think I've been a bit naive to expect that these econometric efforts would make much of a difference in reducing our marginalization within the economics profession. Looking back over a decade's such efforts, I've come to conclude that the sources of the mainstream's neglect of and disrespect for left economics lie elsewhere. My hopes that enhanced dialogue might result from playing by the rules of standard "normal" science now seem credulous.

A few examples may help illustrate the problem.

I've already described our efforts to project our "social" model of the productivity slowdown into the prevailing debate. At the time, the exercise seemed to have been successful by the standards we had set ourselves. We had carefully formulated some econometric tests in which the conventional "technical" explanations could be seen to be nested within our more inclusive "social" analysis. We were able to publish our results in a widely circulated mainstream journal. At the time, the discussants and others participating in the Brookings Panel discussion seemed both to appreciate our efforts at opening up dialogue and to take our efforts fairly seriously. We dared to assume that future mainstream discussions of the productivity slowdown would at least refer to and take into account our strand of explanation — especially since, judged by a number of relatively conventional econometric standards, we had carefully compared our approach with more conventional analyses and concluded by accepted criteria that we were better able to "account for" the slowdown than other prevailing explanations.

Our hopes have not been realized in the least. Our analysis appears to have dropped into the professional pond without leaving a ripple in mainstream discussions. In the ensuing decade, I have not yet seen a *single* mainstream catalog of "leading" explanations of the productivity slowdown that has mentioned our contribution even in passing. Despite our model's brief moment in the sunlight, and despite our own continuing efforts to update and reassert the analysis, it appears to have disappeared without a trace in the world of neo-classical economics.

The explanation is not easy to identify or articulate, but I think here have been at least two operative factors.

One has to do with what's considered respectable (read established and conventional) and what's not. Some kinds of work "matter" and some kinds don't. One of my most direct confrontations with these sorts of judgments, however veiled they may sometimes be, came with my first effort to secure funding from the Economics Program of the National Science Foundation — the principal public source of research support within economics in the United States. I had never bothered to apply until my work had turned toward more formal econometric analysis because until then I assumed application wouldn't have made much sense.

My first application, submitted in the mid-1980s for the initial stages of my macroeconometric modeling project, was fairly detailed but obviously left lots of questions underspecified since I hadn't yet done the work. The proposal was rejected even though a couple of outside reviewers had given it very high marks and some members of the Advisory Panel had supported it. Some of the outside reviewers' comments were so hostile and dismissive that I decided not to revise and resubmit it; it appeared on the basis of many of the responses that I would have had to complete the entire project before I would have enough detail of specification and evidence to persuade the skeptics.

But one of the program staff at NSF, who had already been very supportive and had himself expressed concern about the difficulties that other nonneoclassical economists had previously experienced in securing funding from the Economics Program, strongly urged me to resubmit — stressing that it appeared to him that most of the objections to my initial proposal could reasonably be answered. Despite my instinct that no amount of rewriting would persuade the Advisory Panel, I agreed to revise the proposal and resubmit it — at least partly in order to try to push the Advisory Panel to reveal its preferences more clearly.

So, working under a very tight deadline, I doubled the length of the text of the proposal, included considerably more detail of specification in appendices, and sought to respond to every objection that had been mentioned in the first-round written comments by outside reviewers. As I had expected, the second-round reviewers and advisers were unmoved. The outside ratings remained largely bimodal, with one mode expressing strong opposition, and, as far as I could tell, the critics on the Advisory Panel remained at least as hostile as before, if not more so — judging from what little I could surmise from the terse written summary of the Advisory Panel's discussion.

It turned out to have been even worse than I had imagined. One Advisory Panel member, a leading mainstream macroeconomist, breached the standard confidentiality of the NSF review procedure and wrote me a separate letter about the deliberations before the final staff decision was conveyed to me. Although it seems circumspect to withhold the name of this informant, he made clear that he did not regard the letter as confidential and so I feel comfortable quoting from it. "I will not reveal any confidences," he wrote, "by reporting that your proposal was beat up on, and that I was one of the few supporters." He characterized the general reaction as a "sea of intolerance." He continued:

> It was obvious, in reading your second proposal, that you did an enormous amount of work to respond conscientiously to the earlier objections, even though you were asking for a pittance. My view was that if NSF was going to support any radical economics within a 20-year metric, your proposal was it. Now I know better, and so write to advise you not to waste your time further. When you talk to the NSF panel as currently constituted, you are talking to a stone wall.

The subsequent official reaction confirmed the informant's report. My proposal was, of course, rejected. But the staff person within the Economics Program expressed considerable embarrassment about the virulence of the opposition to my proposal. He was sufficiently concerned about the appearance (to him, at least) of ideological and/or paradigmatic bias that he arranged for me to receive a token grant from the discretionary budget of the Director of the Social Science Division, within which the Economics Program is situated, as much to compensate me for the effort I had put into revising the proposal (at his encouragement) than for anything else. I very much appreciated this generosity beyond the call of duty, as I made clear to him, but it is some measure of how unusually this proposal was being handled that I had to attest orally over the phone that I understood that this token grant was not renewable "under any circumstances" — that it could not be treated as a potential candidate for renewal as would be true of any standard NSF project. I gratefully received my token research money, learned my lesson, and moved on. That was the last time I applied for research support from the NSF Economics Program.

A second source of neglect and dismissal seems to come from a simple lack of interest in the questions of power and institutional determination that frame much of our recent work. If they find the directions of academic work uninteresting, scholars can find any number of grounds on which to dismiss its rigor or coherence. If by contrast they find it intriguing, then a wide variety of peccadilloes may conceivably be forgiven.

This, at least, is how I interpret recent experiences with article submissions to mainstream economics journals. Take a paper on investment that Bowles, Weisskopf, and I have, at the time of writing this essay, been trying fitfully to get published in established economics journals for a number of years. The paper develops a formal model, with econometric tests, to link our work on the postwar SSA in the United States with the standard literature on aggregate investment functions, aiming to provide a more complete explanation of the continued stagnation of net fixed nonresidential investment than (we feel) has been available. We seem to get a consistent response at each doorstep.

Upon first submission, anonymous referees express tepid interest in the basic ideas and considerable hostility to the paper's implementation of its ideas. The paper is then rejected by the journal editor.

But, moved by sympathy or guilt or some other obscure ambivalence, the editor at the same time chooses, as one rejection letter put it, "to leave open the possibility of your submitting a suitably revised version." We don't like the paper, they say in effect, but we don't want to appear to be giving you the complete cold shoulder.

In one case, we responded diligently to all the objections and suggestions, submitted a "suitably revised version," and received yet another rejection. The objections were couched in entirely technical terms, but one couldn't help feeling, in the end, that the basic project seemed so disconnected to the mainstream research program that no amount of technical wizardry in response could possibly overcome their basic indifference.

The Wheel Turns

This neglect and dismissal is frustrating, to be sure, but in the end I remind myself that it doesn't matter all that much.

I continue to pursue economics because I hope that some of my work will help illuminate the obstacles to and possibilities for a more democratic, decent, and egalitarian society. I continue to pursue economics as well because I find many problems just plain challenging and fun to tackle. And I knew nearly thirty years ago that choosing a career path as a heterodox economist would probably mean that I would be excluded from the dominant intellectual and policy debate.

I care most about remaining faithful to my political concerns and scientific standards. Though I sometimes grit my teeth about the politics of the scientific community itself, I let the rest of the chips fall where they may.

NOTES

1. Referring to the economics profession in this piece, I shall use the terms *mainstream* and *neoclassical* interchangeably. I realize that many readers will be a bit nonplused at the idea that the "mainstream" is as monolithic as I appear to suggest in my discussion here. I recognize that there are many differences of view within neoclassical economics, but I also assert for the purposes of discussion that there is a social community of (orthodox) economists who, despite their differences, engage each other in discussion and debate and who refer to each other's work — and that we who characterize ourselves as "left" economists have historically remained outside that community, largely ignored by, and rarely included in, their discussions. I write this not as an expression of complaint but merely as an empirical observation about my own experiences within economics.

2. The Progressive Alliance initiative looked very promising heading into early 1980. But when Teddy Kennedy announced his electoral challenge to incumbent president Jimmy Carter, leaders of the Progressive Alliance worried that the coalition would be seen simply as a "stalking horse" for the Kennedy's campaign, which it most certainly was not, and suspended operations for the duration of the 1980 election campaign lest the principles and politics of the coalition be misinterpreted or compromised. After the right's electoral victories in November 1980, the coalition project was never revived.

ELHANAN HELPMAN

Doing Research

My encounter with economics took place in a most unlikely setting: a military base of the Israel Defense Force (IDF). In high school I was interested in mechanical engineering. My additional interests included mathematics, physics, and Hebrew literature. But engineering was my obvious choice for a future career.

When I was about eighteen, a soldier who served with me in the IDF took evening classes in economics, at what used to be the Hebrew University's extension in Tel Aviv. One day I discovered on her desk a thick volume that was the Hebrew version of Samuelson's textbook. The translation was terrible. It employed convoluted Hebrew terms for simple economic concepts. Nevertheless, I fell in love with the book's content. What struck me most was the realization that one can in fact think systematically about complex social phenomena and describe them in precise language. All this was new to me, and my fascination grew with every page.

There was no one around me to share my enthusiasm, including the woman whose book I was reading. But I kept thinking about demand and supply curves, consumption and saving, and comparative advantage, for hours, day after day. At that point I decided to study economics.

And so I did. Upon completion of my military service, I enrolled in Tel Aviv University, majoring in economics and statistics. During the first year in college I found the study of economics extremely difficult. Mastering a variety of analytical techniques and linking them to relatively loose verbal arguments proved to be much harder than I had expected. But this mix also captured my imagination; I was constantly searching for ways to translate verbal descriptions of economic phenomena into analytical forms. This search has proved to be central to much of my subsequent research. I am still fascinated by our ability to tell economic stories analytically, in ways that enable us to see far beyond the obvious. And I judge much of applied theory in this light.

Two of my teachers who had the largest impact on my education were Eitan Berglas and Menachem Yaari. Their methods of deliberation in class were very different, as were their research styles. In my mind, however, their approaches were complementary. They molded my approach to economics.

The late Eitan Berglas saw economic considerations everywhere. He was always ready and willing to explain them in simple terms and to argue about them passionately. For him, to use a verbal argument, complemented by a simple diagram or an equation and a piece of empirical evidence or institutional detail to support a specification, was as natural as speaking Hebrew. His intuition was so powerful that he felt wholly at ease with this mix of methods. And this is how I was introduced to public finance and to international trade. I admired his style but I never felt comfortable using it myself. In fact, it became clear to me soon enough that I needed to find my own way of doing economics. But it also became clear to me that in addition to theory I needed to study the available evidence and the nature of institutions. Although I myself have not done much empirical research and no work at all on institutions, this early experience induced me to spend much time reading about them.

I took my first course in price theory from Menachem Yaari. This was an experimental course, designed to teach graduate microeconomics to undergraduate students. It included the axiomatic foundations of utility theory on the one hand and the dual approach to consumer theory on the other. Yaari presented the arguments with great precision, devoting much time to the discussion of the meaning of axioms and the restrictiveness of assumptions. And he elevated the Hebrew language, as used in economic discourse, to new heights.[1] I was thrilled. And in those early days of my education I became obsessed with a need to see economics through the lens of this type of theory. I recall spending endless hours in the library, reading journal articles, in an attempt to understand in this way the topics that I was studying in other classes. Little did I know at that time that not all of economics is viewed this way.

Berglas and Yaari were my intellectual heroes. Each one of them planted a seed that grew into a different passion; to understand economics as an applied subject on the one hand and to frame it in elegant theory on the other. For many years, as I went through graduate school and beyond, I struggled to reconcile the differences between these passions. And this struggle led me to focus on applied theory.

In graduate school I had little difficulty with the core courses. On the other hand, I felt ignorant about many areas of economics. My education at Tel Aviv University notwithstanding, the diversity of economics as a scientific discipline appeared to me to be overwhelming (as it still does). As a result I attended many classes, with the aim of broadening my education. Harvard was a perfect place for this purpose. First, the program allowed the student (almost) unlimited flexibility, of which I took full advantage. Second, not only did I have the opportunity to take classes from some of the profession's greatest scholars, but I also had wonderful classmates with whom I studied and with whom I collaborated on my first papers. Those years were a true intellectual treat, strengthening my desire to broaden and deepen my understanding of economics. Some of my early research efforts (in economic theory, public finance, urban economics, and macroeconomics), both in graduate school and upon my return to Tel Aviv University, were driven by this desire. I learned a great deal from my collaborators in those days, and that experience was important for my future work.[2]

For a number of years I had no clear research agenda. In retrospect, it appears that—as far as my evolution as an economist is concerned—I spent the first few years as a faculty member at Tel Aviv University extending my graduate education. Except that then, rather than attending classes, most of the education consisted of writing papers and voraciously reading the related literature. The many term papers that I had submitted to my teachers at Harvard prepared me quite well for this task.

Graduate students on the American job market get points for having a research agenda that they can eloquently describe to their interviewers. I do not know whether this was also true in 1974. But if I had gone on the American job market at that time, I would most likely not have done well on this score. On the other hand, the young department of economics at Tel Aviv University cheerfully tolerated my nonfocused research style.

My first major research project was undertaken jointly with

Assaf Razin. We were both familiar with international finance and with international trade. And we were puzzled by the fact that assets play an important role in the theory of international finance and hardly any role in the theory of international trade. Where did this dichotomy come from? We discussed this issue at some length and concluded that trade in assets may interact in important ways with trade in goods and services. As a result it would be interesting to develop a theory that clarified these interactions. If such a theory could be developed, we reasoned, it should also help in understanding the effects of capital-market policies on trade in goods and services. With these goals in mind, off we went to work on a theory of international trade under uncertainty in which asset markets play a significant role. The result was a series of papers in which we constructed such a theory and applied it to a variety of policy problems. Eventually, we wrote a book that synthesized the papers and provided a systematic exposition of the theory. Little did I know then that this pattern — writing a sequence of papers that build up a theory, and eventually producing a book that provides a synthesis — would repeat itself.

Although I have written a number of books, I have to admit that I never enjoyed writing them. In fact, I find the process of writing a book very painful. This is partly the result of the fact that I write slowly and have to rewrite sentences and paragraphs many times before I am satisfied with the outcome.[3] And it is partly a result of the fact that books require a broader coverage as compared to journal articles. As a result, much time is spent filling in gaps that are not very interesting but that need to be included for completeness. Finally, writing a book entails a severe mental strain. When I am writing a paper or a book, the content of the piece never leaves my mind. It usually requires intense concentration during the actual writing hours, but I also keep thinking about it during meal times, during faculty and committee meetings, and, unfortunately, even in class. I therefore have a strong preference for writing during a span of time in which I have few other commitments. This can often be arranged for a paper, but not for a book, the writing of which lasts a year or more. And this mental pressure rises over time as more and more chapters are completed. I cannot focus exclusively on the new chapter being written. It is as if all the chapters are stored in my mind, and I keep going over them time and again, examining the arguments, the clarity of exposition, and the links between the chapters.

So why write a book? I am not absolutely certain about the answer to this question. The urge to do it builds up gradually. It happens after working on a subject for a number of years, when a distinct perception crystallizes that the papers do not do justice to the subject in the sense that there is a wider truth embodied in this line of work that the readers of the papers may miss. Next comes a cooler calculus. Are the results of this project ripe enough to justify the effort? Justify not only in terms of the amount of time it takes to write a book, but primarily in terms of the benefits to prospective readers. I view a book as a major statement by its writers. Therefore, as a reader I would like to know that at least the authors have faith in its content. As a result I do not wish to write a book unless I am convinced that its messages are important.

Let me give an example. While still working on the theory of international trade under uncertainty, Assaf Razin and I began to ponder the broader relationships between international finance/ macroeconomics and international trade. One particularly acute problem that struck us at the time (and which has still not been resolved) is how to evaluate alternative exchange rate regimes. We had analytical tools to compare the efficiency of competition with monopoly, or free trade with tariff-ridden trade. But we had no comparable tools to compare fixed with flexible exchange rates. This was just one example of the difficulties encountered in dealing with problems in which the interaction between monetary and real features of an economy are central. And this was, we thought, an extremely important example worth studying.

We first wrote an exploratory paper that prompted us to dig deeper into this problem. Then I went on leave to the University of Rochester, during which time I examined the cash-in-advance approach as a building block for a theory of exchange rate regimes. Although I believed at the time that a satisfactory theory needs to take explicit account of the structure of financial institutions, I was sufficiently pleased with the outcome to feel justified in pursuing a simplified model without financial institutions. Upon my return to Tel Aviv University, Assaf Razin and I continued this line of research, exploring complications that result from uncertainty and incomplete markets and from restrictions on payments in different currencies. We wrote a series of papers with a common theme and a common analytical structure. Other researches addressed related issues in much the same spirit. But at the end of the day I did not feel justified in writing a book synthesizing this line of work. The reason was simple: I did not have enough faith in the theory. To be sure, I thought at the time, as I do today, that our effort was worthwhile. However, I viewed it as a preliminary step in the construction of a more elaborate theory that should incorporate financial intermediation as a central element in the determination of exchange rate movements. One purpose of this theory would be to evaluate alternative exchange rate regimes in the context of existing financial institutions. But we were not able to take the next step, and not for lack of trying. It just happened that we had an overambitious research agenda that we could not carry through to a satisfactory conclusion.

This brings me to an important point about research strategy. In my experience, it pays to pursue a far-reaching research agenda, even if the chances of completing it successfully are slim. Setting far-reaching goals releases energies and capabilities of whose presence we are otherwise unaware. With goals like these before us, even partial success often proves more valuable than complete attainment of a simple goal. And last but not least, the pursuit of a distant target brings with it prolonged periods of excitement (that often needs to be controlled in order not to disturb family and friends) and incomparable satisfaction with the attainment of every intermediate target.

There is, of course, a downside to this strategy. It brings with it periods of slow progress and frustration, bad moods, and low spirits. One has to get accustomed to the idea that months will pass with no visible progress. This does not necessarily mean that no progress has been made. Sometimes incubation periods for ideas are very long. Then, all we can write in our report cards is that we have been thinking but have no results to report. Nevertheless, these periods are not a waste of time; they are just part of the creative process. When I find myself in one of these moods, I turn to the library. I collect readings on the subject that is keeping me awake at night, and I read endlessly. The process of reading does not disturb the thinking; in fact, it reinforces it. And often something that comes up in the reading triggers a thought that helps resolve the difficulty.[4]

While still in Rochester, I began to think about the need to integrate international trade with industrial organization; there were too many industrial sectors that did not fit into the Heckscher-Ohlin framework. It was not clear to me, however, which of the many forms of market structures to study first. I spent much time considering various alternatives, weighing their advantages and disadvantages in terms of the types of questions that they might help to address, and I could not make up my mind. This state of flux changed when I encountered Kelvin Lancaster's new book *Variety, Equity, and Efficiency.* Chapter 10 in particular, in which he applied monopolistic competition to international trade in a one-sector framework, convinced me that this could be an extremely useful approach. Afterward I became acquainted with Paul Krugman's paper, which was published at about the same time, and which also employed a one-sector framework. Equipped with these insights, I proceeded to extend the Heckscher-Ohlin theory to economies with product differentiation and monopolistic competition. My immediate purpose was to examine which elements of the Heckscher-Ohlin theory survive this type of generalization and what new insights it can provide. First and foremost, I expected insights into the determinants of the share of intraindustry trade and the volume of trade. However, my longer-run goal was to develop a more general theory of trade in the presence of economies of scale and imperfect competition.

Back in Tel Aviv, I continued to work on this project, my excitement growing with each new result. This excitement peaked in 1980, when I presented my paper in a summer workshop in Warwick. There I was introduced to related work by Dixit and Norman, and by Krugman, who also attended the workshop. It became apparent there that the theory of international trade was changing its face.

I continued to work on monopolistic competition for a number of years. At the same time I was working on a chapter for the *Handbook of International Economics,* which gave me the opportunity to review the literature on economies of scale and imperfect competition. Handling this literature only strengthened my feeling that important elements of the Heckscher-Ohlin theory are not necessarily related to constant returns to scale or to perfect competition, and that each form of imperfect competition may provide distinct insights on particular issues. I felt uncomfortable relying on a taxonomic approach and kept wondering how to avoid it. The opportunity to address this set of issues seriously arose when I took leave at MIT in 1983.[5] Paul Krugman had just returned from the Council of Economic Advisers, and we agreed that the time was ripe for a synthesis of the theory of international trade under imperfect competition and economies of scale. Our challenge was to fill in a number of major gaps and to provide a unified treatment of the subject. A year later we had a draft of *Market Structure and Foreign Trade.*

Coauthors have played an important role in my life. Assaf Razin early on; Paul Krugman, with whom I wrote two books but not a single paper, later on; and Gene Grossman, with whom I wrote a number of papers and a book, more recently.[6] With each one of them I worked in different ways, and from each I learned a great deal. Common to these collaborations was a sense of purpose: the choice of important goals, and the design of paths to reach them that are both interesting and worth exploring even part way. Doing research is a lonely enterprise. And although I very much like to spend at least several hours a day shut up in my study—reading, writing, and thinking—I also like to share the burden of a major research effort with a person whose intellectual outlook is close to mine. Research leads to many hours of hard internal reflection. It also raises questions that stick in the mind for long periods of time while we have to go about doing our daily chores. A successful collaboration provides a channel of intellectual exchange that eases these pressures. And it provides the pleasure of company and moments of fun.

I have been lucky with my collaborators. I have enjoyed watching the workings of their minds, and I have seen them in moments of sheer brilliance. A collaboration is often like a Ping-Pong game, where ideas are tossed back and forth. Except that no matter who scores, you end up winning.

One of my most successful collaborations has been with Gene Grossman, with whom I have been working for more than seven years at the time of this writing. We started our research effort with an attempt to construct a dynamic trade theory. In models of monopolistic competition, the fixed cost of a brand was often interpreted as R&D costs. By treating R&D as an investment that precedes manufacturing, we reasoned, we should be able to develop a dynamic trade theory that will explain the evolution of man-made comparative advantage in industrial products and the timing of important events, such as the emergence of multinational corporations. The idea was simple, but in 1986 there was little experience with these type of models. We began to struggle with this problem in Tel Aviv and continued to struggle with it in the United States, when I went on leave to MIT a year later. The result was a paper on product development and international trade.

In that paper we had to rely on rather restrictive assumptions in order to characterize the dynamic trajectory of two trading economies. Nevertheless, in the course of that investigation we acquired some expertise — via learning by doing — in working out dynamic trade models with monopolistic competition, and we developed a methodology that served us well in later work. Encouraged by that experience, we moved on to a truly ambitious project: to construct a theory that would clarify the links between international trade and economic growth, in which industrial innovation serves as a major engine of productivity gains. There were many questions we hoped to address with this theory. In a way, it looked like an open-ended agenda. This research effort, lasting for several years, led to the publication of *Innovation and Growth in the Global Economy.*

Close collaborations used to rely almost entirely on face-to-face meetings. With the advent of new technologies, however, the amount of time required for this purpose has significantly declined. During the many years of working jointly with Grossman, we have been communicating almost daily by means of electronic mail. With e-mail, the fax machine, and the telephone, most of the necessary communication between Princeton and Tel Aviv was feasible. Now, with the ability to transfer documents over e-mail, writing joint papers and revising them has become easier than ever before. For these reasons face-to-face meetings may seem to be unnecessary. But are they?

My experience has been that much as the new technologies have greatly reduced the need for personal meetings, they have not eliminated those needs altogether. There exist critical stages that do require face-to-face meetings. These are mostly stages in which a problem is formulated, in which questions to be addressed have to be formulated, and in which alternative ideas have to be explored in order to form a judgment as to which will be most useful for the purpose at hand. At these critical stages the personal touch plays a preeminent role. Good chemistry between collaborators produces conversations in the course of which suggestions by one party trigger new ideas in the mind of the other. This type of exchange, which is fascinating in itself, helps to solve the most difficult problems.

Doing research is a lifestyle. And like other forms of lifestyle, each one of us has to find out what suits him best.

NOTES

1. For me this was a great relief after the experience I had had with the translation of Samuelson's *Economics.*

2. In graduate school, and during the early years at Tel Aviv University, I collaborated with Robert Cooter, June Flanders, Arye Hillman, Jean-Jacques Laffont, David Pines, Assaf Razin, and Efraim Sadka.

3. Satisfaction is used here as a relative term, because upon rereading a text I almost always have the urge to change something.

4. The reading items do not necessarily consist of technical articles. Often, these will be works of historians, political scientists, or business commentators, who describe real-world phenomena that we are trying to model. These sources are important for the applied theorist.

5. I spent the preceding year at Harvard, working primarily on the theory of multinational corporations.

6. Other coauthors, whom I have not mentioned so far, include Shmuel Ben-Zvi, Eitan Berglas, Eli Borukhov, Gil Bufman, David Coe, Michael Dooley, Allan Drazen, Harry Flam, Leonardo Leiderman, and Manuel Trajtenberg.

PAUL KRUGMAN

How I Work

My formal charge in this essay is to talk about my "life philosophy." Let me make it clear at the outset that I have no intention of following instructions, since I don't know anything special about life in general. I believe it was Schumpeter who claimed to be not only the best economist, but also the best horseman and the best lover in his native Austria. I don't ride horses, and have few illusions on other scores. (I am, however, a pretty good cook.)

What I want to talk about in this essay is something more restricted: some thoughts about thinking, and particularly how to go about doing interesting economics. I think that among economists of my generation I can claim to have a fairly distinctive intellectual style — not necessarily a better style than my colleagues, for there are many ways to be a good economist, but one that has served me well. The essence of that style is a general research strategy that can be summarized in a few rules; I also view my more policy-oriented writing and speaking as ultimately grounded in the same principles. I'll get to my rules for research later in this essay. I think I can best introduce those rules, however, by describing how (it seems to me) I stumbled into the way I work.

Origins

Most young economists today enter the field from the technical end. Originally intending a career in hard science or engineering, they slip

This essay was previously published in *American Economist* 37, no. 2 (fall 1993): 5–16.

down the scale into the most rigorous of the social sciences. The advantages of entering economics from that direction are obvious: one arrives already well trained in mathematics, one finds the concept of formal modeling natural. It is not, however, where I come from. My first love was history; I studied little math, picking up what I needed as I went along.

Nonetheless, I got deeply involved in economics early, working as a research assistant (on world energy markets) to William Nordhaus while still only a junior at Yale. Graduate school followed naturally, and I wrote my first really successful paper — a theoretical analysis of balance-of-payments crises — while still at MIT. I discovered that I was facile with small mathematical models, with a knack for finding simplifying assumptions that made them tractable. Still, when I left graduate school I was, in my own mind at least, somewhat directionless. I was not sure what to work on; I was not even sure whether I really liked research.

I found my intellectual feet quite suddenly, in January 1978. Feeling somewhat lost, I paid a visit to my old adviser Rudi Dornbusch. I described several ideas to him, including a vague notion that the monopolistic-competition models I had studied in a short course offered by Bob Solow — especially the lovely little model of Dixit and Stiglitz — might have something to do with international trade. Rudi flagged that idea as potentially very interesting indeed; I went home to work on it seriously; and within a few days I realized that I had hold of something that would form the core of my professional life.

What had I found? The point of my trade models was not particularly startling once one thought about it: economies of scale could be an independent cause of international trade, even in the absence of comparative advantage. This was a new insight to me but had (as I soon discovered) been pointed out many times before by critics of conventional trade theory. The models I worked out left some loose ends hanging; in particular, they typically had many equilibria. Even so, to make the models tractable I had to make obviously unrealistic assumptions. And once I had made those assumptions, the models were trivially simple; writing them up left me no opportunity to display any high-powered technique. So one might have concluded that I was doing nothing very interesting (and that was what some of my colleagues were to tell me over the next few years). Yet what I saw — and for some reason saw almost immediately — was that all of these features were virtues, not vices, that they added up to a program that could lead to years of productive research.

I was, of course, only saying something that critics of conventional theory had been saying for decades. Yet my point was not part of the mainstream of international economics. Why? Because it had never been expressed in nice models. The new monopolistic-competition models gave me a tool to open cleanly what had previously been regarded as a can of worms. More important, however, I suddenly realized the remarkable extent to which the methodology of economics creates blind spots. We just don't see what we can't formalize. And the biggest blind spot of all has involved increasing returns. So there, right at hand, was my mission: to look at things from a slightly different angle, and in so doing to reveal the obvious, things that had been right under our noses all the time.

The models I wrote down that winter and spring were incomplete, if one demanded of them that they specify exactly who produced what. And yet they told meaningful stories. It took me a long time to express clearly what I was doing, but eventually I realized that one way to deal with a difficult problem is to change the question—in particular by shifting levels. A detailed analysis may be extremely nasty, yet an aggregative or systemic description that is far easier may tell you all you need to know.

To get this system or aggregate level description required means, of course, accepting the basically silly assumptions of symmetry that underlay the Dixit-Stiglitz and related models. Yet these silly assumptions seemed to let me tell stories that were persuasive, and that could not be told using the hallowed assumptions of the standard competitive model. What I began to realize was that in economics we are always making silly assumptions; it's just that some of them have been made so often that they come to seem natural. And so one should not reject a model as silly until one sees where its assumptions lead.

Finally, the simplicity of the models may have frustrated my lingering urge to show off the technical skills I had so laboriously acquired in graduate school but was, I soon realized, central to the enterprise. Trade theorists had failed to address the role of increasing returns, not out of empirical conviction, but because they thought it was too hard to model. How much more effective, then, to show that it could be almost childishly simple?

And so, before my twenty-fifth birthday, I basically knew what I was going to do with my professional life. I don't know what would have happened if my grand project had met with rejection from other economists — perhaps I would have turned cranky, perhaps I would have lost faith and abandoned the effort. But in fact all went astonishingly well. In my own mind, the curve of my core research since that January of 1978 has followed a remarkably consistent path. Within a few months, I had written up a basic monopolistic competition trade model — as it turned out, simultaneously and independently with similar models by Avinash Dixit and Victor Norman, on one side, and Kelvin Lancaster, on the other. I had some trouble getting that paper published — receiving the dismissive rejection by a flagship journal (the *QJE*) that seems to be the fate of every innovation in economics — but pressed on. From 1978 to roughly the end of 1984 I focused virtually all my research energies on the role of increasing returns and imperfect competition in international trade. (I took one year off to work in the U.S. government; but more about that below.) What had been a personal quest turned into a movement, as others followed the same path. Above all, Elhanan Helpman — a deep thinker whose integrity and self-discipline were useful counterparts to my own flakiness and disorganization — first made crucial contributions himself, then talked me into collaborative work. Our magnum opus, *Market Structure and Foreign Trade,* served the purpose of making our ideas not only respectable but almost standard: iconoclasm to orthodoxy in seven years.

For whatever reason, I allowed my grand project on increasing returns to lie fallow for a few years in the 1980s and turned my attention to international finance. My work in this area consisted primarily of small models inspired by current policy issues; although these models lacked the integrating theme of my trade models, I think that my finance work is to some extent unified by its intellectual style, which is very similar to that of my work on trade.

In 1990 I returned to the economics of increasing returns from a new direction. I suddenly realized that the techniques that had allowed us to legitimize the role of increasing returns in trade could also be used to reclaim a whole outcast field: that of economic geography, the location of activity in space. Here, perhaps even more than in trade, was a field full of empirical insights, good stories, and obvious practical importance, lying neglected right under our noses because nobody had seen a good way to formalize it. For me, it was like reliving the best moments of my intellectual childhood. Doing geography is hard work; it requires a lot of hard thinking to make the models look trivial, and I am increasingly finding that I need the computer as an aid not just to data analysis but even to theorizing. Yet it is immensely rewarding. For me, the biggest thrill in theory is the moment when your model tells you something that should have been obvious all along, something that you can immediately relate to what you know about the world, and yet which you didn't really appreciate. Geography still has that thrill.

My work on geography seems, at the time of writing, to be leading me even further afield. In particular, there are obvious affinities between the concepts that arise naturally in geographic models and the language of traditional development economics — the "high development theory" that flourished in the 1940s and 1950s, then collapsed. So I expect that my basic research project will continue to widen in scope.

Rules for Research
In the course of describing my formative moment in 1978, I have already implicitly given my four basic rules for research. Let me now state them explicitly, then explain. Here are the rules:

1. Listen to the Gentiles

2. Question the question

3. Dare to be silly

4. Simplify, simplify

Listen to the Gentiles
What I mean by this rule is "Pay attention to what intelligent people are saying, even if they do not have your customs or speak your analytical language." The point may perhaps best be explained by example. When I began my rethinking of international trade, there was already a sizable literature criticizing conventional trade theory. Empiricists pointed out that trade took place largely between countries with seemingly similar factor endowments, and that much of this trade involved intraindustry exchanges of seemingly similar products. Acute observers pointed to the importance of economies of scale and imperfect competition in actual international markets. Yet all of this intelligent commentary was ignored by mainstream trade

theorists—after all, their critics often seemed to have an imperfect understanding of comparative advantage and had no coherent models of their own to offer; so why pay attention to them? The result was that the profession overlooked evidence and stories that were right under its nose.

The same story is repeated in geography. Geographers and regional scientists have amassed a great deal of evidence on the nature and importance of localized external economies, and organized that evidence intelligently if not rigorously. Yet economists have ignored what they had to say, because it comes from people speaking the wrong language.

I do not mean to say that formal economic analysis is worthless, and that anybody's opinion on economic matters is as good as anyone else's. On the contrary! I am a strong believer in the importance of models, which are to our minds what spear-throwers were to Stone Age arms: they greatly extend the power and range of our insight. In particular, I have no sympathy for those people who criticize the unrealistic simplifications of model-builders and imagine that they achieve greater sophistication by avoiding stating their assumptions clearly. The point is to realize that economic models are metaphors, not truth. By all means express your thoughts in models, as pretty as possible (more on that below). But always remember that you may have gotten the metaphor wrong, and that someone else with a different metaphor may be seeing something that you are missing.

Question the Question

There was a limited literature on external economies and international trade before 1978. It was never, however, very influential, because it seemed terminally messy; even the simplest models became bogged down in a taxonomy of possible outcomes. What has since become clear is that this messiness arose in large part because the modelers were asking their models to do what traditional trade models do, which is to predict a precise pattern of specialization and trade. Yet why ask that particular question? Even in the Heckscher-Ohlin model, the point you want to make is something like, "A country tends to export goods whose production is intensive in the factors in which that country is abundant"; if your specific model tells you that capital-abundant country Home exports capital-intensive good X, this is valuable because it sharpens your understanding of that insight, not because you really care about these particular details of a patently oversimplified model.

It turns out that if you don't ask for the kind of detail that you get in the two-sector, two-good classical model, an external-economy model needn't be at all messy. As long as you ask "system" questions like how welfare and world income are distributed, it is possible to make very simple and neat models. And it's really these system questions that we are interested in. The focus on excessive detail was, to put it bluntly, a matter of carrying over ingrained prejudices from an overworked model into a domain where they only made life harder.

The same is true in a number of areas in which I have worked. In general, if people in a field have bogged down on questions that seem very hard, it is a good idea to ask whether they are really working on the right questions. Often some other question is not only easier to answer but actually more interesting! (One drawback of this trick is that it often gets people angry. An academic who has spent years on a hard problem is rarely grateful when you suggest that his field can be revived by bypassing it.)

Dare to Be Silly

If you want to publish a paper in economic theory, there is a safe approach: make a conceptually minor but mathematically difficult extension to some familiar model. Because the basic assumptions of the model are already familiar, people will not regard them as strange; because you have done something technically difficult, you will be respected for your demonstration of firepower. Unfortunately, you will not have added much to human knowledge.

What I found myself doing in the new trade theory was pretty much the opposite. I found myself using assumptions that were unfamiliar, and doing very simple things with them. Doing this requires a lot of self-confidence, because initially people (especially referees) are almost certain not simply to criticize your work but to ridicule it. After all, your assumptions will surely look peculiar: a continuum of goods all with identical production functions, entering symmetrically into utility? Countries of identical economic size, with mirror-image factor endowments? Why, people will ask, should they be interested in a model with such silly assumptions — especially when there are evidently much smarter young people who demonstrate their quality by solving hard problems?

What seems terribly hard for many economists to accept is that all our models involve silly assumptions. Given what we know about cognitive psychology, utility maximization is a ludicrous concept; equilibrium pretty foolish outside of financial markets; perfect competition a howler for most industries. The reason for making these assumptions is not that they are reasonable but that they seem to help us produce models that are helpful metaphors for things that we think happen in the real world.

Consider the example that some economists seem to think is not simply a useful model but revealed divine truth: the Arrow-Debreu model of perfect competition with utility maximization and complete markets. This is indeed a wonderful model — not because its assumptions are remotely plausible but because it helps us think more clearly about both the nature of economic efficiency and the prospects for achieving efficiency under a market system. It is actually a piece of inspired, marvelous silliness.

What I believe is that the age of creative silliness is not past. Virtue, as an economic theorist, does not consist in squeezing the last drop of blood out of assumptions that have come to seem natural because they have been used in a few hundred earlier papers. If a new set of assumptions seems to yield a valuable set of insights, then never mind if they seem strange.

Simplify, Simplify

The injunction to dare to be silly is not a license to be undisciplined. In fact, doing really innovative theory requires much more intellectual discipline than working in a well-established literature. What is really hard is to stay on course: since the terrain is unfamiliar, it is all too easy to find yourself going around in circles. Somewhere or other Keynes wrote that "it is astonishing what foolish things a man thinking alone can come temporarily to believe." And it is also crucial to express your ideas in a way that other people, who have not spent the last few years wrestling with your problems and are not eager to spend the next few years wrestling with your answers, can understand without too much effort.

Fortunately, there is a strategy that does double duty: it both helps you keep control of your own insights and makes those insights accessible to others. The strategy is: always try to express your ideas in the simplest possible model. The act of stripping down to this minimalist model will force you to get to the essence of what you are trying to say (and will also make obvious to you those situations in which you actually have nothing to say). And this minimalist model will then be easy to explain to other economists as well.

I have used the "minimum necessary model" approach over and over again: using a one-factor, one-industry model to explain the basic role of monopolistic competition in trade; assuming sector-specific labor rather than full Heckscher-Ohlin factor substitution to explain the effects of intraindustry trade; working with symmetric countries to assess the role of reciprocal dumping; and so on. In each case the effect has been to allow me to tackle a subject widely viewed as formidably difficult with what appears, at first sight, to be ridiculous simplicity.

The downside of this strategy is, of course, that many of your colleagues will tend to assume that an insight that can be expressed in a cute little model must be trivial and obvious — it takes some sophistication to realize that simplicity may be the result of years of hard thinking. I have heard the story that when Joseph Stiglitz was being considered for tenure at Yale, one of his senior colleagues belittled his work, saying that it consisted mostly of little models rather than deep theorems. Another colleague then asked, "But couldn't you say the same about Paul Samuelson?" "Yes, I could," replied Joe's opponent. I have heard the same reaction to my own work. Luckily, there are enough sophisticated economists around that in the end intellectual justice is usually served. And there is a special delight in managing not only to boldly go where no economist has gone before, but to do so in a way that seems after the fact to be almost child's play.

I have now described by basic rules for research. I have illustrated them with my experience in developing the "new trade theory" and with my more recent extension of that work to economic geography, because these are the core of my work. But I have also done quite a lot of other stuff, which (it seems to me) is also in some sense part of the same enterprise. So in the remainder of this essay I want to talk about this other work, and in particular about how the policy economist and the analytical economist can coexist in the same person.

Policy-Relevant Work

Most economic theorists keep their hands off current policy issues — or if they do get involved in policy debates, do so only after the midpoint of their career, as something that follows creative theorizing rather than coexists with it. There seems to be a consensus that the clarity and singleness of purpose required to do good theory are incompatible with the tolerance for messy issues required to be active in policy discussion. For me, however, it has never worked that way. I have interspersed my academic career with a number of consulting ventures for various governments and public agencies, as well as a full year in the U.S. government. I have also written a book, *The Age of Diminished Expectations,* aimed at a nontechnical audience. And I have written a pretty steady stream of papers that are motivated not by the inner logic of my research but by the attempt to make sense of some currently topical policy debate — for example, Third World debt relief, target zones for exchange rates, the rise of regional trading blocs. All of this hasn't seemed to hurt my research, and indeed some of my favorite papers have grown out of this policy-oriented work.

Why doesn't policy-relevant work seem to conflict with my "real" research? I think that it's because I have been able to approach policy issues using almost exactly the same method that I use in my more basic work. Paying attention to newspaper reports or the concerns of central bankers and finance ministers is just another form of listening to the Gentiles. Trying to find a useful way of defining their problems is pretty much the same as questioning the question in theory. Confronting supposedly knowledgeable people with an unorthodox view of an issue certainly requires the courage to be silly. And of course, ruthless simplification is worth even more in policy discussion than in theory for its own sake.

So doing policy-relevant economics does not, for me, mean a drastic change in intellectual style. And it has its own payoffs. Let's be honest and admit that these include invitations to fancier conferences and speaking engagements at much higher fees than an academic purist is likely to get. Let's also admit that one of the joys of policy research is the opportunity to shock the bourgeoisie, to point out the hollowness or silliness of official positions. For example, I know that I was not the only international economist to have some fun pointing out the absurdities of the Maastricht Treaty, and was not above some wicked pleasure when the ERM crisis I and others had long predicted actually came to pass in the fall of 1992. The main payoff to policy work, though, is intellectual stimulation. Not all real-world questions are interesting — I find that almost anything having to do with taxation is better than a sleeping pill—but every couple of years, if not more often, the international economy throws up a question that gives rise to exciting research. I have been stimulated to write theory papers by the Plaza and the Louvre, by the Brady Plan, NAFTA, and EMU. All of them are papers that I think could stand on their own, even without the policy context.

There is, of course, always a risk that an economist who gets onto the policy circuit will no longer have enough time for real research. I certainly write an awfully large number of conference papers; I am a very fast writer, but perhaps it is a gift I overuse. Still, I think that the big danger of doing policy research is not so much the drain on your time as the threat to your values. It is easy to be seduced into the belief that direct influence on policy is more important than just writing papers—I've seen it happen to many colleagues. Once you start down that road, once you begin to think that David Mulford matters more than Bob Solow, or to prefer hobnobbing with the Ruritanian finance minister to talking theory with Avinash Dixit, you are probably lost to research. Pretty soon you'll probably start using *impact* as a verb.

Fortunately, while I love playing around with policy issues, I have never been able to take policymakers very seriously. This lack of seriousness gets me into occasional trouble—like the time that a gentle parenthetical joke about the French in a conference paper led to an extended diatribe from the French official attending the conference—and may exclude me from ever holding any important policy position. But that's OK: in the end, I would rather write a few more good papers than hold a position of real power. (Note to the policy world: this doesn't mean that I would necessarily turn down such a position if it were offered!)

Regrets
There are a lot of things about my life and personality that I regret—if things have gone astonishingly well for me professionally, they have been by no means as easy or happy elsewhere. But in this essay I only want to talk about professional regrets.

A minor regret is that I have never engaged in really serious empirical work. It's not that I dislike facts or real numbers. Indeed, I find light empirical work in the form of tables, charts, and perhaps a few regressions quite congenial. But the serious business of building and thoroughly analyzing a data set is something I never seem to get around to. I think that this is partly because many of my ideas do not easily lend themselves to standard econometric testing. Mostly, though, it is because I lack the patience and organizational ability. Every year I promise to try to do some real empirical work. Next year I really will!

A more important regret is that while the MIT course evaluations rate me as a pretty good lecturer, I have not yet succeeded in generating a string of really fine students, the kind who reflect glory on their teacher. I can make excuses for this failing—students often prefer advisers who are more methodical and less intuitive, and I all too often scare students off by demanding that they use less math and more economics. It's also true that I probably seem busy and distracted, and perhaps I am just not imposing enough in person to be inspiring (if I were only a few inches taller . . .). Whatever the reasons, I wish I could do better and intend to try.

All in all, though, I've been very lucky. A lot of that luck has to do with the accidents that led me to stumble onto an intellectual style that has served me extremely well. I've tried, in this essay, to define and explain that style. Is this a life philosophy? Of course not. I'm not even sure that it is an economic-research philosophy, since what works for one economist may not work for another. But it's how I do research, and it works for me.

WILLIAM M. LANDES

The Art of Law and Economics: An Autobiographical Essay

Introduction

In his essay "How I Work," Paul Krugman points out that the increasing formalism of modern economics leads most graduate students in economics today to acquire the necessary mathematical skills before they enter graduate school.[1] I strongly suspect the converse holds as well: the student who lacks a technical background will be deterred from choosing a career in economics. This was not always the case. Like Krugman, I came to economics from a liberal-arts background, picking up technical skills as needed both during and after graduate school. My journey, however, was more circuitous and unplanned than Krugman's. That I ended up a professor of economics and law is the outcome of an unlikely chain of events.

I started out as an art major at the High School of Music and Art in New York City. Although art majors also were required to take the standard fare of academic courses, it was not a strenuous academic program, and it was possible to do reasonably well without much effort. The emphasis was clearly on the arts, and many graduates went on to specialized art and music colleges in the New York area. I

I would like to thank Elisabeth Landes, Martha Nussbaum, and Richard Posner for very helpful comments. As the reader will see the term "art" in the title bears on the subject of this essay in several ways.

This essay was previously published in *American Economist* 41, no. 1 (spring 1997): 31–42.

ruled that out since I was only an average art student. I also experimented with architecture in high school. But here I fared no better and decided not to pursue it further, in part, because my closest friend had far more talent than I.[2]

When I entered Columbia College at seventeen I was not well prepared for its demanding academic program (which remains largely intact to this day). I had a good background in the arts but undeveloped study habits. Playing tennis and piano, frequenting jazz clubs, and just hanging around Greenwich Village with my high school friends held my interest more than studying Western civilization and humanities. But in one respect Music and Art taught me a valuable lesson. It impressed upon me the importance of being creative and imaginative in one's work. I have carried that lesson with me throughout my academic career. I strive to be imaginative both in my choice of topics and my approach to them. Rarely have I come up with a topic by sifting through the economics literature or scouring footnotes hoping to find loose ends to tidy up. I have often stumbled upon a good topic while preparing my classes, participating in seminars and workshops, auditing law school classes, talking to colleagues, or just reading the newspaper. The trick is to recognize what one has stumbled upon, or as Robertson Davies writes in his latest novel: "to see what is right in front of one's nose; that is the task."[3]

Early Training as an Economist

I took my first economics course in my junior year at college. Two things still stand out in my mind about that course. One was that little effort was made to show that microeconomics could illuminate real-world problems. I and my classmates came away from the course believing that the assumptions of microeconomics were so unrealistic that economics couldn't have any bearing on real-world problems. The other was the professor's condemnation of advertising as a monstrous social waste, a view shared by most of the economics profession at that time. By default, I became an economics major in my senior year at Columbia and took courses in public finance and money and banking, and a seminar for economics majors. After graduation I went to work on Wall Street at a brokerage firm producing colorful charts (my art background helped) tracking the movements in earnings per share, net working capital, and so on, of different companies in the hope that I or one of the senior members of the research department could detect likely trends in stock prices. I soon realized that school was more fun and challenging than work, so after four months on Wall Street I returned to Columbia on a part-time basis. My intention was to get a master's degree in economics and ultimately work for some government agency. Becoming an economics professor or even getting a Ph.D. was not on my radar screen.

Unlike more selective graduate schools, Columbia had pretty much an open-door policy, admitting large numbers of students and letting Darwinian survival principles operate. There were always a few exceptional students at Columbia who went on to get their doctorates in four or five years, but most didn't survive. They either got a master's degree or lost interest after a year or two and dropped out. (At the other extreme, Columbia was also home to a number of professional students who had been around for ten or fifteen years working on a thesis they were unlikely ever to finish.) After my first year of graduate school, in which I continued to work half-time on Wall Street, I realized I had a talent for economics and asked to be admitted to the doctoral program. The chairman of the department looked over my grades and pronounced that "my prognosis was good," and so I became a full-time doctoral student.

Success in graduate school requires brains, sustained effort, and hard work. Exceptional success at Columbia required a little luck as well. Luck to be plucked from the mass of students by a great economist and placed under his wing. I was lucky.

In the spring semester of my second year at graduate school, I audited Gary Becker's course on human capital, which covered his still unpublished manuscript on that subject. Since Becker had been on leave at the National Bureau of Economic Research during my first year, I had not taken his "price theory" course or what is now more commonly termed microeconomics. In class, Becker called on me regularly (sometimes I thought "ruthlessly," for I was only an auditor) and referred to me as "an eager beaver." If I didn't come up with the answer at first, Becker would tease it out of me. Having been a member of a law school faculty for over twenty years, I am still struck by the difference between Becker's teaching style (unusual even in economics departments) and that of the typical law school professor. As in law classes, Becker called on students who did not volunteer. But Becker would work with the student for a few minutes until (hopefully) he came up with the right answer. In contrast, the law school professor practicing the Socratic method calls on different students in rapid succession, playing one off against another ("Ms. Y, do you agree with Mr. X's answer?"). To push the students to think more clearly, the professor will often vary the hypothetical until the reasoning behind the earlier answer collapses. A premium is placed on verbal agility and thinking quickly on one's feet. A series of questions may end without a definite answer, and the teacher moves on to the next case. Indeed, the Socratic method impresses on the student that there is no right or easy answer in law. Yet the fact that the method survives (but in a somewhat gentler form today) is a tribute to its value in training students to become practicing lawyers.

Auditing Becker's course in human capital marked the beginning of my training as a real economist. To be sure, I had already been in graduate school for over a year. Yet, for the first time, I began to appreciate that economics was more than just a set of formal tools but a way of thinking about interesting real-world problems. I began to understand the advantages of simplifying and descriptively un-realistic assumptions, and how a person with imagination could de-velop a simple model to illuminate a real-world problem. Such mod-els provided an approach to thinking systematically about public policy and law. Instead of saying policy X was good or fair, one could use economic principles to spell out the consequences of that policy.

During my third year at graduate school, I completed my course requirements, audited Becker's price theory course, and passed my comprehensive oral examinations. For three or four months before the oral exams I was part of a small group of students (we called ourselves "Becker Bombers") who met regularly to review questions from Becker's prior exams and problems from Milton Friedman's soft-cover textbook.[4] Working through this material made it clear to me the difference between knowing economics and thinking like an economist. The former comes from mastering the language and for-mal principles of economics that are found in graduate textbooks and articles in professional journals, the latter from applying these tools with varying degrees of sophistication to solving problems. The par-ticular problem might be a conventional economic one (e.g., will a price ceiling on lumber lower the price of new construction) or a problem not ordinarily viewed as an economic one (e.g., do laws protecting privacy lead to more unconventional behavior). Any prob-lem involving competing goals and choices constrained by limited resources and available opportunities is fair game for economics. The problem need not involve explicit markets or observable prices, for one can derive shadow prices that function like market prices. Frequently, simple economic concepts applied in an imaginative way yield subtle insights. All this may sound commonplace today, but thirty years ago it was not. It is a tribute to Gary Becker's pioneering efforts that we now take for granted that the domain of economics is not confined to explicit markets but is a "way of looking at life."[5]

My next stroke of good luck was quickly settling on a dissertation topic. Becker proposed that I study whether state fair-employment laws improved the economic position of nonwhites in the United States.[6] I eagerly agreed both because I wanted to work with Becker and because the topic was intrinsically interesting. To get me started, Becker gave me a copy of an unpublished paper by George Stigler and Claire Friedland that used regression analysis to estimate the effects of state utility regulation.[7] At that time, it was highly novel for an economist to employ multiple regression analysis to estimate empirically the actual effects of a law or regulation. The paper by Stigler and Friedland was one of the first. Before undertaking the empirical analysis, I set out to develop a model to explain the likely effects of fair-employment laws. Here I added sanctions against firms that discriminated against nonwhites to Becker's theory of discrimination. I assumed that an employer violating a fair-employment law faced a probability rather than a certainty of being caught and a sanction if caught. The greater that probability and the greater that sanction, the greater the cost of discriminating and the more likely the employer would increase its demand for nonwhite relative to white workers. Thus, I had a thesis that not only lent itself to imaginative modeling (by using the expected-utility model to analyze law enforcement) but was capable of answering empirically an important public-policy question.

Developing a model was the easy part compared to carrying out the empirical analysis. Acquiring empirical skills requires a good deal of "learning by doing." Graduate school had not prepared me for the many months I would have to spend meticulously gathering data state-by-state from census volumes, calculating state averages by race for earnings, years of schooling, and other variables, fitting Pareto distributions to open-ended census intervals, and collecting data from state fair-employment commissions on the number of prosecutions, enforcement expenditures, sanctions, and so forth. I was my own research assistant, and I carried out most of these calculations on a mechanical calculator that frequently jammed. Fortunately, computers make it possible today to avoid this kind of tedious work, although I don't have the impression that this has increased the frequency of empirical dissertations in economics.

Getting Started in Law and Economics

In its broadest sense, "law and economics" is coextensive with a large part of the field of industrial organization. Both cover, among other things, the study of the legal regulation of markets, including economic analysis of the business practices described in antitrust cases. These cases provide a rich source of material on such practices as tie-in sales, exclusive dealing, vertical restrictions, and information exchanges among competitors. Both fields also include research on the theoretical and empirical consequences of different types of government regulations and laws. Thus, the most recent issue of the *Journal of Law and Economics* (a leading journal in both industrial organization and law and economics) includes articles by economists on the anticompetitive effects of most-favored-nation clauses, the effects on stock prices of regulatory drug recalls, the performance of the airline industry under deregulation, and the impact of collective-bargaining legislation on labor disputes in the public sector. For my purposes, however, I want to define law and economics more narrowly. I want to limit it to what is called the "new" law and economics, a field that essentially began with Ronald Coase's article on social cost over thirty years ago[8] and where most work has been carried on in law schools rather than economics departments.

The "new" law and economics applies the tools of economics to the legal system itself. It uses economics to explain and illuminate legal doctrines in all fields of law, including the common-law fields of torts, contracts and property, intellectual property, corporate law, bankruptcy law, criminal law, and the legal process itself (e.g., the effects of fee-shifting statutes, discovery rules, and legal precedent on litigation). The "new" law and economics is not limited to areas of law that only impact explicit markets. It is a theory of both the legal rules themselves and their consequences for behavior. The former is the more controversial of the two. It treats legal rules and doctrines as "data" in order to test the hypothesis that the law is best explained as efforts by judges, often implicitly, to decide cases as if they are trying to promote economic efficiency.

I got started in the "new" law and economics by chance rather than by any well-thought-out plan to work in this area.[9] Shortly after finishing my thesis on the effects of fair-employment laws (the "old" law and economics) I came across a newspaper article on plea bargaining in criminal cases. The article pointed out that only a small fraction (probably less than 5 percent) of criminal defendants actually went to trial. The rest pleaded guilty, often to substantially reduced charges. Investigating a little further, I learned similarly that only a small fraction of civil cases ended up in trial. Most were settled out of court before trial. Not only did these issues seem like a natural subject for economic analysis (an example of "seeing what is right in front of one's nose") but no one had previously examined it from the standpoint of economics — maybe because economists believed that people were more likely to behave emotionally than rationally in a litigation setting.

But as Becker's former student, I had no trouble assuming that parties behaved rationally in nonmarket settings. The ultimate test was whether rational behavior was a useful assumption, not whether it was descriptively realistic. I reasoned (using Coase's theorem) that the prosecutor and defendant would reach a plea bargain on a sentence if both could be made better off compared to risking an uncertain trial outcome. Similarly, parties would prefer to settle a civil lawsuit out of court provided one could find a settlement that made both better off than their expected trial outcomes. Assuming that trials were more costly than plea bargains or settlements, I showed that if the parties agreed on the probabilities of winning and losing at trial, they would always settle (unless they had strong preferences for risk) because each party's utility from a settlement would be greater than his or her expected utility from a trial. Further, trials would be more likely to occur when the parties were mutually optimistic (i.e., each party believed he or she had a greater probability of winning a trial than the opponent believed), were risk preferrers, where the cost of trials were low relative to the cost of reaching a settlement, and where the stakes in litigation were greater (for that magnified the difference in expected outcomes for mutually optimistic parties). My paper also has implications for law enforcement, for I showed that criminals as a class could be made worse off by plea bargains even though any particular offender was made better off by avoiding a trial (a true prisoner's dilemma) because settlements freed resources that enabled the prosecutor to pursue more criminals.

I presented a preliminary version of this paper[10] in 1967 to the labor workshop at the University of Chicago. At the time I was an assistant professor in the economics department at Chicago. My talk was not greeted with much enthusiasm. Afterward, one of my senior colleagues in the department took me aside for some friendly advice. He said I was making a career mistake by doing research on problems like the courts that were only of marginal interest to other economists. Professional success, he emphasized, required working on problems of the latest interest to other economists. I asked him how one knew what was of the "latest interest." He replied that one could gauge interest by seeing what problems other economists were currently working on. In short, see what your colleagues are working on and try to take it a step further. I decided to ask Gary Becker what he thought (though I suspect I already knew what he would say). Becker had just finished his paper on the economics of crime, and one of Becker's students, Isaac Ehrlich, was completing a thesis at Columbia on the deterrent effects of conviction rates and sanctions on crime. Becker disagreed with my Chicago colleague. His advice was simple: law enforcement and litigation are interesting and important social issues that can be illuminated by economics; don't worry so much about whether your work is part of the latest fad in economics; and ultimately good work will be recognized. Fortunately, I listened to Gary Becker.

In 1968 I moved from Chicago to New York City to accept a fellowship at the National Bureau of Economic Research, and a year later I joined the NBER's research staff. At that time, members of the NBER's staff resided almost entirely in New York City. Although I also had academic appointments in the economics departments at Columbia and later at the Graduate Center of the City University, my intellectual life centered on the NBER. The NBER offered me the freedom to choose projects interesting to me and to avoid the distractions associated with student turmoil at Columbia during this period. The bureau had a professional and no-nonsense attitude toward research — projects were undertaken with the expectation that they would be completed, rough deadlines were imposed, progress reports were required, and research directors took a strong interest in the work under their direction. But there was also the give-and-take and informality of a university that I cherished. The bureau was an ideal place for conducting serious empirical research.

When I joined the NBER it was best known for its empirical research in traditional economic subjects such as business cycles and national-income accounting, but it was beginning to branch out into other areas of economics. For example, Becker and Jacob Mincer ran projects on the economics of education and human capital, and Victor Fuchs directed a program in health economics. The bureau formally established a program in law and economics in 1971 that was funded by a grant from the National Science Foundation. The program included Becker, myself, Isaac Ehrlich, and Richard Posner (then professor at the University of Chicago Law School and now chief judge on the U.S. Court of Appeals of the Seventh Circuit). Adding Posner filled a critical hole in the program. In order to apply economics to areas of law other than crime and the courts we needed some expertise in law. Posner seemed ideal. He had a strong interest in economics, had already published several widely regarded papers in antitrust, and was starting to apply economics to torts and judicial administration.

It should be mentioned that the early applications of economics to law at the NBER (pre-Posner) and elsewhere required almost no knowledge of law. This was true of Becker's paper on crime, Ehrlich's pioneering studies of deterrence and law enforcement, and my own work on the courts, plea bargaining, and the bail system. That this should be so is not surprising. We were economists applying the theoretical and empirical tools of economics to the systematic study of enforcement.[11] To be sure, we had to develop some basic understanding about the relevant legal terms and institutions under investigation, but that requires far less knowledge of law than becoming familiar and comfortable with legal rules and doctrines in order to analyze them from an economic standpoint.

An Economist on a Law School Faculty

Although the bureau provided a superb research environment, it could not match the intellectual excitement of the University of Chicago. Chicago was home to the economists I most admired — Becker, Coase, Friedman, and Stigler. Plus it offered me the opportunity to work more closely with Posner. So in 1973 I eagerly accepted a tenured appointment at the University of Chicago Law School. The Law School had a long tradition of having an economist on its faculty, starting with Henry Simons, Aaron Director, and Ronald Coase. When I arrived, Coase was still an active member of the faculty but taught only an occasional course. Still, my appointment was somewhat unusual. I was genuinely interested in explaining legal rules and doctrines from an economic perspective. Coase was not. He believed that knowledge of law and legal institutions was valuable because it helped one understand how explicit markets truly worked. But Coase had little interest in showing, for example, that the various legal doctrines governing liability for accidents or contract damages had an implicit economic logic. It is one of the ironies of law and economics that the person whose pioneering work (cited by the Nobel committee) provided the foundation for the subject has been less than enthusiastic about its development. Coase believed that much of law and economics was outside the domain of economics and that, in any event, lawyers rather than economists were better suited for the enterprise. Most law professors went even further. They believed that lawyers would also fail in explaining law from an economic perspective.

At the few law schools with an economist on their faculty in the 1970s (as opposed to a law professor who happened to have a graduate degree in economics), the economist was hired to teach price theory, coteach with a law professor a course on business regulation such as antitrust, and serve as a resource to the few law professors who thought economics might have something to contribute to their particular area of law. The economist did not mess with law, nor was he expected to do so. And even when he stuck to economics, the results could be unsettling. One only has to recall the often-told story of the antitrust course at Chicago in the 1950s cotaught by Professors Edward Levi, later attorney general of the United States, and Aaron Director. During the first four classes of each week, Levi would carefully go over the cases and struggle to make sense of the judge's economic reasoning. On the fifth day, Director would explain why everything that went on during the previous four classes was wrong.

Research Interests
Twenty years ago there were two options open to an economist who wanted to contribute to the "new" law and economics. A person could collaborate with a law professor interested in economics or immerse himself or herself in law and, given enough time and effort, become sufficiently comfortable with legal materials to work solo. (Today there is a third way. By studying the substantial law-and-economics literature, one may be able to find promising but often technical problems to work on.) I chose to do both. I collaborated with Posner and I

immersed myself in the study of law. Not that I wanted to be a lawyer, but I wanted to know enough about different areas of law to see where economics would be most useful. Unlike most other economists, I actually enjoyed reading law cases. I read them with an economist's eye, however. I looked for and often found an implicit economic logic in the outcome of a case. And if I didn't quite get the law right or misinterpreted what the judge said, neither of which was unusual, I always had Posner or one of my other colleagues at the law school to straighten me out.

My first paper with Posner started out as a theoretical comment on Becker and Stigler's paper on private enforcement. We showed that private enforcement could lead to overenforcement relative to (optimal) public enforcement because a higher fine would lead private enforcers to step up rather than reduce their enforcement activity.[12] But the paper quickly developed into a more ambitious project. We tested the predictions of the analysis against real-world observations. We explained why there is a greater reliance on private enforcement in contract, torts, and other "private law" areas compared to criminal law; why victims rather than others have the exclusive rights to sue and redress violations; why the budget of public enforcement agencies tend to be small relative to what private profit-maximizing enforcers would spend; and why public enforcers nullify particular laws by declining to prosecute whereas private enforcers would not. We also applied the model to blackmail and bribery as forms of enforcement and the legal rules governing rewards for lost or stolen property — also a method of compensating private enforcers.

In an important sense the paper on private enforcement represented a sharp departure from my earlier work. It systematically applied economics to a large number of legal rules and showed that these rules promoted economic efficiency. Of course, this was mainly due to Posner, for I lacked the necessary knowledge of law. But I was determined to remedy this deficiency by auditing law courses — particularly, basic first-year courses such as civil procedure, contracts, and torts — and by jointly teaching law courses and seminars with law professors.

Over the next twenty years, Posner and I coauthored more than twenty-five articles and a book on tort law. Our work was truly a joint effort and continues to this day. I have had greater responsibility for the economic modeling and Posner for the law, but each of us contributed substantially to both the economics and the law. True, there were substantial gains from trade because we each brought different skills to the enterprise, but the final product greatly exceeded the sum of the individual parts. We each raised the marginal product of the other. Looking over the papers, it would be misleading to say, "Posner did this" or "I did that," for the ideas, choice of topics, approaches to them, and execution were always joint efforts. The topics we collaborated on covered a broad range of legal subjects including legal precedent, the resolution of legal disputes, laws governing rescue such as salvage in admiralty law, antitrust, torts, the role of an independent judiciary, trade secrets, trademarks, and copyright. Our best-known work, *The Economic Structure of Tort Law,* showed that a relatively simple economic model of wealth maximization could explain and organize what at first appeared an incomprehensible array of unrelated rules and doctrines governing tort liability. We covered all the important areas of torts from simple problems such as the choice between negligence and strict liability rules for ordinary accidents, to more complicated questions involving defenses to liability, causation, joint torts (two or more injurers), catastrophic injuries (many victims), and intentional torts.

Although I have also worked on a number of projects on my own, including papers on litigation and copyright law, I continue to do collaborative work both with Posner and more recently with Larry Lessig, a recently appointed law professor at Chicago.[13] I am surprised that collaboration between lawyers and economists is not more common because the gains from trade seem so substantial. Aside from Posner and myself, the only other long-term collaboration involves Charles Goetz, an economist, and Robert Scott, a law professor and now dean, of the University of Virginia Law School.[14] On the other hand, an increasing phenomenon at law schools is the lawyer who also has a Ph.D. in economics. Most of these are recent law school graduates. Their work is a form of collaboration between a lawyer and economist but involves one person.

The Changing Role of the Law School Economist
Over the years I have become much more comfortable with law and pretty much have become assimilated into the law school culture. That is also true for other economists who have full-time positions at law schools. We spend much more time with our colleagues at the law school than we do with economists in the economics department

or business schools. Proximity is one reason, but there are more fundamental forces at work.

One is that economics departments have become less interested in applied economics such as law and economics. Economics has become more formal and theoretical. Research is increasingly aimed at demonstrating technical skills and solving technical problems rather than at analyzing social problems. Consequently, the law school economist feels less comfortable intellectually on the other side of the campus. Fortunately, this is less true at Chicago, and I continue to attend economics and business school workshops with Becker, Sam Peltzman, Sherwin Rosen, and others. But Chicago is unusual.

Another is that economists at law schools have more in common with law professors today than twenty years ago because economics has transformed legal scholarship in torts, contracts, securities, antitrust, corporations, environmental law, intellectual property, and other business-related areas. There are large numbers of law professors who consider themselves members of the law-and-economics movement.[15] Another indication of the growing importance of economics at law schools is the appointment of economists (but virtually no other nonlawyers) to full-time positions at all major and many other law schools. Twenty years ago, the economist at a law school was a peripheral figure. Today he or she occupies a central position.

A related factor is the increasing importance of economics in the teaching of law. Law schools are professional schools that view their primary mission as educating future practitioners. For economics to be more than of marginal importance, it must demonstrate its relevance to the education of future practicing lawyers. It has done this by making significant contributions to the practice of law. Economics has altered antitrust; plays a significant role in securities, pension, environmental, unfair competition, and discrimination litigation; and is important in valuation and damage calculations in virtually all large-scale commercial lawsuits. Law students are quick to recognize the value of economics in the practice of law. Knowing economics gives them an edge over their competitors. As a result, law-and-economics courses are increasingly popular at law schools, as are our courses jointly taught by lawyers and economists in a variety of subjects. Moreover, it is not uncommon today for an economist to teach a law course alone, which was unheard of thirty years ago. Consider my teaching responsibilities. Although I run the law-and-economics workshop, I teach copyrights, trademarks and unfair competition, and (my favorite) art law. These are not law-and-economics courses but regular law school courses. To be sure, I add a heavy dose of economics not only because I am an economist but because the cases explicitly discuss and recognize the importance of economic factors and because the use of economics (by lawyers) in private-law subjects has become commonplace. Indeed, I have become so assimilated into the world of academic law that I am now a professor of law and economics, not just a professor of economics (my original title at the law school).

The Future

I have been struck by comments made to me on several occasions from young scholars starting out in law and economics today. The gist of their remarks is that "when you started out, there were lots of areas of law open to economics, but you and others have taken all the interesting problems, so now there is nothing left." There is, of course, an element of truth to this, but it is greatly exaggerated. Early on, an economist auditing a law school course in torts or contract was like a child in a candy store — there was an interesting topic to be discovered in almost every class. Indeed, the difficulty was not finding topics, but deciding which ones to work on. My torts book with Posner is a good example. While auditing Posner's tort course, I worked up economic notes on the cases and doctrines discussed in class and in the casebook. Then I refined and expanded this material in connection with a course I taught in law and economics. These notes became the starting point for our tort book. But today economic analysis of common-law fields like torts and contracts have been so picked over that it would be a mistake for a young scholar to concentrate on them. The same is probably true for litigation models, though I am less confident here because recent applications of game theory to litigation has yielded some interesting new scholarship.

What is left? Law-and-economic scholars have only recently applied the tools of game theory to understanding how legal doctrines may overcome strategic behavior and asymmetrical information.[16] This remains a promising area for future work. Turning to particular fields of law, one observes that constitutional law has been barely touched by economic analysis. And family law, criminal law (as distinct from empirical studies of deterrence), legal procedure, and intellectual property have been relatively neglected compared to torts, contracts, and corporate law. These fields also remain promising for future work. But the most neglected side of law and economics is empirical. In most areas of law and economics there is a dearth of empirical studies that are surely worth doing. Recently, I surveyed all articles published in the *Journal of Legal Studies* (the leading "new" law-and-economics journal) during the last five years and found that only about 20 percent had some empirical content. Contrast this with the *Journal of Political Economy,* where more than 60 percent of articles published in the past year contained substantial empirical analysis.[17] This difference cannot be accounted for solely by differences in data availability. There are substantial bodies of data on the number and disposition of criminal and civil cases at both the trial and appellate levels, awards in civil cases, sentences in criminal cases, earnings of lawyers, accident rates, and so forth. Moreover, computerized legal databases make it possible at relatively low cost to extract significant amounts of information from cases in order to develop data sets relevant to the problems at hand.

Finally, there are different approaches to research. One can work productively and imaginatively at either the intensive or extensive margin. The first approach is illustrated by Coase's work on problems such as marginal cost pricing, the organization of firms, social cost, and durable-goods monopolies. Before Coase, economists had worked on these problems for many years. Yet Coase was able to say something new and novel about these problems and ultimately to change the way economists think about them. Becker, on the other hand, works primarily at the extensive margin, showing the relevance of economics to a wide range of social issues usually considered beyond economics. These include marriage, divorce, bringing up children, education, altruism, crime, addiction, and preference formation. As Becker and Coase have shown, Nobel Prizes can be won at either margin. The fact that there now exists a substantial body of literature in law and economics makes it simultaneously more difficult to work at the extensive margin but easier to work at the intensive margin.

Consulting or Law and Economics in Action
Describing my career in law and economics would be seriously incomplete without considering consulting or what I call "law and economics in action." In 1977, Posner, Andrew Rosenfield, then a third-year student at the law school, and I founded the firm Lexecon, Inc.

Economics was just starting to catch on in antitrust litigation and regulatory proceedings. We were confident that it was going to play a bigger role in the future. At the same time, law firms and their clients often expressed dissatisfaction with the quality of economic consulting services they were receiving. Their main complaint was that, in the end, they weren't getting good value for their money. The economic analysis and empirical studies were costly and rarely provided much help. But part of the problem rested with the lawyers who had so little understanding of economics that they did not know how to deploy it effectively.

The idea behind Lexecon was a simple one. There existed a market niche for a firm that supplied high-quality economic consulting services that would be relevant and helpful in litigation and regulatory matters. We brought unique qualities to this venture. Posner was a lawyer who knew economics, I was an economist who knew how to explain economics to lawyers, and Rosenfield, who had graduate training in economics to go along with his law degree, was willing to devote himself full time to building up Lexecon, as we were not. Together we could figure out what economic studies should be done, direct and supervise them efficiently, and, when needed, bring in other academic economists who had expertise and specialized knowledge in the areas being litigated.

Lexecon played an educational role as well. Many exceptionally talented and experienced attorneys felt at sea when it came to economics and statistics. But they were fast and eager learners. We explained basic economics (and even econometrics) and showed them how they could use economics to help structure and strengthen legal arguments. With this panoply of services we were able to convince law firms to turn over to Lexecon the economic side of many large cases. We had another selling point. We did not pose an economic threat to law firms. We were not competing for their clients because we didn't practice law. Indeed, Lexecon became a competitive tool in the hands of law firms because it enabled them to offer their clients a superior product.

As they say the rest is history. Lexecon became enormously successful and spawned many imitators. It is a source of great personal satisfaction to me that I helped create and develop Lexecon. Today Lexecon has about 125 full-time employees in Chicago (although Posner left in 1981 when he became a judge and I have significantly reduced my role in the past few years),[18] including a large staff of extraordinarily able economists with Ph.D.'s, and affiliations with a number of leading academic economists, including several Nobel Prize winners.[19]

Economic consulting has become an increasingly attractive option for some of the brightest Ph.D.'s in economics. It offers the prospect of considerably greater financial rewards than academics (but not the prospect of formal tenure) and a wide range of real-world problems to work on because the role of economic evidence, once largely limited to antitrust cases and calculating damages in personal-injury cases, has expanded to embrace virtually all kinds of large-scale commercial litigation. Economists are routinely employed in areas such as securities and corporate law, pension law, environmental and safety regulation, and discrimination litigation. Indeed, it would verge on legal malpractice not to use an economist in these areas.

There is, of course, an important difference between academics and consulting. Academics set their own agenda. They have the luxury to choose whatever problem catches their fancy and the pace at which to pursue it. Not so in consulting. There, the problem is placed before you, and you face the press of time, the tension of litigation, long hours, and travel away from home. Moreover, millions of dollars may be at stake, and your role may be crucial. Not surprising, one tends to get caught up in the excitement of litigation and relish the satisfaction from having done a first-rate job. Rewards come more slowly, if at all, to the academic economist.

There is a common misconception about litigation among academic economists who have little or no consulting experience. They assume that the pressures of litigation compel an economist who testifies as an expert witness to slant his or her analysis, present only favorable results, and massage the data in order to come up with the answers the client wants. The flaw in this argument is it ignores how litigation works. Both the data the expert relies on and his or her analysis are turned over to the opposing party way before any testimony in court is given. The opposition, armed with their own economists, will check the opposing expert's calculations, reestimate equations, analyze the sensitivity of the estimates to alternative specifications, see how the results change if other variables are added, and so forth. The combination of high stakes and the workings of the adversary system means there is a very high probability that any mistakes, whether intentional or inadvertent, will be unmasked. The same holds for economic presentations before regulatory agencies such as the Antitrust Division of the Department of Justice or the Federal Trade Commission. They have their own professional staff of economists to analyze the expert's work. Contrast this with academic work. A well-refereed journal will often catch theoretical mistakes. But it is far easier to get away with sloppy and even intentionally misleading empirical analyses in academic studies than in litigation because it is rare that other economists will take the trouble to check the earlier work.

Concluding Remarks

In describing his evolution as an economist, Ronald Coase wrote: "I came to realize where I had been going only after I arrived. The emergence of my ideas at each stage was not part of some grand scheme."[20] That phrase captures my journey as well. I had no particular career path in mind when I started graduate school. I chose economics rather than something else because I had taken a handful of economics courses as an undergraduate. I got started in law and economics by chance because I came across a newspaper article on plea bargaining. True, I wanted to apply economics to important social issues, but law was just one of many possibilities. I worked on a wide range of topics in law that, on looking back, evidence a common approach but not an overall scheme to remake legal scholarship. I never thought I was part of a movement, but now it is commonplace to hear about how the "law-and-economics movement" has transformed legal scholarship and teaching.

I was also extraordinarily fortunate to have worked with Becker and Posner. Becker opened my eyes as a student to the power of economics to illuminate social issues and has been a source of inspiration ever since. Posner is probably the most influential legal scholar and certainly the most prolific in this century. It is hard to imagine that law and economics would have been anywhere near as successful had he chosen another career.[21] I also had another extraordinary bit of luck. I married an economist more than twenty-five years ago who has been my best critic and the source of countless ideas. I met Lisa when I was an assistant professor and she was a first-year graduate student in the economics department at Chicago. Had the current rules and policies governing sexual harassment at universities and the like been in place in 1968, I would never have dated a graduate student. Many believe the benefits (e.g., reducing coercion by men) of sexual-harassment policies exceed the transaction and other costs such policies may impose on the dating and marriage markets. In my case, however, I would have been a big loser. But the general subject of sexual harassment is a great topic for future work in law and economics.

NOTES

1. Paul Krugman, "How I Work," in this volume.
2. That friend, Charles Gwathmey, went on to become one of the leading architects in the United States today.
3. See *The Cunning Man* (New York: Viking, 1995), 142. The doctor who speaks these words adds, however, that it is not so easy a task, for the full quote reads "to learn to see what is right in front of one's nose; that is the task and a heavy task it is." Martha Nussbaum points out that Robertson Davies was not the first to make this point. It was made earlier by Greek philosophers as well. For example, in an essay on Heraclitus, David Wiggins writes, "But the power of Heraclitus — his claim to be the most adult thinker of his age and a grown man among infants and adolescents — precisely consisted in the capacity to speculate, in the theory of meaning, just as in physics, not where speculation lacked all useful observations, or where it need more going theory to bite on, but where the facts were as big and familiar as the sky and so obvious that it took actual genius to pay heed to them." See David Wiggins, "Heraclitus' Conceptions of Flux, Fire, and Material Persistence," in *Language and Logos: Studies in Ancient Greek Philosophy Presented to G. E. L. Owen,* ed. M. Schofield and M. Nussbaum (Cambridge: Cambridge University Press, 1982), 32.
4. The textbook, *Price Theory: A Provisional Textbook,* was based on Friedman's graduate course at Chicago, and a number of problems in that book had been suggested by Aaron Director, an economics professor at the University of Chicago Law School.
5. See Becker's Nobel unpublished lecture entitled "The Economic Way of Looking at Life."
6. In 1963 (when I started my dissertation) thirteen states had passed fair-employment legislation. The major federal civil rights legislation was not enacted until 1964.
7. George Stigler and Claire Friedland, "What Can Regulators Regulate? The Case of Electricity," *Journal of Law and Economics* 5 (1962): 1–16.
8. R. H. Coase, "The Problem of Social Cost," *Journal of Law and Economics* (1960): 1–44.
9. Hereafter I use the phrase *law and economics* also to denote the "new" law and economics.
10. The paper was initially titled "Rationing the Services of Courts." A substantially revised version, which contained an empirical analysis of the frequency of both criminal and civil cases tried across different jurisdictions in the United States, was eventually published in the *Journal of Law and Economics* in 1971. That paper plus papers by Richard Posner, Jack Gould, and Steven Shavell have

stimulated a voluminous law-and-economics literature on the resolution of legal disputes. In a somewhat dated survey article, Robert D. Cooter and Daniel L. Rubinfeld, "Economic Analysis of Legal Disputes and Their Resolution," *Journal of Economic Literature* 27 (1989): 1067–97, discuss more than one hundred such articles. I suspect that the number of articles has at least doubled since the year of the survey article.

11. Coase was an exception. He had taken some business law courses, and his social-cost paper discusses a number of important early English nuisance cases.

12. Optimal enforcement (following Becker's earlier paper) typically involved a low probability of apprehension and conviction and a high fine that produced the same level of deterrence at lower costs.

13. Lessig and I are completing a large-scale project estimating empirically the influence and reputation of federal court judges by counting citations to their opinions. Viewing citations as "output," we borrow from the human-capital literature and estimate equations of citations on experience and a variety of other variables. Not only do we rank judges but we examine factors that may explain differences in influence among judges (race, sex, quality of law school, law school performance, prior experience, etc.).

14. As a rough measure of the benefits from collaboration, Landes and Goetz accounted for more than 45 percent of the citations in law journals to the articles and books of economists at the top fifteen law schools. (See Landes and Posner, "The Influences of Economics on Law: A Quantitative Study," *Journal of Law and Economics* 36 (1993): 385–424.

15. A pretty good measure of this is that lawyers comprise about 50 percent of four hundred or so members of the recently formed American Law and Economics Association.

16. For an excellent start in this direction see Douglas Baird, Robert Gertner, and Randal Picker, *Game Theory and the Law* (Cambridge, MA: Harvard University Press, 1994).

17. The reason there are relatively few empirical articles in law and economics is an interesting question in itself. I recently addressed this issue in a presentation on law and economics at the annual meetings of the American Economics Association in 1994. I advanced several explanations, including the fact that the initial success of law and economics at law schools came not from empirical studies but from the light that economics shed on legal doctrines; that the law school culture values verbal quickness and analytical skills but not painstaking empirical analysis; that law and economics has been centered at law schools rather than economics departments or business schools; and that law professors, the major contributors to law and economics, are selected for verbal not quantitative skills. Equally puzzling is why economists on law faculties also tend to avoid empirical analysis. But again this is related to both the reward structure at law schools and the kind of economists who have been attracted to law and economics.

18. I might add that Lexecon's offices were designed by Charles Gwathmey (see note 2).

19. Rosenfield is now president but is also a senior lecturer at the University of Chicago Law School, where he teaches antitrust, securities, and evidence.

20. R. H. Coase, "My Evolution as an Economist," unpublished version of a

lecture in the Lives of the Laureates series, given at Trinity University, San Antonio, Texas, on April 12, 1994.

21. It would be more accurate to say "had he not chosen economics as *one* of his careers." Posner is also a federal court of appeals judge (whose opinions are cited more frequently than any other appellate court judge) and a significant contributor to other fields such as law and literature and jurisprudence.

N. GREGORY MANKIW

My Rules of Thumb

My assignment is to describe how I work. I take on this task with mixed feelings. One can easily become vain in the process of public introspection, and vanity is a trait best left private. It is not entirely clear to me why anyone should care about my idiosyncrasies — except, perhaps, for my colleagues, students, and family, who have no choice but to live with them.

Yet when other economists write essays of this sort, I enjoy reading them. I like to think that these essays edify me in some way, but at the very least they appeal to the voyeur in me. So, I figured, others may learn from a brief essay about how I work. Or, at least, they may be amused by it.

I have organized this essay around six rules of thumb that I follow as I go about my working life. I have chosen these rules largely for their positive value — they describe my behavior. I do not pretend that the way I work necessarily holds any prescriptive value for anyone else. But it may. If these rules of thumb ring true to others and help them to run their lives, so much the better.

Rule No. 1: Learn from the Right Mentors
I learned how to practice my trade from four distinguished economists. Perhaps the reason was good career planning on my part. More likely, it was just good luck.

This essay was previously published in *American Economist* 40, no. 1 (spring 1996): 14–19.

In the spring of 1977, as a freshman at Princeton, I took Principles of Microeconomics from Harvey Rosen. Harvey was an excellent teacher. I remember finding the material easy and, at the same time, feeling that I was learning a tremendous amount. Each lecture was filled with insights that were novel, profound, and so stunningly obvious that it seemed I should have known them all my life. But, of course, I didn't. Principles of Microeconomics was the most eye-opening course I have ever taken. All subsequent courses in economics have exhibited the property of diminishing returns.

For reasons that are a mystery to me now, Harvey hired me as a research assistant for the summer after my freshman year. I knew very little economics, for I had taken only the two principles courses. I did know something about computer programming (a fact that surprises my own research assistants, for changes in technology have made this human capital long obsolete). For whatever reason, Harvey did hire me, and the experience proved invaluable. I knew so little that Harvey had to teach me whatever he needed me to know. Spending a summer being tutored by a top teacher and scholar is the best learning experience I can imagine. To this day, I have never learned so much in so short a period of time.

Eventually, my interests drifted toward macroeconomics. As a senior at Princeton, I took graduate macroeconomics from Alan Blinder, another excellent teacher. At the same time, I wrote my senior thesis under Alan's supervision. In the thesis, I tried to make sense of the cyclical behavior of the real wage, which has puzzled macroeconomists at least since the publication of Keynes's *General Theory*. Part of my senior thesis became a paper coauthored with Alan, which we later published in the *Journal of Monetary Economics*. More important, as I worked on the thesis, I became convinced that imperfections in goods markets were at least as important as imperfections in labor markets for understanding the business cycle. This conviction eventually led to my involvement in a line of research now called New Keynesian Economics.

When I entered MIT's graduate program in the fall of 1980, Larry Summers was a young assistant professor. Larry's enthusiasm, breadth of knowledge, and quick mind attracted me, and we spoke together at MIT during the year and at the NBER during the following summer. When Martin Feldstein brought Larry to work at the Council of Economic Advisers in September 1982, Larry brought me along with him. I was fortunate to be able to work closely with Larry during the brief period when Larry was already a great economist but not yet a famous one.

When I returned to MIT, Stanley Fischer served as my dissertation adviser, as he did for a remarkable number of students in my class. Stan was a model of professorial balance. As a lecturer, he gave clear and evenhanded presentations in a field that can be confusing and divisive. As an adviser, he encouraged students to pursue their interests with the highest standards of rigor without imposing his own intellectual agenda on them. My dissertation, like most in recent years, was a collection of loosely related papers bound together for the sole purpose of getting a degree. It bore the soporific title "Essays on Consumption."

When I look back at these four mentors—Rosen, Blinder, Summers, and Fischer—I see in them various characteristics that I have developed over time. They are prolific writers. Their research tends to be empirical and policy oriented. They take teaching seriously.

All of my mentors have shown interest in reaching a broader audience than can be found writing in academic journals. All four of them have taken time away from academia to work in policy jobs in Washington. Three out of four have written textbooks, and two of them have written more than one textbook.

It is easy to see why mentors matter. Mentors determine your professional outlook in much the way that parents determine your personal outlook. Mentors, like parents, give you your values. They teach you what kind of behavior to respect and what kind to avoid. And they teach these lessons indirectly, more often through their actions than through their words.

The major difference is that your parents are predetermined. You get to choose your mentors.

Rule No. 2: Work with Good Coauthors

I have been lucky to be able to work with many talented coauthors. In approximate order of appearance, they include Alan Blinder, Bryan Boulier, Larry Summers, Julio Rotemberg, Matthew Shapiro, David Runkle, Avery Katz, Bob Barsky, Steve Zeldes, Jeff Miron, Mike Whinston, John Campbell, Andy Abel, Richard Zeckhauser, David Romer, Larry Ball, Miles Kimball, David Weil, Olivier Blanchard, Susanto Basu, Robert Barro, Xavier Sala-i-Martin, Bob

Hall, Niko Canner, and Doug Elmendorf. Some of these coauthors were my mentors, others were my contemporaries (often fellow students at MIT), and still others were students of mine at Harvard. In recent years, I have done most of my research with these coauthors.

Why are coauthors so important for the way I work? One reason is found in Adam Smith's famous story of the pin factory. Smith observed that the pin factory was so productive because it allowed workers to specialize. Research is no different—it is just another form of production. Doing research takes various skills: identifying questions, developing models, proving theorems, finding data, analyzing data, expositing results. Because few economists excel at all these tasks, collaborating authors can together do things that each author could not do as easily alone. In manufacturing knowledge, as in manufacturing pins, specialization raises productivity. (The puzzle is why Adam Smith chose to ignore his own analysis and write *The Wealth of Nations* without the benefit of a coauthor.)

The second reason I work with coauthors is that it makes my job less solitary. Research and writing can be a lonely activity. It is easy to spend endless hours with pad and pencil or in front of a computer without human contact. Some people may like that kind of work, but not me. Arguing with my coauthors makes my day more fun.

The third reason I work with coauthors is the most important: a good coauthor improves you forever. In the most successful collaborations, both coauthors learn from the experience. A coauthor can help you expand your knowledge, improve your skills, and expose your biases. Even after the collaboration is over, you take these benefits with you to future projects. To a large extent, as I have grown older, my coauthors have become my mentors.

Rule No. 3: Have Broad Interests
Throughout my life, I have been blessed with broad interests. (Or, perhaps, I have been cursed with a short attention span.)

As a child, I had numerous hobbies. I collected coins, stamps, shells, rocks, marbles, baseball cards, and campaign buttons. For pets, I had turtles, snakes, mice, fish, salamanders, chameleons, ducks, and, finally, a cocker spaniel. In high school, I spent my time playing chess, fencing, and sailing. I have long since given up all these activities (although I do have a border terrier named Keynes).

As a college student, I committed myself to a new major several times each semester, alternating most often among physics, philosophy, statistics, mathematics, and economics. After college my path was indirect and largely unplanned. In chronological order, I spent a summer working at the Congressional Budget Office, a year studying at the MIT economics department, a year studying at Harvard Law School, a summer working at a law firm, a year working at the Council of Economic Advisers, a second year at MIT finishing my Ph.D., another semester studying at Harvard Law School, and then another semester at MIT, this time as an instructor teaching statistics and microeconomics. In 1985, I gave up my studies in law and became an assistant professor at the Harvard economics department, where in my first year I taught principles of economics and graduate macroeconomics.

Remarkably, I have been at Harvard now for about a decade. Harvard is a wonderful place to work. Yet I often get the itch to leave, just for the sake of doing something different. One thing that keeps me at Harvard is the proximity of the National Bureau of Economic Research. Every year the NBER holds dozens of conferences on various topics with prominent economists from around the world. Having an office at the NBER is a bit like moving to a new university every few days.

My broad interests (short attention span) help to explain my diverse (incoherent) body of work. My research spans across much of economics. Within macroeconomics, I have published papers on price adjustment, consumer behavior, asset pricing, fiscal policy, monetary policy, and economic growth. I have even ventured outside of macroeconomics and published papers on fertility with imperfect birth control, the taxation of fringe benefits, entry into imperfectly competitive markets, and the demographic determinants of housing demand. None of this is part of a grand plan. At any moment, I work on whatever then interests me most.

Coming up with ideas is the hardest and least controllable part of the research process. It is somewhat easier if you have broad interests. Most obviously, broad interests give you more opportunities for success. A miner is more likely to strike gold if he looks over a large field than over the same small field over and over again. More important, thinking about one topic can generate ideas about other topics. I started thinking about menu costs and macroeconomic price adjustment, for instance, as I sat in a law school seminar that was discussing monopoly pricing and antitrust policy. Research ideas pop up in unexpected places.

Of course, breadth has its costs. One is that it makes writing grant proposals more difficult. I am always tempted to write, "I want to spend the next few years doing whatever I feel like doing. Please send me money so I can do so." Yet, in most cases, those giving out grant money want at least the pretense of a long-term research plan.

The greatest cost of breadth, however, is lack of depth. I sometimes fear that because I work in so many different areas, each line of work is more superficial than it otherwise would be. Careful choice of coauthors can solve this problem to some extent, but not completely. I am always certain that whatever topic I am working on at that moment, someone else has spent many more hours thinking about it than I have. There is something to be said for devoting a lifetime to mastering a single subject.

But it won't be my lifetime. I just don't have the temperament for it.

Rule No. 4: Allocate Time with Care

This is a rule of thumb I have been slow to learn. I used to go to every school that invited me to give a seminar, comment on every paper that a conference organizer asked me to discuss, referee every paper that a journal editor sent me, write every letter of recommendation that a department chairman requested of me, and sit on every committee that a dean asked me to attend.

But no more. Over time, the number of such requests has increased exponentially. Within a few years of going on the Harvard payroll, the cost of saying yes became intolerable. I came to realize that too much professional responsibility can be irresponsible, for it takes time away from the most important tasks — teaching and research. I now turn down the overwhelming majority of offers from seminar organizers, conference organizers, journal editors, department chairmen, and deans.

Deciding which research projects to pursue is the most difficult problem I face in allocating my time. I find it almost impossible to predict how any project will turn out before it is done. And even when I have finished one of my papers, I cannot predict with much accuracy how other people (such as editors and referees) will react to it. My strategy, therefore, is to choose research topics based on what interests me most and, to some extent, on whether I have a good coauthor who shares my enthusiasm. Sometimes I work on a topic for a while and decide that I have nothing new to say. I then force myself to remember the irrelevance of sunk costs and move on to another topic.

One way that I spend quite a bit of time is writing textbooks. I have written an intermediate-level textbook on macroeconomics, which is now in its third edition, and I have just finished writing a textbook on the principles of economics. Writing a textbook is a lot of work, and I am sometimes asked why I choose to spend my time this way. So let me explain.

Textbook writing is a form of teaching. As such, it has all the pluses and minuses of teaching. The major minus is that it takes time. And time is an academic's most valuable resource.

Despite the cost, I view textbook writing, like classroom teaching, as a good use of my time. One benefit is pecuniary. Few people in the world earn a living just creating knowledge. Most academics spend some of their time imparting knowledge as well. Giving lectures is one way of imparting knowledge; writing textbooks is another. So far, I have been able to make enough money imparting knowledge to students that I have not had to spend time on other activities, such as paid consulting, to put food on the table.

Of course, the most immediate benefit of classroom teaching and textbook writing is that they allow you to mold the minds of students. Economics is not a straightforward discipline like Newtonian mechanics or Euclidean geometry. Whenever you teach economics, you have wide latitude in choosing what material to include and how to present it. In making these choices, you give your own "spin" to the subject and help determine the views of your students. Although classroom teachers and textbook writers share this responsibility, textbook writers reach a larger audience. For those who want to bequeath their view of economics to the next generation, textbooks are the most efficient medium. Indeed, because textbooks are so important in shaping the field, many of the most prolific writers in academic journals are also textbook authors: Samuelson, Baumol, Blinder, Stiglitz, Barro, Dornbusch, Fischer, and on and on.

A less obvious benefit of classroom teaching and textbook writing is that they stimulate ideas for research. Whenever you have to explain something to someone, either in person or on a printed page, you have to think it through more thoroughly than you otherwise would. Preparing a lecture or drafting a textbook chapter reveals holes in your understanding. And, sometimes, as you try to fill these holes, you get ideas for research. Put simply, imparting knowledge and creating knowledge are complementary activities. That is why these two forms of production take place in the same firms, called universities.

The final benefit to spending time writing textbooks is that it makes you a better writer. But that brings me to my next topic.

Rule No. 5: Write Well

I think of myself as a mediocre writer. I do not come by my mediocrity naturally. It is the result of hard work and determination. This may seem like a small accomplishment, but I reassure myself with the fact that most economists do not live up to this standard.

Economists tend to underestimate the value of good writing. The reason, I believe, is that we like to think of ourselves as scientists. Scientific truths are as valid in run-on sentences as in well-written prose, so why bother trying to write well? Of course, no one would actually endorse bad writing, but this subconscious attitude pervades the profession and explains why economics is a more dismal science than it needs to be.

Despite our profession's bad attitude toward writing, good writing is in fact extraordinarily helpful to achieving success. Everyone knows that Robert Solow and Robert Lucas are important economists. But they are also superb writers, and this fact helps explain their prominence.

Whenever a person sits down to write something about economics, he or she is engaged in a form of joint production. Each article has two key attributes: style and substance. For producers of articles, style and substance are substitutes. The more time is spent avoiding the passive voice and replacing a *which* with a *that,* the less time is left to spend thinking new thoughts about the economy. But if you want to succeed as a producer, you have to think about your consumers. For consumers of articles, style and substance are complements. When I see an article by Solow or Lucas, I want to read it, not just because I will learn something about economics, but also because I will have fun doing so. An article that offers both style and substance is far more appealing than an article that offers one without the other. So if you want to sell your substance, you have to worry about your style. In other words, if you want to be read widely, you have to write well.

Writing is a craft, like carpentry. Some people are naturally better at it than others. But anyone can get better at it by devoting enough time and effort.

The first step to writing better is deciding to write better. After that, it is like acquiring any skill. Just as you can learn how to run regressions by reading a RATS manual, you can learn how to write better by reading books on style. I often recommend Strunk and White's *The Elements of Style* to my students, and I am surprised at how many have never heard of it. (It is the perfect book to leave in the bathroom. Whenever you have a spare minute, open it to a random page and start reading.) I also recommend that students read William Zinsser's *On Writing Well* to learn how to write and Donald McCloskey's *The Rhetoric of Economics* to learn how to persuade.

Becoming a good writer also takes practice. Reading the RATS manual will tell you how to run a regression, but you cannot easily run a regression after just reading about it. You have to turn on the computer and try it several times. You see what mistakes you make, what bugs show up unexpectedly, what things the manual forgot to tell you. The same is true with writing. The more you write, the better you get. When I look back on my own education, one thing that stands out is how often I had to write in the (private) high school I attended. I always had some writing assignment hanging over my head. At the time the school's policy seemed oppressive, but now I am grateful for the oppression. It prepared me perfectly for my current job.

Writing well is hard work. It requires that you revise, revise, and revise. Then, when you think you are done, you should revise again. Good writing is fun to read, but it is often not fun to do. (I once asked John Kenneth Galbraith the secret to his success as a popular writer. He said that he revises everything many times. Around the fifth draft, he manages to work in the touch of spontaneity that everyone likes.)

Fortunately, modern technology has made writing much easier. I write directly in Wordperfect. Pen, paper, and secretary are not necessary, which surely makes me more productive. But modern technology has also made it easier for people to produce bad writing. The supply of good writing and the supply of bad writing have both increased over time. The demand for bad writing remains low, however, so in equilibrium there is not much reward for producing it.

By contrast, good writing has substantial rewards. Writing something well attracts readers and gives your ideas a better chance to be heard. But there is also another payoff: good writing brings personal satisfaction. An author should get pleasure from looking back and finding that he or she has presented ideas well. I do not like writing, but I do like having written.

Rule No. 6: Have Fun

A book I read long ago revealed to me the secret to a happy life: find out what you like to do, and then find someone who will pay you to do it.

I learned this secret as a teenager. At the time, I liked racing small sailboats. So, when I looked for my first summer job, I found one giving sailing lessons. (My employer charged fifteen dollars for a one-hour lesson and paid me the minimum wage of $2.25. This was my first lesson in the economics of monopolistic competition.) Yet I knew that this advice would not always be easy to follow. I had no idea how to find someone to pay me to race sailboats for the rest of my life, and this was a source of some adolescent distress. Luckily, my tastes changed as I aged.

I now keep the secret to a happy life in mind when selecting topics for research. Editors and conference organizers often invite me to write papers on specific topics of their choosing. I turn down most of these offers. (This essay is one of the few exceptions.) Unless the editors happens to propose a topic in which I am already interested, I will not enjoy writing the paper and, most likely, will not do a good job. My approach to research is to decide first what I want to think about. I then see if I can get someone to publish the result. If my current interests happen to coincide with a conference someone is organizing, that's great, for the conference is a convenient outlet. And a conference invitation might help me to choose among several projects that I have in the back of my mind. But the most important question for me when beginning any project is whether the topic gets me excited.

Graduate students starting work on their dissertations often ask me for strategic advice. What are the hot research areas? What topics will get them jobs at the top universities? It is easy to understand why students ask these questions, but these are the wrong questions for someone embarking on a research career. I tell students that they should be asking themselves more personal questions. What would they like to learn about? What do they observe in the world and find puzzling? What topics get them excited?

Doing research is not like digging a ditch. A person can dig a perfectly fine ditch without enjoying his job for a minute. By contrast, research requires a certain passion about the topic being studied. Passion goes hand in hand with creativity. No one can manufacture this passion for strategic reasons of career advancement.

Most people who pursue an academic career do so because they are fascinated by their subject. It is for this reason that professors report among the highest rates of job satisfaction of all professions. Professors have found what they like to do, and they have found someone to pay them to do it.

DEIRDRE N. McCLOSKEY

Duty and Creativity in Economic Scholarship

How do I work? Messily, cleaning up in dull moments. And I imitate my betters. And I cherish my little flame.

Academic life, like any other, has a full in-box. A professor can stay busy answering his or her mail. Professors, after all, are employed by bureaucracies, and it is the way of bureaucracies to generate tasks to fill the time allotted. The committees of a modern college or university grow yearly. They are too many and too large by a factor of about three, but you can make a career on them, attending to what appears to be your duty. And they are socially pleasant. Serving on a committee is a chance to get to know your colleagues, a chance strangely rare in academic life.

The requests that come from outside by mail or phone or e-mail grow steadily. Some grow because colleges are part of the 20 percent or so of national income in the course of being absorbed by the federal government without actually becoming government offices, above the 40 percent now supplying alleged goods and services as some level of government. Will the professor kindly fill out this report of how he or she spent his or her time, suitably jiggered to keep the feds happy? Some grow because the time of professors at *other* universities is a common pool, which academic institutions have become careless in exploiting. Will he or she kindly act as referee for a paper generated by fear of tenure review? Will he or she kindly be one of a dozen or so people solicited to write meaningless letters of recommendation, interpretable only by the people in the identical field who know that Ken Arrow always exaggerates or that Stan Engerman always understates, but read by committees of people in other fields who know nothing of this?

I am not recommending irresponsibility. Some refereeing needs to be done, and who better to do it than you or me? Some committees need to meet, even though the VP will then do what she already planned to do. Most first-class mail, and even some third-class, warrants a reply, if only a scribbled note on the bottom. Books should be reviewed. The students must be graded. I seldom miss a class, even for really important matters like shopping the post-Christmas sales.

Many bureaucratic jobs really do need to be done, and it is shameful not to do them when asked, if you can. Everyone with gifts that way should be chair of the department for a while, poor though the job is (it is like being a foreman in a factory — neither labor nor management, chewed up by both). The work has to be done. The journals do have to be edited (though the task would be lighter if we did not need ten pieces for tenure). I still growl at a friend who twice turned down the editorship of the *Journal of Economic History* for what seem selfish reasons. He was willing to take honors from the profession but not to do the dirty work. Finally I shamed him into doing it.

And yet. Harry Johnson and Robert Mundell are paired in my mind, both at Chicago in the early 1970s. Both were Canadians, both heavy drinkers, both world famous in trade theory. Harry was the most responsible academic I have known, the very soul of professional care. His capacity for routine work was amazing. I came into the department once on a Saturday morning to find him with a pile of fifty Ph.D. core examinations on one side of the desk and a full bottle of scotch on the other. When I left a few hours later the pile and the scotch, both finished, had traded positions. Johnson inspirited hundreds of other economists, traveling incessantly to universities off the main track, commenting on everyone's work, synthesizing, editing, teaching (his classes were models of preparation and clarity), attending committees (while opening his mail, all of which he answered promptly), running the invisible college. Bob Mundell, on the other hand, is among the least responsible academics I have known (the competition is stiff). His office at Chicago looked like the result of a terrorist bombing. He never prepared classes. He was editor of the *JPE* for a while, but was so negligent that Harry had to take over and straighten things up. And yet. Who remembers Harry?

And who can forget Bob's contribution to international monetary theory, in a brief flurry of creativity from 1965 to 1970?

If you are going to do creative work, you have to cherish the flame. You have to protect it from the puffing of bureaucracy. The examples from art are impressive, the most extreme case being Gauguin, who one day (it is said: the true story must be more complicated) left his bureaucracy and his family for a life of painting in Tahiti. That is a terrible thing to do, morally indefensible, and as a woman I am truly appalled. And yet.

The literary critic Edmund Wilson had late in life a postcard printed up, which he would use to reply to requests not relevant to his current projects. It said, "Edmund Wilson regrets that he does not (1.) Write testimonials for books (2.) Attend conferences (3.) Comment on unsolicited manuscripts" and so on through the dozen ways of snuffing the flame. He would check off the relevant item and drop it in the mail to the person soliciting him. The technique is harsh, but you see the point.

I learned how to cherish my flame from experts. My mother's passions for painting, singing (she started a promising career in opera), Greek, poetry, and remodeling the house have been a model of how to work for me. In 1995 I attended a conference at Temple University on writing, and some woman gave a paper called "Writing on the Bias" ("on the bias" is a term in sewing, guys). She said she learned to write by watching her mother make beautiful clothing. The inspiration to work is the same, whatever the medium. It fits me. My mother's way of tearing down a wall and rebuilding it is a way of doing science.

My father was a professor, too (as is my kid sister, a psychologist; professing is the family business). He was well known in political science in the 1950s and 1960s, a fine scholar. I watched him goof off a lot between deadlines. He would read two mystery novels a night, for example, and read many other books not on his professional list (his profession was the American Supreme Court). I say "goofing off," but that's not right, because he showed me that wide reading makes a flexible scholar. From him I learned to make time for reading outside British iron and steel 1870–1914, my dissertation subject, or British economic history, my specialty. The result was for example that in early middle life I had a way of learning something about the humanities, in order to see the "rhetoric" of economics; and in late middle life I could see the relevance to economics of ethical reflection.

My mentor early in graduate school was John Meyer, whose graduate course in transportation economics I had taken as a senior in college. He supported me for a couple of summers, and in part during the year, in exchange for incompetent assistance on the economics of slavery and the Colombian Transport Project. I saw him as an academic entrepreneur, more businesslike than my father. But "businesslike" does not mean "methodical, orderly, time-keeping." The word is "businesslike," not "bureaucracy-like." It is what foreign academics can learn from American academics, using the best values of a commercial civilization for the study of economics or Greek.

Meyer's force and business reminded me of my mother, or her father, an electrical contractor in Michigan. I noticed in particular that Meyer was ruthless about his research time, as an electrical contractor had better be ruthless about his wiring time. One day for example I was standing in Meyer's office waiting to be told what to do (research assistants are like that, unfortunately) when his secretary brought in a new book from the mail. Meyer tore open the package, turned at once to the index, scanned the pages he had looked up, and tossed the book aside, probably forever. In retrospect it's possible he was looking up (1) his own name and (2) sex. But at the time it struck me as an emblem of how a businesslike scholar works. Get right to the point. Dig out what you need. Don't *read* books; use them. From Meyer I learned to *use* the books relevant to a particular project.

Read for pleasure, use for work. Since then I've rarely read a nonfiction book cover to cover, though I've used thousands of books. As it was put by Francis Bacon: "Some books are to be tasted, others to be swallowed, and some few [very few, and mainly if written by your scientific opponents] to be chewed and digested." Good advice (though, it should be noted, from a scoundrel: Bacon was for instance the last man to use torture in England for official purposes).

But in my father's way the "pleasure" reading kept becoming work reading. I would read about astronomy for pleasure, but then find ten years later that I was using what I had absorbed about the scholarly attitude of astrophysicists to compare with economics and its math-department values. I would read about linguistics for pleasure—if I had it to do over again, I think I would become a linguist, although probably unhappily, linguistics in my day being one of the most violently contentious fields around. But then ten years later I found that the linguistics illuminated how an economy operates. In the early 1980s I read Thomas Mann's first big novel, *Buddenbrooks,* because I was ashamed I had not read it. I found it enthralling and recognized that it was one of the few sympathetic portraits of a businessman in modern literature (another is David Lodge's recent *Nice Work*). It started me thinking, at Arjo Klamer's urging, about the role of persuasion in the economy, and then of ethics and our times.

My Ph.D. dissertation at Harvard was supervised, if that is quite the word, by Alexander Gerschenkron, the economic historian. One learned about cherishing one's creative flame in many ways from Gerschenkron. For one thing, he did not believe in spending a lot of time leading advanced graduate students through their work step-by-step. His neglect appears to have arisen from conviction, not sloth, since he would spend many hours talking to each first-year student in his large required course in economic history about their term papers. But from him no one got advice on how to write a thesis. Stop whining. Go read and write. In this I contrast Gerschenkron with the labor economist the late H. Gregg Lewis, long a colleague at Chicago, whom I watched extract the best from students by working with them closely, sometimes daily. By contrast, Gerschenkron got the best out of us by not working with us at all. You just wanted to do it right. Both models produced a lot of good scholarship.

I recall only one conversation with Gerschenkron about the thesis. Mostly we talked about baseball or literature. A *doktorbruder* of mine, Knick Harley, had exactly two conversations about his thesis, one of which consisted of Gerschenkron saying of Knick's long work on British shipbuilding, "It doesn't have an argument, does it?" Knick went back and worked for another year, giving it an argument.

Gerschenkron made his first impression on many people through his office, another lesson in cherishing the flame. It was an appalling mess, books and papers piled high, a long tunnel of stacked tomes to the desk itself, bottles of brandy littered within reach (he had a heart condition). Gerschenkron claimed that he knew where everything was because once a year he spent a day going through the stacks. It was one of the great messes of academic life. The prize in this regard goes in fact to Leo Goodman, the sociologist and statistician at Chicago, whose office had when I saw it a ton of unopened mail covering the entire floor, tilting up to the walls at the angle of repose of mail. Al Harberger's office at Chicago, despite the work of a super secretary,

Elyce Monroe, was only an order of magnitude or two below Goodman's entropy scale. Gerschenkron's lay somewhere between Harberger's and Goodman's.

The messy academic offices make the point. These were brilliantly creative people, masters in their field and beyond. The moral is given by the joke: "If a messy desk is a sign of a messy mind, what's an empty desk a sign of?" I recently saw at the University of Virginia the office of Ralph Cohen, a great student of literature, and it reminded me so strongly of Gerschenkron's that I told him so. Cohen, Gerschenkron, and the rest did not waste time being neat about inessentials. They were neat when it mattered, for this footnote or that equation — and then fanatically neat, willing to go to absurd lengths of precision — but not as a rule in matters far from the creative flame. Being neat about inessentials is like attending all committees and answering all mail or, in the modern mode, reading the manual from start to finish before starting up the computer. In the way of John Meyer or my father, Gerschenkron was businesslike and neat when it mattered, for compiling a table on Russian agriculture in the late nineteenth century or for writing English better than most native English speakers. But for the rest, well: clean up in a dull moment.

In the way of my father, too, who was a friend of his for this reason, Gerschenkron read widely, showing that the creative flame burns best in the open air. He wrote papers on the theory of index numbers, but also on the translations of Shakespeare. It was said implausibly but not impossibly that when the great critic Roman Jakobson retired from his chair in Slavic Literature at Harvard that Gerschenkron from Economics was on the short list to fill it. Waiting in Gerschenkron's chaotic office for a chat about baseball one day I received from the nearest of numerous stacks of books and magazines a lesson in the scholarly life, the sort of lesson that professors forget they give. The stack contained a book of plays in Latin, a book on non-Euclidean geometry, a book of chess problems, numerous statistical tomes, journals of literature and science, several historical works in various languages, and, at the bottom of it all, two feet deep, a well-worn copy of *Mad* magazine. Here was a scholar.

Above all I learned how to cherish the flame from Robert Fogel, who hired me at Chicago and was my colleague there for seven or eight years before he decamped for a stint at Harvard. One learned from Fogel, as I had learned in a smaller way from my mother, my father, from Meyer, and from Gerschenkron, the nitty-gritty of cherishing the flame.

The nitty-gritty does not mean isolating oneself from the scholarly conversation. For example, Fogel sends draft papers out for comment on a massive scale. His students have adopted the practice. Invite criticism and take advantage of it. Mail is cheap. "I'd rather be criticized in private by a friend," says Fogel, "than be savaged in public by an enemy," and unlike most of us he actually believes it. (He also believes he has more friends than he in fact does, but that is another matter.) He believes deeply in the conversation of scholarship, often starting a new project by writing long, sweetly reasonable letters to other scholars, whether or not he has been introduced. I have since learned how unusual is Fogel's attitude toward criticism. A few years ago, for example, I sent fifty pages of confidential comments to a historical demographer, reckoned a friend, who did not thank me but instead got angry. She treated me with hostility even when I was being harassed by my sister about my gender change, and all the other women academics at the Social Science History Association supported me warmly (they threw a party for me with balloons reading "It's a girl!"). A couple of years ago I replied at length to a request by a well-known experimental economist to criticize a draft, ending by telling him he needed to read more. He got angry, too, like a bush leaguer. Fogel is a major leaguer.

Fogel does not spurn the nitty-gritty of administration, either, so long as it too feeds the scholarly flame. He has assembled research teams, larger and larger and larger with each successive project (each project, admittedly, less interesting than the last: he seems to be a lone scholar who wants nonetheless to run research teams). He has repeatedly created new institutions and taught his students the desirability of doing the same. His workshop in economic history was one of many in the Chicago Department of Economics — the institution of workshops is Chicago's main contribution to the culture of the field — but his was suffused with warmth as well as rigor. Some of the other workshops at Chicago seemed to spring more from the dark side of the Force. Chicago had a stream of foreign visitors coming to study with Fogel, because Fogel does not view demographers and historians as engaged in some other enterprise that we economists can safely ignore. Like most economists he believes in intellectual specialization. But unlike most economists he is consistent in his economics: after the specialization he also believes in trade, rather than piling up exports unsold in the backyard.

Fogel embraced with enthusiasm the nitty-gritty task of financing his little flame of scholarship. He taught us that a scholarly life was worth paying for. He got fellowships for his visitors, he argued for appointments, and he paid for much of the resulting intellectual activity out of his own pocket. He spent what seemed like enormous sums on cameras and tape recorders and other equipment, using them to record first drafts of papers in seminars and to photograph participants quarreling with each other at conferences. A tape of the last seminar ran as background music for the famous annual Indoor Picnic at Bob and Enid's.

All these unifications of Fogel's life with his work were corollaries of The Great Nitty-Gritty, which I learned from my parents and Meyer and Gerschenkron, too: *put scholarship first.* Always, always scholarship came first. Moses Abramovitz, a student of Simon Kuznets as Fogel was, tells how terrifying it was to encounter Kuznets, because the older scholar would invariably ask, as though to a graduate student who was not making very good progress on his dissertation, "Well, Moses, what are you working on?" Fogel acted always as though Kuznets was going to show up in a few minutes and pop the overwhelming question, "Well, Robert, what are you working on?" He worked, and works, incessantly, to a plan that Kuznets would recognize as the most serious of scholarly work. When the Nobel committee called Fogel to announce his Nobel Prize, in the wee hours Chicago time, Fogel was awake and working, working, working.

So I try to work like these people, watching them cherishing the flame. Flame-cherishers are rare, so you have to pay attention when you run into one. I watch how the best people work and then try to imitate them. That's how you learn a sport and that's how you learn scholarship. Watch how the tennis player lines up her backhand. Watch how Bob Solow brings a personal tone into his scholarly writing. Keep your eyes open for hot tips.

For example, from the world historian at Chicago, William McNeill, whose office was across the hall from mine, I learned that you should never complain about teaching. He combined his teaching with his research, as we all should — anyone who can't learn a lot about economics from teaching Economics 1 is intellectually dead. McNeill said it this way:

> A university promotes scholarship less through the leisure it confers
> upon faculty and students than through the routines of classroom per-
> formance that require student and teacher to have something to say at
> a fixed point in time, ready or not. By compelling initial formulations
> of a given subject matter in this way, ideas are literally forced into
> existence, to wither or to flourish under subsequent examination as the
> case may be. (McNeill 1980, vii)

Or as another example, from Milton Friedman I learned how to keep
theory connected with fact, by asking myself Milton's most terrifying
seminar question, "How do you know?" Milton is always ready to
listen to some fool's answer. At the first cocktail party I attended at
Chicago as an assistant professor in 1968 I was holding forth to a group
including Milton on the monopoly of professional sports, the existence of which I had learned from reading Milton's writings. He asked
mildly, "How do you know? How do you know that professional
sports is a monopoly?" Gak. Jessum. I dunno. Milton told me so.

Now the problem is that it is hard to arrange to be around world-
class scholars every day, right? After all, most of us are not at MIT,
and even those who are there don't chat daily with Paul Samuelson
or Peter Temin or Franklin Fisher, right?

No, wrong, You can learn from writings, without a presence,
whether you are in Cambridge, Massachusetts, or at the North Pole,
if you give it a serious try. This entails, though, reading, which most
economists do not do enough of. Books, especially. I am often depressed by how few books economists have in their houses. An economist who thinks that economics, "like physics" (as they'll always say,
without knowing physics), requires one merely to read the latest
articles is not going to be much of an economist. (It should be noted
that most fields in physics are not "like physics" in this sense, and
that anyway physicists have famously wide interests. The definition
of a string quartet at the Institute for Advanced Study at Princeton is
three physicists and a mathematician.)

I learned most about The Great Nitty-Gritty, more even than
from Fogel or Gerschenkron or Meyer or my parents, by reading
books. I learned to pay attention to Bill McNeill by being a colleague, true, but I learned the idea about teaching from one of his
books. Milton (Friedman, and the poet John) has taught me more in
print than in person.

There's an enormous literature on How to Cherish Your Flame,
in as much detail and specificity as you could want. You've just got to

read beyond the *Journal of Economic Theory.* If you're going to be anything but a routine scholar, you need to learn that people outside of economics are not all misled dolts. You can learn from them, if you'll just start buying and reading their books. Listen up.

An important example for me was the essay by the American sociologist C. Wright Mills (I do not recommend his views on economics), "On Intellectual Craftsmanship." It is an appendix to a collection of his essays called *The Sociological Imagination* and tells in detail how one fine scholar went about his work. Books on writing are good places to learn about flame cherishing. After all, a scholar is a writer. I read style books the way other people read econometrics books. Writing paragraphs well is just as important as inverting matrixes well. The *Paris Review* interviews of creative writers are the very type of flame-cherishing literature. They've been published now in successive collections, a half-dozen or so. Jay Woodruff has edited an amazing book of five interviews with the likes of Joyce Carol Oates and Robert Coles on how successive drafts change: *A Piece of Work: Five Writers Discuss Their Revisions* (1993).

Another good source of flame-cherishing advice is the academic biography. I read them compulsively. You need to know how other brain-workers have lived their lives. The *Autobiography of Edward Gibbon* (1796) tells how to write *The Decline and Fall of the Roman Empire. The Education of Henry Adams* (1907) tells how to continue to educate oneself into old age. I especially like mathematical biography, such as S. M. Ulam, *Adventures of a Mathematician* (1976), Paul Halmos, *I Want to Be a Mathematician: An Automathography* (1985), or Constance Reid's books *Hilbert* and *Courant,* though you have to watch out for a worshipful attitude toward math. For economics read James Buchanan's autobiography, *Better Than Plowing* (1992). The two volumes edited by J. A. Kaegel, *Recollections of Eminent Economists,* collected from pieces in the *Banca Nazionale del Lavoro Review,* should be perused by everyone interested in economics, though they show that not all economists are gifted in telling what happened to them beyond their résumé.

The wider point is that the key to scholarly creativity is to combine your life and your work. That's how to cherish the flame: make the passions of your life a part of your work, and your work a passion of your life. My best articles and books have come out of passions in my life — to mention a couple of recent examples, irritation with the stockbroking industry after it had enticed my mother to lose two small fortunes *(If You're So Smart);* or concern about lofty sneering at the midwestern bourgeoisie ("Bourgeois Virtue"); or the experience of gender change *(The Vices of Economists).* The autobiography by the psychologist Jerome Bruner, *In Search of Mind,* contrasts two models of intellectual life: "Alfred Kroeber [the anthropologist] once told me that the difference between him and Clyde Kluckhohn [another anthropologist] is that Clyde wanted to weave everything he knew into one tapestry — anthropology, psychoanalysis, classics. He, Kroeber, was quite content to let them live on their own" (Bruner 1983, 77). I favor the Kluckhohn model (although Kroeber was hardly a barbarian). We should bring everything we know into our economics and our lives.

So read widely, for pleasure, and keep trying to reintegrate what you know with what you do. "To burn always with this hard, gemlike flame, to maintain this ecstacy, is success in life," said the English critic Walter Pater over a century ago. Heady stuff, but also soberly correct. Routine science is satisfactory and pays the bills. Yet we should each of us cherish our hard, gemlike flame, success in the scientific life, however small. Neglect the committee that is not accomplishing anything; avoid the student who is merely buttering you up; do not respond to the nth request for a recommendation of a colleague you don't know or care about. Or, to be exact and economic, watch out for the opportunity cost in cherished flame forgone.

REFERENCES

Bruner, Jerome. 1983. *In Search of Mind: Essays in Autobiography.* New York: Harper and Row.
Buchanan, James. 1992. *Better Than Plowing and Other Personal Essays.* Chicago: University of Chicago Press.
Kaegel, J. A. 1989. *Recollections of Eminent Economists.* 2 vols. New York: New York University Press.
Lodge, David. 1988. *Nice Work.* Harmondsworth: Penguin.
McCloskey, D. N. 1990. *If You're So Smart: The Narrative of Economic Expertise.* Chicago: University of Chicago Press.
———. 1994. "Bourgeois Virtue." *American Scholar* 63 (spring): 177–91.
———. 1997. *The Vices of Economists: The Virtues of the Bourgeoisie.* Amsterdam: University of Amsterdam; Ann Arbor: University of Michigan Press.

McNeill, William H. 1980. *The Human Condition: An Ecological and Historical View.* Princeton, NJ: Princeton University Press.

Mills, C. Wright. 1959. "On Intellectual Craftsmanship." In *The Sociological Imagination.* New York: Grove.

Woodruff, Jay. 1993. *A Piece of Work: Five Writers Discuss Their Revisions.* Iowa City: University of Iowa Press.

RACHEL McCULLOCH

Assembling the
Puzzle Pieces

I find inspiration for my work in the here-and-now of economic life, especially those parts involving international transactions. My goal is always to impose order and logic on the world I see, or at least on a little corner of it. As a young economist I used theoretical models for this purpose. Now (with luck I'm around the midpoint of my research career) my approach is harder to describe simply. My current efforts are usually directed toward integration and interpretation of theory and evidence. In essence, I try to fit together the pieces of an economic puzzle. The process often draws me into the history of ideas. I am particularly intrigued by ideas that become influential for a time yet are fundamentally flawed — ideas so out of sync with the "real world" that even economic theorists are bound eventually to take notice.

Although some of my papers draw heavily on contributions of other economists, they aren't proper surveys. A good survey seeks to impose order on a body of literature. My focus is not a body of literature but a particular phenomenon. Thus, I typically end up citing material from a variety of economics subfields ranging from labor to finance, and perhaps also political science or sociology. I draw on other work mainly when it helps to provide a coherent story, but occasionally also to explain why it doesn't help.

One editor who solicited a proposal from me subsequently

I am indebted to my Chicago classmate Robert Pollard for many comments and suggestions. In a marginal note to my section on the stimulus of deadlines, Bob wondered whether I was just saying that I am not very good at time management. But a second note a little farther down on the page acknowledged that he, with no external deadline, has been working on the same book for fifteen years.

rejected what I sent as too descriptive and journalistic. Although he did not intend this as a compliment, I think he was on the right track. Since my focus is a phenomenon, accurate description is often an essential element. I differ from the typical journalist not in my goal (piecing together a coherent story) but in my training and that of my typical reader. Even when I write papers specifically aimed at the "lay reader," they still end up finding their best audience among other economists and their students.

Given the goal of integrating observation and literature, it is not hard to imagine my office. As well as a place to work, it serves as a sort of physical extension of my brain, stuffed with disparate bits of information on all kinds of subjects that interest me. I have always been somewhat of a generalist; the only element of specialization to be detected in my list of publications is that every paper deals with some variety of international transaction.

My office is a minilibrary, crammed from floor to ceiling with research materials of every kind: specialized journals, newsletters, working papers, government documents, data sources, photocopies of key passages from books, masses of clippings from periodicals of all sorts. Mine is decidedly not a "paperless office," although the computer revolution has added floppy disks and CD-ROMS to the clutter. Because I am interested in the way ideas wax and wane in their influence, I often keep old editions of books even after I have acquired the new ones. Other things equal, I would prefer not to have papers and books stacked on every horizontal surface, but I have yet to find an effective alternative system. The top of my desk does become visible — briefly — between bouts of writing.

The Stimulus of Deadlines

Given my goal of integrating facts and analysis from many sources, I inevitably find myself working under pressure. Or perhaps I should say that I *write* under pressure, and almost only under pressure. Once I commit to a project, I am constantly *thinking* about the research, reading related material, sorting through ideas, integrating bits of new information, trying out arguments on a collaborator or colleague. This is an open-ended activity that lends itself to procrastination, albeit of a scholarly sort. Since there is always an unbounded set of potential resources to investigate, the final product doesn't start to take shape until the deadline looms. Without the externally imposed discipline of a deadline, I'm sure I would find it difficult to declare anything complete.

There are other reasons for last-minute writing that are less linked up to a specific research style. Most senior faculty have in common an excess of commitments relative to time available to meet them. Research is just one of a long list of must-do items on the weekly calendar. For many (I am surely one) the hardest part is the writing; it requires that scarcest of resources, big chunks of uninterrupted time. As a conscientious faculty member, I must prepare and give lectures, meet with students and visitors, answer mail and return phone calls (eventually), review manuscripts and grant proposals, and attend too many seminars, meetings, and conferences. Only when that deadline is looming do I ruthlessly push all else aside and start to write.

It wasn't always this way. As a young economist writing theoretical papers, I did sometimes need a deadline for inspiration. Usually, however, there were enough hours in the week to do everything I wanted to do. At the time I did not sufficiently appreciate the major benefit of my junior faculty status at Chicago and Harvard: administrative duties were almost nonexistent. With no children, I was free to continue the graduate-student norm of the seven-day workweek. This wasn't a hardship. Many of my friends were doing the same, and the long working hours were enlivened by camaraderie and even the junior faculty's idea of fun. Contrary to what some publish-or-perish types may have told their long-suffering spouses, those hours "at the office" were sometimes taken up by activities not easily interpreted as work. On any given weekend afternoon, the faculty lounge at the Chicago Business School was likely to be occupied by junior scholars watching a ball game on our large-screen color TV. Of course, that was before computer games and more recently the Internet made it so easy to waste time without even getting up from the desk.

According to my calculations, it has been about twenty years since I completed any project more than seconds before the deadline. The day my first child was born in December 1977 I was correcting the (overdue) proofs of a forthcoming monograph on the then-obscure topic of international competitiveness. Since then, the time squeeze has only gotten worse, and by now I fear that working to the deadline may have been established as a lifelong habit. Lest I frighten any young readers, I hasten to add that I am very satisfied with my life as it is — even if I would be delighted to have a few extra hours in each day!

Planning versus Serendipity

Does any child dream of becoming an economist?[1] Even as an undergraduate at the University of Pennsylvania, I wouldn't have enrolled in a single economics course without the pressure to satisfy certain "distribution requirements" for graduation. As it was, I did take an economics course in my last year; it was economics rather than sociology or political science because I wanted to be in the same class as my boyfriend. To my good fortune, the professor was Irving Kravis, not only a fine economist but also a dedicated and inspiring teacher. Despite my lack of initial motivation, I enjoyed the course and found the new way of thinking congenial. But economics still failed to emerge as a likely vocation. The principles course remained bracketed in my mind with philosophy, art history, music, and biology, all good things for a liberally educated person to know something about.

Unlikely though it may seem to those familiar only with my recent work, I eventually came into economics by way of mathematics. But even math was not my first love. I entered college as a student of engineering. In our rather inept family, I had been legendary for my mechanical aptitude. In retrospect, I suppose my true aptitude was for extracting information from instruction booklets and how-to-fix-it manuals. In my current household, I am still the person who, book in hand, programs the VCR and replaces the hard drive. Alas, the results of freshman year brought home the difference between what I would later know as comparative and absolute advantage. I rarely completed a lab without breakage, injury, or other disaster. On the positive side, for an engineering student I was unusually good at math. A new career path soon beckoned.

After earning a master's degree in math at Chicago, I worked first as a high-school math teacher and then as an applied mathematician and programmer in the Department of Aeronautics and Astronautics at MIT. Finding applied math congenial but nose cones, wind tunnels, and trajectories boring, I cast about for a new field of application. A college friend, Joe Ostroy, told me that mathematical models were becoming increasingly important in economics. With the encouragement of Karl Shell, who had entered economics by the same route, I enrolled in MIT's Ph.D. program in economics.

For purely personal reasons, I stayed at MIT only one year and completed my graduate education in economics at the University of Chicago. This was in the late 1960s, when MIT (along with Harvard and Yale) and Chicago represented opposite intellectual poles. Thus, my training was highly eclectic. At MIT I had learned about optimal intervention. At Chicago, I learned that intervention was rarely optimal. As a graduate student, I remained agnostic. Later, and as I learned more about the world, I leaned increasingly to the Chicago viewpoint.

Oddly enough, I can't recall how I came to write a thesis on international trade. I certainly didn't enter graduate school with the thought of specializing in this, or indeed any, particular field. My strong background in math made theory and econometrics likely areas, and my first Chicago mentors were Hirofumi Uzawa and Zvi Griliches. However, both left Chicago before I began a dissertation. In the late sixties, very few Americans chose to specialize in international economics, but with Harry Johnson and Robert Mundell (both Canadians) on the faculty, Chicago was probably the best place in the world to make a start in this field. My Chicago cohort included many of today's best-known international economists, including Rudiger Dornbusch, Jacob Frenkel, and Michael Mussa.

A Research Trajectory

I began my research career as an applied trade theorist. My first paper, written in 1969 while I was still a graduate student at Chicago, was inspired by the U.S. oil import quotas then in effect. Working in Washington for the U.S. Cabinet Task Force on Oil Import Control, I had become intrigued by an unusual method used to distribute import licenses for oil. This led to a series of theoretical papers evaluating alternative trade policies, not in the usual terms of effect on aggregate national welfare but in terms of the implied cost of achieving possible underlying objectives, such as an induced increase in producer surplus or government revenue.

As a junior faculty member at Harvard, I continued with theoretical research, now branching out from trade to other types of international transactions (capital flows, migration, technology transfer) and usually in the context of conventional two-sector general-equilibrium models. Several of these Harvard papers I wrote in collaboration with Janet Yellen, a brilliant but also fun-loving colleague who served on the Board of Governors of the Federal Reserve System and then as chairman of the Council of Economic Advisers in the Clinton administration. Although Janet and I were successful according to one standard — publications in leading journals — I was increasingly dismayed to find that even in published form, these papers seemed to sink out of sight within months of their completion.

In contrast, my first paper of a different type made me famous, or maybe I should say notorious, even before it was published. In 1974, Karl Brunner had asked me to write a background paper on oil and OPEC for a West German television broadcast. My task was to explain what had made the huge OPEC price increase possible, and whether the same scenario might be repeated for other commodities such as copper. I concluded not, and explained why. The gratifying response to the paper, "Commodity Power and the International Community," contrasted sharply with my experience writing on trade theory. But Harry Johnson, my ever-practical thesis adviser and mentor, cautioned me to continue with the theoretical research — "at least until you get tenure."

I followed this advice, partly because Harry almost always knew what he was talking about, and partly because I still had hopes of writing a theoretical paper that would make some impact on the profession. The result of this continuing effort, along with a few empirical studies, was that I became tenured but remained intellectually frustrated. Almost the only acknowledgment of the theoretical papers was a trickle of letters from graduate students at obscure places asking about mathematical derivations or, worse, pointing out errors.

In addition to the disappointing response from the profession, a more fundamental problem was that the theoretical work never managed to achieve my own objectives. While the papers always began from an idea that seemed important and interesting, the exigencies of mathematical modeling seemed inevitably to leave the initial spark on the cutting-room floor. Maybe I wasn't a good enough mathematician, or maybe I wasn't audacious enough in stripping away the inessentials. Whatever the reason, I gradually found myself doing less theory and more of the integrative or interpretive papers. Although these were often published in conference volumes or other relatively obscure outlets, they seemed to fill a real need. I was pleased to find some of the newer papers on reading lists or reprinted in collections. Economists I met for the first time sometimes mentioned a paper they had found helpful when beginning work in a new area. Perhaps I was actually writing very brief and specialized textbooks.

Finding Inspiration

As a graduate student, I worried about running out of ideas. I knew that many economists never published any papers beyond ones based on dissertation research — in fact, only half of all Ph.D.'s ever publish even a single article. As I worked on my dissertation, I began to note down ideas for postdissertation research. This precaution proved unnecessary. In the area of trade policy, researchable questions seemed to be thick on the ground. One reason was the success of the Kennedy round of GATT negotiations, completed in 1967, in slashing tariff rates around the world. The unanticipated result of this success was the proliferation of nontariff barriers, less-transparent policies used to achieve the same protective objectives as the tariffs. However discouraging to free traders, the emergence of nontariff barriers proved to be a research gold mine for trade economists. The collapse of the Bretton Woods system in the early 1970s yielded a similar treasure trove of researchable ideas on the financial side. These milestones also provided the first of many lessons in the way real-world events perversely fail to conform to the predictions of economic modelers.

My concern about running out of research ideas may have been a legacy of my days in mathematics, where it is quite possible for a field to be mined until there is literally no theorem left to prove. Mathematics is a young person's game in part because young mathematicians begin their labors in new fields rich with open questions. At Chicago, however, I was impressed by the large number of middle-aged and even elderly mathematicians who had evidently learned the secret of eternal scholarly life. One older mathematician, I believe it was Saunders MacLane, told us that he devoted a sizable fraction of his time to learning new fields. As an aging economist I find that plan laudable but hard to follow. The closest I have come to expanding rather than simply updating my own stock of intellectual capital is a modest investment in game theory, a subject unknown to me in graduate school but today essential for any international economist.

Fortunately, economics differs from mathematics in a very basic way, one that may account for the large number of economists who remain productive well into their "retirement" years. Mathematicians can answer a question only once; after a theorem is proved, it stays proved. In economics the situation is different because the economic world never stops changing. As economists we can answer the same question over and over. Indeed, we are likely to become the experts best positioned to provide the updated answer to any given question.

An important offset to the documented disadvantages of increasing age comes from the attendant additions to one's mental data bank. As a trained on-the-spot observer of more than three decades of important economic happenings, I have gained a perspective on today's events and the economic questions they raise that I doubt could be duplicated through the most assiduous library digging. From the vantage point of middle age, I am amazed at how utterly ignorant I was when I left graduate school. And I am horrified to recollect being the young referee who rejected several truly innovative papers. Happily, these gems eventually found their way to their rightful place in the literature despite my lack of appreciation.[2]

Another consequence of increasing age is a heightened awareness of the history of ideas. Of my own papers, my favorite is called "Surprising Real Consequences of Floating Exchange Rates." Other people seem to agree; this is by far the most often cited and reprinted of my papers. The paper was originally prepared for the 1982 Wingspread conference organized by my former teacher and colleague, Robert Z. Aliber of the Chicago Business School. It was also my first paper dealing with exchange rates rather than the "real" goods-and-services side of international transactions.

The inspiration came from the astonishing contrast between the academic debate on the merits of floating exchange rates that raged while I was a graduate student in the 1960s and the actual performance of the post-1973 international monetary system. The volatility of floating rates vastly exceeded even the most pessimistic predictions of the 1960s, yet, far from bringing trade and investment to a screeching halt, the unprecedented volatility was accompanied by continued growth in every type of international transaction.

The Economist as Writer

A successful economist is necessarily a professional writer. For this profession I had a very unpromising start. My parents emigrated from Europe during World War II. Neither had graduated from the European equivalent of high school, and neither ever learned the subtle points of English. *The Reader's Digest* and a daily newspaper constituted the main printed matter in our home. Until graduate school, my formal education entailed few demands in terms of writing. I attended a rather seedy neighborhood high school where even "honors" students were never required to write a research paper. In college, I consciously avoided courses where papers were likely to be assigned. I recall writing a few short papers on philosophy and French literature, but with a schedule filled by math and science courses, my academic labors were devoted mainly to problem sets and lab reports.

In graduate school I eventually did start to do some writing. As a rank beginner, I found the process intimidating and arduous. Friends helped me with tips. One I especially liked and still use in modified form entailed setting a daily writing quota. After a while, I would arrange all the pieces on a big table and see if anything fit. This is not an economical way of writing economics—so much ends up in the wastebasket—but it does wonders to fend off writer's block.

Completing my dissertation seemed such a monumental feat that I immediately made three photocopies to keep in different places— at home, at my office, and in my briefcase. I felt I could never do it a second time. Once I had managed to produce a draft, my thesis committee did their part through intensive use of the red pencil. Bob Aliber gave me a copy of Strunk and White's small classic, *The Elements of Style*. Today I still keep it handy, and I have passed along countless copies to my own students.

With my first journal submission, I learned the awful truth about publication: most of the work comes *after* the author considers the paper done. First come revisions, sometimes multiple revisions, to meet the demands of the referees. Then come negotiations with editors, who at best help you say clearly what you mean, and at worst take the liberty of changing what you mean, but perhaps fail to say clearly, to what you don't mean. From the good editors I have learned much about how, and how not, to write. I could probably make a book-length manuscript from all the passive constructions I have deleted from my papers over the years. From the bad editors I have learned to ask, politely, to have the edited copy returned to me before the article goes to the printer.

Writing is still an uphill battle. As one editor told me, "You're a pretty good writer—for an economist." I remain envious of those who write economics effortlessly, or at least as if it were effortless.

Although I often disagree with what they write, I never fail to envy the easy expository style of Paul Krugman and Bob Aliber. And I am in awe of Milton and Rose Friedman for their ability to make truths (as they see them) so seductively simple. Perhaps my favorite economics writer remains George Stigler. His short treatise *The Theory of Price* may be the sole example of a witty textbook. Consult his treatment of consumer's surplus for an example of vintage Stigler.

Perils of Publishing

One day in class Bob Mundell told us what may have been the single most important thing I learned in graduate school. He remarked in an offhand way that every one of his significant papers had been rejected by at least one journal before being published. What vital information for a graduate student to hear![3] I have never figured out whether there is truly a marketplace of ideas, or whether it is just that refereeing is a random process. My own experience confirms that even among the major journals, a paper's rejection from one by no means precludes publication in another of at least equal status. But I wish I had known at an earlier age how to distinguish an outright rejection from a noncommittal "revise and resubmit," and that it does sometimes pay to argue with a referee or an editor who is simply wrong.

At least in retrospect, my funniest experience along these lines concerned a theoretical paper (jointly authored by Janet Yellen) that had been accepted by the referees and one coeditor of an appropriate journal, only to be rejected by the second coeditor on the grounds that he himself had already published a paper that proved the same thing. Armed with this abstruse and far from user-friendly paper, Janet and I eventually figured out what he actually *had* proved, and then amended the original paper to include a discussion of his result and an explanation of how it related to our own.

Refereeing is a nearly unavoidable responsibility of those who hope to publish in refereed journals. Experiences as both a referee and an author lead me to pass along an important caution. Lapses on the part of editors or editorial assistants are frequent enough that no referee should ever write anything in the report or in the usually franker covering letter that he would not want the author to know he had written. The same applies to an author's correspondence with the editor concerning the refereeing process.

One referee wrote in his covering letter to the editor that he would not even use the submitted paper for a classroom exercise on a rainy afternoon. His formal report, however, was so circumspect that the editor, in rejecting our paper, felt compelled to send along a copy of the covering letter to bolster his case. Another editor forwarded a copy of a referee's apology for losing our manuscript behind the file cabinet and his hope that the long delay did not mean that the paper had to be accepted. In both cases, the paper in question was eventually published in an equally prestigious journal, although I will never feel quite as much warmth toward the offending referees or the indiscreet editors. In yet another egregious breach of confidentiality, an editor forwarded to me a copy of a rejected author's irate attack on the referee — in this case me.

The Gender of Economists
In writing the above section, I have referred to the unnamed editors and referees as *he*. This is appropriate since all were male. Happily, being female has become less of an anomaly in economics since I entered graduate school. My Chicago class contained four women and fifty-six men. In those days (circa 1967) Chicago discriminated openly against female applicants for financial aid. The "rational" argument was that women would soon marry and leave the profession to raise a family; the anticipated social return on their education was thus lower than for their male counterparts. But what doesn't actually kill you makes you stronger. It is probably not a coincidence that my classmate Claudia Goldin became the first tenured woman on the Harvard economics faculty.

Until the profession looks very different from today, a woman will never be just another colleague. Throughout my career, being a woman in a male-dominated profession has made a difference. As a woman, I am bound to be more conspicuous professionally than my peers; this magnifies both achievements and shortcomings. Affirmative action further complicates the situation. As a woman, I have found some opportunities foreclosed and others extended simply on account of my sex. Since I can usually do nothing about the opportunities that do not come my way, I never hesitate to accept any that do, even when they positively reek of affirmative-action considerations. One dark side of affirmative action is its perverse effect on the self-assurance of its supposed beneficiaries. I still remember my great pleasure as a new Ph.D. in receiving an offer from the University of Maryland, which already had three women on the economics faculty. They loved me for myself!

Another potential pitfall for women and members of "underrepresented" minorities is committee work. In these politically correct times, anyone charged with appointing a committee must strive for some measure of diversity. That means a few of us are asked much more often than the rest. Say yes to all of these offers and there is no time left for anything else. As with other opportunities, I don't waste time agonizing about underlying motives. I accept the memberships that have professional appeal or promise to be fun (exotic travel is my favorite), plus as much of the rest as represents my fair share of the work.

Specialization, Diversification, and Collaboration
There is great professional reward to narrow specialization. There is great fun in diversification. I lean toward the fun of doing new things. I usually feel most satisfied with my first or second paper on a particular subject. After that, my ability to contribute new insights seems to be spent; it may need a few years to revive unless the territory itself is changing rapidly — as has been the case with international capital flows.

The problem is that new opportunities tend to be shaped by past contributions. As soon as I publish a paper that contains all my good ideas on a subject, I am likely to receive an invitation to write another one along the same lines. For me, a way out of this dilemma is through collaboration, which expands both the set of interesting opportunities and the set of good ideas on any given subject.

Although fewer than half my papers have been written with a coauthor, I consider myself to be an inveterate collaborator. Collaborative research has the potential to be fun in a way that solitary scholarship never can be. But it also requires a meshing of approaches, priorities, working styles, and professional standards. This means inevitable conflict and possible acrimony and pain. After working with ten collaborators, I can say that each collaboration had its payoff. Even with my one "collaborator from hell" the final product was unambiguously superior to what I would have written on my own.[4]

Heroes and Role Models

I have many heroes among my fellow economists, and I will name only a few of them. Some have done the sort of work to which I aspire. In this category I include Charles Kindleberger, Albert Hirschman, Max Corden, and Harry Johnson. Harry's death in 1977 cut short a monumentally prolific career. Someone recently commented on the virtual disappearance of references to Harry's work, concluding that his contributions were thus shown to be ephemeral. As Harry's student, I must register a dissent from this interpretation. Much of what Harry wrote has become part of the standard training of any international economist. Because many of his ideas and interpretations are now so universally accepted, they no longer seem to require a citation.

Other heroes are wonderful economists in their own way but a way that will never be mine, even in my dreams. The list is too long to include here, but I give special mention to Irving Kravis, my first teacher in economics, and Robert Baldwin, my valued colleague at Wisconsin. Three other heroes are Robert Fogel, Robert Stern, and Richard Freeman. They are similar in their unusual success in turning ordinary garden-variety students into highly productive independent researchers. In each case an important ingredient is the ability to conceive, finance, and implement a broad research agenda that generates apprenticeship opportunities for many fledgling scholars. Although many of my former teachers have now become Nobel laureates, I felt a special pleasure in learning of Bob Fogel's prize.

I have also drawn inspiration from role models, by which I mean women who have succeeded on their own terms in a field dominated by men. In my own subfield of international economics, Anne Krueger stands out as an extraordinarily versatile contributor who has made her mark on both the academic science and its application to policy. I esteem my Brandeis colleague Anne Carter as one whose life demonstrates the possibility of balancing successfully all the demands confronting a spouse-parent-teacher-administrator-scholar. She even cooks.

Tying Up Loose Ends

Paul Krugman concludes his essay in this volume with a section titled "Regrets." As I pondered this, I realized that I don't have very much in the way of regrets. Over the years I have made many choices and many mistakes. Nonetheless, things always seem to turn out rather well, although often not at all in the way that I might have expected. It was my good fortune, not to be confused with smart planning, to enter a subfield of economics that has enjoyed steady growth over the subsequent years. If there is any "secret" to whatever success I have enjoyed, I suppose it is being open to new opportunities and, even more important, not being crushed when things don't go according to plan. In my experience, things rarely do go according to plan.

NOTES

1. My daughter, the offspring of two economists, was once asked by a visitor whether she also planned to take up economics. She looked at me tentatively, then replied, "I hope this won't hurt your feelings, Mummy, but I want to do something interesting when I grow up." Yielding to parental pressure, she enrolled in one economics course at Yale, where she has otherwise studied interesting things.

2. After writing this confession, I read "How Are the Mighty Fallen: Rejected Classic Articles by Leading Economists," by Joshua S. Gans and George B. Shepherd, *Journal of Economic Perspectives* 8 (winter 1994): 165–79, and learned that I am far from alone in having failed to appreciate the merit of contributions to the economics literature later viewed as seminal. None of the authors and papers that prey on my own conscience are even mentioned.

3. I have always repeated the Mundell story to my own graduate students. Now I will also pass along copies of "How the Mighty Have Fallen" (see n. 2).

4. I trust my failure to name the name will not leave the other nine worrying.

PHILIP MIROWSKI

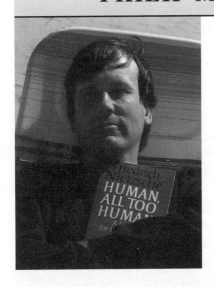

Confessions of an Aging Enfant Terrible

How This Essay Works

It is the nature of an enfant terrible to be obstreperous, so perhaps I can begin by quibbling with the terms of the mandate so generously tendered by Professor Szenberg. He requested essays on the theme "How I Work," but I find the format of this particular type of autobiography so suspect and its "lessons" so treacherous, that with his indulgence I should like to alter the terms of the mandate slightly to read, "How Things Work." This is my oblique way of saying: "Don't take anyone's anecdotes at face value — even my own." With your own postmodern indulgence, perhaps you will let me briefly explain.

Anyone who has kept up with literary theory over the past two decades would probably quail at the idea that simple heartfelt *apologiae pro sua vitae* contain the keys to success in any walk of life, but most emphatically would deny that they play any pedagogical role in academe. Indeed, I myself have been very taken with some work done on the genre of the autobiography, turning a somewhat jaundiced eye on the history of their common structures (Furbank 1993; Sturrock 1993). Briefly, and crudely, there are two classes of autobiography: let us call them the Academy Award Speech and the Adventures of a Self-Made Man, respectively. In the first, you are put at great pains to thank everyone from your kindergarten teacher to your shrink for their wonderful communal effort in bringing you to the brink of success and recognition; all hints of envy and

This essay was previously published in *American Economist* 38, no. 2 (fall 1994): 28–35.

struggle and despair and randomness are banished in a warm diffusion bath of responsibility and self-congratulation. Morals are of course drawn, but they inevitably verge on the platitudinous. Anyone who has ever sat through such testimonials realizes immediately that this genre never will be art. At best it can be minor grist for the mills of those who will construct our narrative histories after we are gone.

And then there are the second class of autobiographies, those more substantial *Confessions,* from Augustine to Rousseau to De Quincy to Hobson to Verlaine to Richard Rorty: the ones that, to varying degrees, can be elevated to the status of art. Here the pattern is decidedly different. Its topos is the story of someone fearlessly opting out of staid convention and the fellowfeeling of mankind to wander in the wilderness and, with success, to return preaching strange and novel doctrines. Intrinsic to the narrative is the conviction that the author is self-made or self-taught (men write these much more often than women: feminists, take note!). "They are likely to tell us of some turn in their experience when they were thrown back on their own resources (like Descartes, alone in his stove-heated room) . . . rendering them unsociable for the moment, with a need one day to make their terms again with humankind. . . . As a class, they have a tendency to megalomania. . . . For all their self-castigation and earnest proclamations of indebtedness, [these] autobiographers are an arrogant and autarkic bunch" (Furbank 1993, 6).

Economists, it seems, inevitably find themselves torn between these two genres. Insofar as they are wont to be team players and happy campers (not to mention reinforcing their reputations as dull and dismal souls), they should opt for the first narrative, pretending that there are uncontentious transpersonal rules and an orderly structure to their discipline, a functional meritocracy of incremental normal science. Yet however much this would seem to be the harsh imperative of academic etiquette (Hamermesh 1992), economists' own social theories tell them that this communal conception of social life is bunk, that everything that is law-governed springs directly from individual consciousness, that the lonely genius is the only real font of innovation, and that aggressive self-promotion is the law of the jungle. The commonplace fallback of a competitive "marketplace of ideas" best captures this latter temptation to apply their own theories to their own economistic lives, with the coda that the inevitable reintegration into the society of scholars comes in the stylized format of chastened vanquished opponents acknowledging on bended knee the prophet's property/ideas as coin of the realm.

I couldn't possibly produce a plausible version of either narrative; I just can't summon sufficient faith in either genre, much less the requisite enthusiasm. Because I am not a product of a successful socialization into the economics profession, lots of things that economists say strike me as funny. The idea that we are paid according to our marginal productivity, for instance, rocks me as risible; the tendency to suggest the economy "overheats" is a richly wrought satire. The doctrine that the market maximizes the freedom of a set of agents identical in all relevant respects is a joke worthy of Nietzsche. At the University of Michigan, where I did my graduate degree, the people who worked in the econometric forecasting unit used to call tinkering with unsatisfactory predictions "adding the bump constants." These are fine as harmless entertainments, but turn to ashes in my mouth when I am forced to render an account of my own life.

I have resisted becoming integrated into the "normal science" practices of the discipline, and I know this has been one common thread connecting the diverse areas within which I have labored. Others sense this instinctively: I am frequently reprimanded in print for my style and tone; some of my teachers in graduate school warned me ominously that I would not fit in; and fellow faculty at Yale cautioned graduate students to keep an assured clear distance from any of my projects while I was a visiting professor there. Now, in retrospect, I can appreciate the kernel of wisdom in all this unsolicited advice. The ingrained stodginess of the social structures of science does serve certain cognitive functions. Asking me now to write on how I feel about economics journals is like asking a lamppost to write a memoir on dogs. But the alternate narrative portrayal of myself as a Nietzschean *Übermensch,* performing the magic trick of conjuring myself out of thin air, or even more incongruously, the idea of some of my writings as somehow becoming valorized in the marketplace of ideas, is just ludicrous. Anyone who had actually read any of my other stuff would immediately detect an inauthentic note from page one.

Another thread that binds my diverse writings together is an attempt to understand myself as a product of my age through trying to understand economics as a product of the social conditions of its production. This may sound an impossibly misplaced motivation, rather like trying to understand Mozart by studying Freemasonry, or to take the comparison down a notch, Charles Manson by studying the lyrics of the Beatles. Perhaps a surfeit of incredulous reactions will one day convince me of that fact. Yet, until that day dawns, I will continue to be taken with Nietzsche's notion that philosophical discourse is actually a species of veiled autobiography, "the personal confession of its author and a kind of involuntary and unconscious memoir; also that the moral (or immoral) intentions in every philosophy constituted the real germ of life from which the whole plant had grown" (1966, 13). Thus, when I read a particular economist's advocacy of regarding children as consumer goods, or another insists that Third World countries should be dumping grounds for toxic industrial wastes since life is cheap there, or a third proclaims that no sound economist would oppose NAFTA, or a fourth asserts confidently that some price completely reflects all relevant underlying fundamentals in the market, or a fifth pronounces imperiously that no credible theorist could recommend anything but a Nash equilibrium as the very essence of rationality in a solution concept, I do not view this as an occasion to dispute the validity of the assumptions of their "models"; rather, for me, it is a clarion call to excavate the archaeology of knowledge that allows such classes of statements to pass muster, as a prelude to understanding what moral presuppositions I must evidently hold dear, given that I find them deeply disturbing. However unpopular it may be, I find it hard to understand economics as anything other than a subset of moral philosophy, even though this definition of "philosophy" awaits explication. Thus, by learning about economists and their peccadillos, I learn about myself; discovering how these things work helps me understand How I Work.

Living in the Material World

> I'm an economist. I don't think in historical terms.
> — Polish government official, on the erstwhile
> *MacNeil-Lehrer News Hour*

The separation of *is* from *ought,* the positive from the normative, is of course the byword of our stridently secular discipline. I am also perfectly aware that political economy traces its lineage out of moral philosophy, essentially renouncing the terms of that earlier discourse in favor of the instrumentalist terminology of Science in order to assert its novel identity as "economics." For most of my colleagues, this dictates that the language and concepts of moral philosophy are an anathema, the province of confused and conflicting claims and counterclaims. Although they might differ as to whether it happened in 1776 or 1838 or 1870 or 1944, at some juncture economics attained its status as a science and said good-bye to all that.

My little epiphany, which occurred quite early in my career, was to decide that I should provisionally accept their ukase regarding philosophy and follow them part of the way into their kingdom of preferred legitimacy, namely, Science. This did not mean for me, as it did for so many of them, starting off with a degree in physics or engineering or mathematics; nor did it imply direct recourse to the self-conscious philosophy of science or its bastard offspring in economics, "methodology." Rather, it meant following my own prior inclinations to learn some history of science and history of economics. In this quest, I was fortunate to be encouraged by a few open-minded individuals along the way: Warren Samuels, Gavin Wright, and Lawrence Sklar.

Because this sounds like such a prescription for disaster in modern economics, I want to stress that the whole thing was not the resultant of some decision-theoretic calculation on my part.

I was only dimly aware that by the early 1970s an interest in intellectual history was tantamount to career suicide in academic economics, though things certainly have gotten worse in the interim. I did it simply out of curiosity. I would never counsel anyone else to follow in my footsteps in this respect, though it has remained an article of faith with me to do at least a third of all my reading well outside of economics, and further, to sporadically read randomly, trusting my instincts and keeping copious notebooks in order to trace my way back to any particular node. In a world where it is cute to think that the only famous Ricardo was the second banana on *Lucy* show, but getting the Euler equation wrong is grounds for getting you booted from the profession, imputing rationality to my actions would be a shameless whitewash. Sometimes I wonder the extent to which my younger self was conscious of living in the material world.

Once I had gained a fair grounding in the history of physics (having also had a few courses in the area), I began to discern a repetitive set of invocations of Science in various economists, and then my ear became attuned to some of their ambivalences and ambages along the way. Luckily, I was living through an era in which belief in any context-independent Scientific Method was being unsentimentally deconstructed, so I did not have to take the various economists' characterizations at face value. I began to understand the extent to which their dependence upon Science was inextricably time-bound, and further, the astounding degree to which they would persistently confuse imitation of the trappings of physics (or lately, biology) with privileged access to the ontological heart of the economy. I still marvel at the extent to which economists openly pride themselves in living in the material world, when they are mostly surrounded by shadows in their own private cave.

Once I had become convinced of the pervasive character of this dependence upon diverse meanings of *science,* I became more and more excited, like a kid in a candy store (or some would say: a bull in a china shop); so many of the things about economics that had nettled and disturbed me now had a context and a frame, inviting detailed clarification through comparison of the history of the sciences. Just one product of this reconfiguration of the history of economics that has subsequently attained a modicum of notoriety is my (1989) argument that the "Marginalist Revolution" of the 1870s was no discovery, but rather a fairly straightforward appropriation of the energetics movement of the mid–nineteenth century, with utility being the direct analogue of potential energy, prices the analogue of forces, and the budget constraint a deformed version of kinetic energy. While some have misunderstood the message of *More Heat Than Light* as "Economics copied physics and that's patently wrong," others have seen that I have tried to raise the issue of what it is that makes certain metaphors and their attendant special mathematics work in some disciplines and fail miserably in others. Images of physics must be separated out from real physics; children's fairy tales about the scientific method must be distinguished from the actual historical practices of real scientists; images of a generic mathematical rigor must be distinguished from actual mathematical arguments. Elsewhere this has led to the compilation of proceedings of a conference that gathered together other detailed documentations of the use (and misuse) of physical and biological concepts in many diverse areas of economics (1994).

It has been difficult not to let this excavation of physical metaphors come to usurp my entire research life, since it has opened up so many new questions and areas of inquiry. Indeed, I am heartened to observe that some others have seen fit to take up the gauntlet, such as Rob Leonard's exploration of the role of structuralism in game theory,

Bruce Caldwell's inquiry into the role of the computer in the socialist calculation controversy, Geoff Hodgson's fine-grained explication of the metaphor of biological evolution in a number of economists, Roy Weintraub's demonstration of the importance of Alfred Lotka and E. B. Wilson for the evolution of the neoclassical stability literature, Michael White's unpacking of the meaning of equilibrium in Jevons, Abu Rizvi's connection of British psychophysics to modern doctrines on the nonrecoverability of neoclassical preferences, Esther-Mirjam Sent's exploration of the importance of artificial intelligence for Tom Sargent's peregrinations, and Paul Christensen's detailed exposition of the importance of Quesnay's training as a surgeon for his innovation of the concept of the circulation of value. But as Arjo Klamer has written in his contribution to the *Natural Images* volume, this work has yet to get much beyond the stage of "Look, Ma—a metaphor!" Certainly no one else has felt the force of this observation more than myself. As someone who has gone on record as skeptical of the McCloskeyesque version of a "rhetorical program" in economics, I have come to appreciate how effortlessly this work might be shrugged off by a profession contemptuous of its history, overtly hostile to philosophy, smug in the trappings of academic success, ready to absorb any intellectual challenge as an analytical special case, and quick to hurl accusations of the genetic fallacy at any of these scholars wishing to reopen consideration of the meanings of Science in practice.

My own response to this situation has been to broaden out the program by constructing specially targeted exercises for very specific subsets of the economics profession. Often this assumes the counterintuitive format of my adopting the persona of the empiricist for the methodologists, the philosopher for the economic historians, the historian for the theorists, and the theorist for disaffected groups of antineoclassicals, such as the Institutionalists. Let me give one example of each. As to the first, I have been much concerned of late to address a common objection to *More Heat Than Light:* perhaps mathematical theory has worked itself into various dead ends due to the original physics inspiration, but, goes this objection, one cannot ignore the rich history of empirical endeavors that provides the real backbone and continuity of the economics profession. Since one of the lessons I have drawn from the comparisons with physics is that neoclassicals have been egregiously lax in their commitments to what is indeed conserved or invariant in their portrait of the economy, I have recently begun to address the econometricians on a related malaise that seems to have infected their own bailiwick of late. Using techniques from physical metrology (especially Birge ratios), I show empirically that the quality of quantitative agreement in econometric estimates of numerical "constants" is far and away inferior to that of parallel endeavors in either physics or psychology. Rather than appeal to inchoate personal conceptions of a "science," we should try to look at its actual track record. This, in an indirect way, calls into question the assumption of existence of the consensual stable empirical base that lies at the center of econometric practice, as well as at the heart of this response to *More Heat.*

In the next case, I have tried to confront the conviction that Cliometricians have rendered the study of history Scientific in their own terms. I have sought to implement this by writing a standard Cliometric paper on the rationality of wages by brewers in nineteenth-century Britain, and then rewritten the same paper showing that the path-dependence of econometric estimation does not at all adequately constrain the historical narrative — in other words, by judicious choice of assumptions, I can render the portrait of the historical actors as rational or irrational as I please — only to then demonstrate that good old-fashioned archival digging serves to restrict the range of interpretation of their behaviors much more perspicaciously than does regression analysis.

An instance of the third presentation would be my recent work on game theory. It is fortuitous to be alive during a juncture when the neoclassical orthodoxy has rapidly shifted its allegiance from Walrasian general equilibrium (I would suggest Marshall was left behind long ago, spooned out only as thin gruel for weak minds in the principles course) to noncooperative game theory as the core doctrine of what it regards as the hallmark of economic expertise. It is during such tectonic shifts that major players feel impelled to comment upon epistemic ruptures, play up or play down the obsolescence of their predecessors, and gear up to rewrite the Whig histories. In the case of game theory, events have moved with such alacrity that no canonical story of the rise and rise of game theory yet exists, though glimpses can be discerned here and there, such as Robert Aumann's essay (1985). What I and a number of others have tried is to intervene in this process at an early stage and make it a little bit harder to write that standard hagiography where the hallowed progenitor has a number of inconvenient appendages amputated in the interests of a progressive narrative. In particular, we have excavated evidence (in Mirowski, forthcoming) of some of the motivations and concerns of John von Neumann and Oskar Morgenstern, showing, for instance, that von Neumann was heavily influenced by twentieth-century physics (especially quantum mechanics), disliked neoclassical theory, and was never favorably disposed toward the solution concept of choice of the modern orthodoxy, the Nash equilibrium. Indeed, he anticipated the present fascination with the theory of automata by a half-century. I am not so deluded as to think this will substantially change the behavior of modern game theorists in their quest for the philosopher's stone of rationality, but it may make it more difficult to present their burgeoning program as a "natural" outgrowth of the prior orthodoxy.

Finally, I must confess that there are a small number of self-consciously "theoretical" papers listed in my vita, though I do not hold that abstract genre appropriated from the rhetoric of the physics journal in very high regard. After all, forcing people to write in such an impoverished style is one of the major instruments by which historical consciousness is exiled and the question of the character of science is repressed. Although it may seem quixotic, I have felt it necessary periodically to counteract the common impression that Institutionalist economics is hopelessly atheoretical (an impression studiously promulgated by the alumni of the Cowles Commission) by insisting that the mathematical character of the practices of economic actors (and *not* economists) needs a rational explanation, something lacking in every formal economic tradition of which I am aware. In pursuit of this goal I have cribbed together a few underutilized bits of mathematics, like abstract algebra, automata theory, and directed graphs, in order to make an argument that economic value is not intrinsic either in the commodity (as in classical political economy) or hardwired in the psyche (as in neoclassicism), but is instead socially constructed by the postulation of mathematical invariants where none truly exist. The purpose of such "models" is not to identify equilibria, or any other such vestigial holdover from physics envy, but rather to give an impression of what it is like for an actor to try and read the "meaning" of a transaction where no single correct reading exists. Rather than persisting in the hallowed Western tradition of regarding the mind as a machine, perhaps a renovated formal Institutional economics could come to portray the set of diverse market institutions as algorithmic, undergoing a process of evolution in which people and cultures constitute the shifting environments.

The titillating title of this essay promises confessions, and I realize that I have only been writing little abstracts of my work until now, so here comes my effort to make good on the initial promise. While playing the outsider with each of these groups of economists in a kind of musical chairs is good fun, it really has addled my sense of audience. Always play-acting the other has made it very difficult to have a very good idea to whom I am talking; sometimes I despair at identifying exactly whom I may be influencing and to what end. Do economists care any longer to understand the forces that propel them willy-nilly across the intellectual landscape? Has intellectual history become anything more than high-toned PR about the Next Big Thing to attract funding in an age of downsizing, or an insignificant diversion in the fin de siècle Science Wars (Horgan 1997)? In my private moments, I envy Marx or Hayek or Keynes or (dare I say it?) Milton Friedman, because they had supreme confidence in where they wanted people to end up and merely adjusted their scientific manner and modalities to get them there in the most efficacious geodesic. (What better way to understand Friedman's essay on methodology?) I, on the other hand, am still struggling to figure out what it is that moral philosophy is or should be, so that economics might endorse some light at the end of the tunnel. I am reasonably sure it will not consist of yet more baroque epicycles on utilitarianism or ponderous academic pronouncements on ethics or another paean to Nature or empty exhortations towards Truth and Honesty; but beyond that, I am as much in the dark as the next Technocrat or Aesthete. Poverty decimates lives; but what are riches?

No Man Is an Island

> I am far from being an enemy to the Writers of Fables,
> since I know very well that this Manner of Writing is not
> only Ancient, but very useful, I might say sacred, since it
> has been made use of by the inspired Writers themselves;
> but then to render the Fable worthy of being received into
> the Number of those which are truly valuable, it must
> naturally produce some useful Moral. . . . but this of
> *Robinson Crusoe* . . . is design'd against . . . publick good.
> — Gildon 1719

The format of the brief autobiography is inevitably allegorical. The writer is a Pilgrim, searching for somebody or something, deflected this way and that, struggling mightily to maintain a narrative thread in a world of chaos and dissociation. Here, for me, is where all the tensions between Science and Art meet. I am enjoined to talk about myself, and all I can manage to do is to hide behind my Science. Neoclassicism wants desperately to be a Science, and yet all it can do is talk in terms of allegories. Unlike some partisans of the "rhetoric" movement, I do not regard this as an occasion to flaunt my (nonexistent) mastery of classical Greek or Vladimir Propp's taxonomy of folktales, with a view to provoking economists to acknowledge that they are telling stories, culminating in a hearty round of self-congratulation that "we are all Artistes now." Alisdair MacIntyre has argued that the only two moral personae available to the intellectual in an era of bureaucratic individualism are the Technocrat and the Aesthete; economists like myself would seem doomed to waver between these poles. Some, such as Richard Rorty, think this dilemma can never be resolved; others like MacIntyre think the answer is a return to earlier Aristotelian conceptions of the moral life. I myself would like to enlist as an advocate of a third position, namely, that the promises of modernity have largely been illusions with respect to the great divide between Science and Art, Objectivity and Subjectivity, Nature and Society (Latour 1993). We spend so much of our intellectual efforts trying to reconcile one to the other, when in fact they may have never been separate in practice. Let me give just one indication of what I mean.

I have been trying to write a narrative of my own wanderings, an allegory of what I am, but this is embedded in a narrative of the history of my profession, an allegory of what economics is all about. Just as I have my literary precursors, neoclassicism has its own allegorical account of its true telos. This account can be found in nearly every textbook: it is the story of Robinson Crusoe. In the middle of an indoctrination of the tyro into our science, we find this story, this artful narrative, of what it means to be a neoclassical rational actor. The isolated individual, alone confronting scarcity on his island with his scant endowments, deliberates as to the appropriate combination of goods to maximize his well-being, imposing order upon the primeval chaos of Nature. As I have intimated before, economists generally don't read, but they think they know this story cold. The English hosier in the eighteenth century and the American academic in the twentieth understand each other perfectly, describing the inherent transcendental logic of their own system as it spreads across the face of the globe.

But economists really don't read, and therefore they don't generally realize that the actual Defoe novel does not underwrite their convictions to any appreciable extent. The man who wrote the following might resist being dragooned into the neoclassical cause:

> The most covetous griping miser in the world would have been cured of the vice of covetousness, if he had been in my case; for I possessed infinitely more than I knew what to do with. I had no room for desire, except it was of things which I had not, and they were but trifles. . . . I learned to look more on the bright side of my condition and less upon the dark side and to consider what I enjoyed rather than what I wanted; and this gave me sometimes such secret comforts that I cannot express them; and which I take notice of here, to put those discontented people in mind of it who cannot enjoy comfortably what God had given them because they see and covet something He has not given them. (Defoe 1941, 126–27)

Some such observation that stories often sprawl outside the conventional interpretation is itself not novel. The few economists who have not lost the habit of reading have periodically tried to embarrass the textbook Robinson in various ways. One notable attempt was a paper by Stephen Hymer in 1971 that reminded us of the repressed character of Friday in order to turn the novel into an allegory of Marxist primitive accumulation. But trading one economic Robinson for another does not quite get at the crux of the problem: that was rather the achievement of Michael White (1982).

As opposed to the conviction that there is one invariant Robinson in our culture, the epitome of Art imitating Science, White showed that there were numerous rereadings of Defoe's novel throughout history, and that the neoclassical textbook Robinson probably dated from the mid–nineteenth century, roughly contemporaneous with the rise of marginalism in the 1870s. We might go further and suggest that not only was Defoe's Robinson Crusoe misread at various junctures for various purposes, but that it has periodically been rewritten in order to codify each generation's revision of the myth. The version to which neoclassicals seem to be inclined to favor most closely resembles that of Johann Heinrich Campe's *Robinson de Juengere* (1779), which was written for children in order to exemplify certain bourgeois virtues. (So the Rational Economic Man is a German folktale!) Indeed, the novel has been rewritten so many times since that there is even a special term for the genre in German, the *Robinsonade*. From Johann Wysse's

Swiss Family Robinson (1812) to Frederick Marryat's *Masterman Ready* (1841) to Jules Verne's *Mysterious Island* (1874) to Jean Giradoux's *Suzanne et la pacifique* (1922) to William Golding's *Lord of the Flies* (1954) to Michel Tournier's *Vendredi: Ou Les limbes du Pacifique* (1967) to Marianne Wiggins's *John Dollar,* the narrative archetype has been bent and reshaped in so many directions to fit so many changes in concurrent images of Nature and Society in so many cultural contexts, that perhaps one might suggest there is no solid Crusoe there to misrepresent anymore.

Isn't this just one of the characteristics of Art, that it is ephemeral and insubstantial, contextual and interpretative, whereas Science is forever? I would like to suggest otherwise. It is no accident that Robinson Crusoe and the mathematics of constrained optimization are yoked together in the same text, for in general they have suffered the same fate. Just as Robinson has been creatively misread and willfully revised, the physics of the field that represented Hard Science to the late-nineteenth century Western mind has been creatively misread as economics and willfully rewritten any number of times, from utility to ophelimity to revealed preferences to convex sets to neural nets, and the beat goes on. All that holds them together is a vague family resemblance (and here mathematics as the bearer of inexplicit analogy plays an important role) that does not depend upon anyone actually *knowing* the physics or understanding the history in order to participate in the tradition. Everyone involved can honestly think that they understand that of which rationality consists and what economics really is about, without ever once having to confront the disturbing fact that their narrative is the most frightful hodgepodge of bits and bobs, a cumulative bricolage that cannot be readily subsumed or sorted into Science or Art, Nature or Society, Objectivity or Subjectivity, Positive and Normative. This pattern of concerted revisionism will undoubtedly continue so long as some alternative narrative does not swoop down out of nowhere (or more likely, out of physics) and relegate Robinson to the dark oblivion of complete and utter neglect.

Where does that leave the poor autobiographer, the person trying to proffer a moral tale or two to those who follow afterward in this curious blinkered profession? Given that any overarching Method has disintegrated into lumps of clay in our hands, disinterested general advice would seem presumptuous, if not downright foolish. Given that Robinsonades are still so popular, one could end on the note of narrative closure that, having wandered far and wide and seen strange and wondrous things, our wayfarer returns from his remote island to peaceful Indiana to regale the locals with tales of his adventures. But, just as equilibrium is a deeply unsatisfying resting place, specifying the ends of autobiography is a prematurely deadening procedure. Perhaps it is better to end as Defoe did: "All these things, with some very surprising incidents in new adventures of my own, for ten years more, I may perhaps give a further account of hereafter."

REFERENCES

Aumann, Robert. 1985. "What Is Game Theory Trying to Accomplish?" In *Frontiers of Economics,* ed. K. Arrow and S. Honkapohja. Oxford: Basil Blackwell.

Defoe, Daniel. 1941. *Robinson Crusoe.* New York: Walter Black.

Furbank, P. N. 1993. "Confessional Claims." *Times Literary supplement,* 13 August, 6.

Gildon, Charles. 1719 [1724]. *The Life and Strange Surprizing Adventures of Mr. Daniel DeFoe,* . . . London: Printed for J. Roberts.

Hamermesh, Daniel. 1992. "The Young Economist's Guide to Professional Etiquette." *Journal of Economic Perspectives* 6:169–79.

Hobson, J. A. 1938. *Confessions of an Economic Heretic.* London: George Allen and Unwin.

Horgan, John. 1997. "The Big Bang Theory of Science Books." *New York Times Book Review,* December 14, 39.

Latour, Bruno. 1993. *We Have Never Been Modern.* Cambridge, MA: Harvard University Press.

MacIntyre, Alisdair. 1984. *After Virtue.* 2d ed. Notre Dame: University of Notre Dame Press.

Mirowski, Philip. 1989. *More Heat Than Light.* New York: Cambridge University Press.

———. 1993. "The Goalkeeper's Anxiety at the Penalty Kick." In *Non-Natural Economics,* ed. Neil de Marchi. Durham, NC: Duke University Press.

———, ed. 1994. *Natural Images in Economics: Markets Read in Tooth and Claw.* New York: Cambridge University Press.

———. Forthcoming. *Machine Dreams.* Cambridge: Harvard University Press.

Nietzsche, Friedrich. 1966. *Beyond Good and Evil,* trans. Walter Kaufmann. New York: Vintage.

Rorty, Richard. 1992. "Trotsky and the Wild Orchids." *Common Knowledge* 1:140–53.

Sturrock, John. 1993. *The Language of Autobiography.* Cambridge: Cambridge University Press.

White, Michael. 1982. "Reading and Rewriting: The Production of an Economic Robinson Crusoe." *Southern Journal* 15:115–42.

ROGER B. MYERSON

Working on Game Theory: A Personal Perspective

In December 1994, I sat with my family to watch a television broadcast of the Nobel Prize ceremonies. We proudly watched as three leading game theorists received the highest award in economics. At the end, memories came rushing back to me from my student days, when I first searched through the Harvard University libraries for books and articles about game theory. In particular, I remembered discovering the work of John Harsanyi, because that was when I really knew that I had found the research program that I wanted to join.

When I was a student in the early 1970s, the development of general game-theoretic solutions concepts did not attract much attention in Cambridge, Massachusetts. So my primary form of intellectual dialogue was scribbling notes into the margins of photocopied journal articles, which were written by the distant leaders of the field: Robert Aumann, John Harsanyi, John Nash, Reinhard Selten, Lloyd Shapley, and others. Their published writings gave me good guidance into the field, and after graduate school I was welcomed into a growing community of game theorists. But still it was deeply moving for me to see the Nobel Prize committee express the same excitement that I had found when I worked alone under the fluorescent lights in the undergraduate library, twenty-two years earlier.

To describe how I have worked in game theory, I should begin by trying to assess what drove me into game theory in the first place.

Concern about the new threat of nuclear destruction was widespread in the 1950s, and like many of my generation I was aware of this terrible threat from a young age. But when I was twelve I was swept away by a classic science-fiction novel (Asimov 1951) that depicted a future where advanced mathematical social science made possible a new utopian civilization. These images from youth have continued to burn bright in my imagination: the threat of conflict in our nuclear world, and the hope that fundamental advances in social science might provide some of the understanding that we need to preserve and protect our civilization. This is the passion that has driven me throughout my career.

In the spring of 1972, as a college student, I took a beautiful course on decision analysis from Howard Raiffa. He taught us to see utility functions and their maximization as parts of real life that are expressed (however imperfectly) in our daily decisions. At the end of the course, he told us that the analysis of interactions among two or more rational decision-makers is called game theory, and he described game theory as a field in which only limited progress had been made. At that point I was hooked, and I started reading Owen's (1968) book on game theory that summer. I felt that if I did not know how to analyze such obviously fundamental models of human decision-making, then how could I pretend to understand anything in social science?

I was first attracted to the work of John Harsanyi by his (1963) paper that defined a general cooperative solution concept that included both the Nash bargaining solution and the Shapley value as special cases. In the early game theory literature, Nash's (1950) bargaining solution was the first solution concept that could identify a single cooperative outcome for two-person games without assuming transferable utility. Shapley's (1953) value was the first solution concept that could identify a single cooperative outcome for multiplayer games with transferable utility. Both of these solution concepts had elegant axiomatic derivations, and their single-point predictions were much more appealing to me than the multiple sets of sets identified by the solutions of von Neumann and Morgenstern (1947). So in the search for a general theory of cooperative games, the outstanding landmark in the field was Harsanyi's (1963) demonstration that Nash's and Shapley's solution concepts could be unified into a single solution theory for multiplayer games, without assuming transferable utility.

But Harsanyi (1967–68) also wrote a series of papers about how to model games with incomplete information (that is, games in which the players have different information at the beginning of the game). And during my student days, Harsanyi and Selten (1972) published a new paper that defined a generalized Nash bargaining solution for games with incomplete information. So in all this pathbreaking work, an obvious hole had been left in the literature: How should we extend the Shapley value to games with incomplete information? That is, what outcomes should we predict when people who have different information try to negotiate cooperative agreements with each other? This was the problem that I set out to solve in my dissertation research.

I did not solve this problem in graduate school, but it was a very good problem to work on. To try to build a theory of cooperation under uncertainty, I first needed to rethink many of the fundamental ideas of cooperative game theory and noncooperative game theory; and along the way I got a reasonable dissertation's-worth of results. Any ideas in the literature that could not be extended to general incomplete-information games were irrelevant to my project, and so this quest for generality gave me a good way of sifting through the wide literature on cooperative game theory.

My work on the revelation principle began with an article (Myerson 1979) that essentially used it only to simplify the feasible set for Harsanyi and Selten's generalized Nash bargaining solution. In Harsanyi and Selten's solution concept, the objective is to maximize a special multiplicative product of the players' expected utility gains. Only later (in discussions with Robert Wilson about auctions) did I realize that the revelation principle could be a general tool of microeconomic analysis, applicable for optimizing any social-welfare function in any situation where there is a problem of getting information from different individuals. In any such situation, the revelation principal allows us to formulate mathematically simple constraints that summarize the problems of incentives for sharing information and coordinating actions. (See Myerson 1981, 1983).

Any kind of creative work generally revolves around a prolonged personal exploration of how to use an idiosyncratically selected combination of structural elements. In this way, the use of informational incentive constraints became a central focus of my thinking in the late 1970s and early 1980s. Economics had previously focused primarily on resource constraints, but I began to see that incentive constraints may be equally important in determining the shape of optimal economic institutions. Thus I worked along with many others, including my coauthors David Baron, Mark Satterthwaite, and Bengt Holmstrom, to develop techniques for analysis of incentive constraints, so that such analysis could become part of the standard toolkit that economists use to think about applied problems (Baron and Myerson 1982; Holmstrom and Myerson 1983; Myerson and Satterthwaite 1983).

On January 1, 1980, I had another technical insight that guided much of my subsequent work. In the previous fall, I had taught linear programming to a large and exhausting class of masters students, and the rest that I had gotten during the Christmas break seemed too brief and unfulfilling. Thus, it was one of those days when one feels a deep emotional need for some satisfying research result; and so I sat alone in my apartment thinking once again about the problem of cooperation under uncertainty.

To say how much each type of each player should deserve in a cooperative solution, we need some kind of pricing system that assigns a value to each possible type of each player. The crucial question was, how to measure the contribution that one possible type of a player makes to the bargaining positions of other possible types of the same player. Suddenly I saw a connection with the basic ideas of duality that I had just finished teaching. In linear programming, each constraint is mathematically associated with a dual variable (or Lagrange multiplier). One of the great ideas of mathematical economics is that, in an economic-planning problem, the dual variables of the resource constraints can be interpreted as prices in a market equilibrium. Given my conviction that incentive constraints may be as economically important as resource constraints, I suddenly wondered whether the dual variables associated with incentive constraints might also be economically important. In particular, these incentive duals might somehow measure the contribution that each type makes to the other types in the bargaining problem.

It is probably true that no economist has yet been convinced that the duals of incentive constraints are even one-tenth as important as prices in economic theory, but that is not the point. The point is that I worked with this insight over the next several years, and with it I found the general theory of cooperation under uncertainty that I had sought since graduate school. (See Myerson 1983, 1984a, and 1984b.) It is also true that this general bargaining solution has not yet found much direct application in economic analysis. Indeed, I was unable to offer any solved example at all for the general case of more than two players (Myerson 1984a). But the long quest for a general theory of cooperation in Bayesian games with incomplete information gave me a perspective that was essential for me to find my way to the more applied papers that I wrote on information economics during the 1980s.

Let me try to explain this last point more concretely. A colleague whom I very much admire once challenged me to defend the proposition that Harsanyi's (1967–68) work on Bayesian games with incomplete information was really essential to the subsequent advances in information economics. The counterexample, my colleague argued, was William Vickrey's (1961) paper on auctions, which introduced many of the fundamental ideas and results of auction theory. But Vickrey wrote this paper six years before Harsanyi's papers on incomplete-information games. If Vickrey already understood how to analyze auctions as a Bayesian game in 1961, then what was the significance of Harsanyi's contribution?

The answer to this question, as I have come to see it, is that Harsanyi's general theory of Bayesian games taught us how to see many different situations with incomplete information (auctions, negotiations, regulation, insurance, job-market signaling, etc.) as examples of a general underlying structure that we can analyze systematically. When traditional price theory provided the only general framework for rigorous economic analysis, then the auctions that Vickrey studied had to be viewed as exceptions to the standard paradigms of the profession; and there is always something disturbing or irritating about such exceptions. Vickrey's work on auctions could be recognized as clever and even as having some practical significance, but its inconsistency with the standard paradigms would make many leading theorists uncomfortable about thinking very long about it. I guess that this tension might be responsible for Vickrey's important paper being published in a specialized finance journal, rather than one of the leading journals of general economic theory.

Later in the 1970s, those of us who had studied Harsanyi's general theory of Bayesian games could approach Vickrey's auction paper from a very different perspective. We could embrace the study of auctions as an important example of the general problem of incomplete information in economics. We could study bidding in auctions (as well as signaling in job markets, and moral hazard and adverse selection in insurance) without fear of losing our intellectual coordinate system, because we could see everything in the context of the general Bayesian game model. Thus, Harsanyi's general framework enabled us in the next generation to appreciate and generalize techniques that could be only recognized by rare genius in 1961.

In this way, work at the most fundamental level in game theory has substantially extended the scope of applied economic analysis over the past twenty years. And in any scholarly endeavor, I believe, there is no higher goal than to help people think more clearly and systematically about situations that had previously seemed confusing or obscure.

REFERENCES

Asimov, Isaac. 1951. *Foundation.* New York: Doubleday.

Baron, David P., and Roger B. Myerson. 1982. "Regulating a Monopolist with Unknown Costs." *Econometrica* 50:911–30.

Harsanyi, J. C. 1963. "A Simplified Bargaining Model for the n-Person Cooperative Game." *International Economic Review* 4 (1963):194–220.

———. 1967–68. "Games with Incomplete Information Played by 'Bayesian' Players." *Management Science* 14:159–82, 320–34, 486–502.

Harsanyi, J. C., and R. Selten. 1972. "A Generalized Nash Solution for Two-Person Bargaining Games with Incomplete Information." *Management Science* 18:80–106.

Holmstrom, Bengt, and Roger B. Myerson. 1983. "Efficient and Durable Decision Rules with Incomplete Information." *Econometrica* 51:1799–1819.

Myerson, Roger B. 1979. "Incentive Compatibility and the Bargaining Problem." *Econometrica* 47:61–73.

———. 1981. "Optimal Auction Design." *Mathematics of Operations Research* 6:58–73.

———. 1982. "Optimal Coordination Mechanisms in Generalized Principal-Agent Problems." *Journal of Mathematical Economics* 10:67–81.

———. 1983. "Mechanism Design by an Informed Principal." *Econometrica* 51:1767–97.

———. 1984a. "Cooperative Games with Incomplete Information." *International Journal of Game Theory* 13:69–86.

———. 1984b. "Two-Person Bargaining Problems with Incomplete Information." *Econometrica* 52:461–87.

Myerson, Roger B., and Mark A. Satterthwaite. 1983. "Efficient Mechanisms for Bilateral Trading." *Journal of Economic Theory* 29:265–81.

Nash, John F. 1950. "The Bargaining Problem." *Econometrica* 118 (1950): 155–62.

Neumann, John von, and Oskar Morgenstern. 1947. *Theory of Games and Economic Behavior.* 2d ed. Princeton: Princeton University Press.

Owen, Guillermo. 1968. *Game Theory.* Philadelphia: W. B. Saunders.

Shapley, Lloyd S. 1953. "A Value for n-Person Games." In *Contributions to the Theory of Games II,* ed. H. Kuhn and A. W. Tucker. Princeton: Princeton University Press.

Vickrey, William. 1961. "Counterspeculation, Auctions, and Competitive Sealed Tenders." *Journal of Finance* 16:8–37.

SUSAN ROSE-ACKERMAN

Work, Family, and Odd Topics: On Being a Female Economist

Is there anything special about being a female economist? I do not think much of the distinction between female and male minds, especially since, within that framework, my mind is male. Probably that is true of most female economists, but that does not mean that being a woman is irrelevant. You are an oddball from the beginning of your graduate career. You can be one of the boys, but it never quite works. Maybe being an outsider is an advantage. One is not oppressed by an excessive number of avuncular role models. You will never really fit in, so why try.

I became an economist by default. I almost became an astronomer. For my sophomore year at Wellesley College I originally registered for astronomy. My father, an accountant and businessman, urged me to shift to economics on the ground that every educated person should learn the basics of the field. I did so, and the profession of astronomy is now one woman short.

Becoming an economist never occurred to me as a child. This wasn't gender bias. I think the problem was that economists, unlike firemen, doctors, nurses, and carpenters, didn't have distinctive uniforms or tools. Economists are not pictured in children's books that recommend alternate life plans. In any case I came to college planning to major in either mathematics or English. Neither satisfied me my freshman year, and I was casting about for an alternative. I spent the summer in an exchange program in Turkey and became interested in the problems of developing countries. Economics looked like a way to pursue that interest and like a good compromise between mathematics and the humanities. I could continue my interest in math, but study a less abstract collection of problems. Also, I was good at it.

I was attracted by the paradox of parsimonious formal models explaining a messy economic and social world. Economics seemed a way to put sentimentality in its place, a way to use logic to explain the seemingly absurd. I liked both the substantive problems and the rationalistic methods.

The Wellesley Department of Economics in the early 1960s was a congenial place to study. It produced more than its share of women who went on to graduate school. Marshall Goldman taught my principles course and nudged me toward graduate school without being overbearing. The department gave its majors good advice — study mathematics even if it means taking fewer economics courses; you can always make up the gaps in graduate school. Although I began thinking seriously about graduate school, I did not want to be a college professor. I refused to apply for one fellowship that required a commitment to college or university teaching. What I wanted to do with my degree, however, was a mystery. I think I had a vague idea of working for the government.

After Wellesley, the graduate program at Yale was something of a shock. I was the only female doctoral student in my year. This meant that I was both isolated and overwhelmed with attention. That wasn't so bad, but, in addition, I was suddenly in an academic environment where most people were at least as competent and well trained in mathematics as I was, and some were obviously superior. I survived and took a comprehensive exam in mathematical economics, but I knew I could never be a pure theorist. By the time I passed my qualifying exams I did not even want to be one.

Something was missing in my graduate training. I mastered the material and became a professional economist, but I had no idea what kind of career I wanted. I had no agenda of issues I wanted to study. I picked my dissertation topic (an empirical study of the demand for used cars), not because it excited me, but because it looked feasible, and I had an adviser, Bill Brainard, who liked automobiles (repairing them, that is). Maybe my method of topic selection was a good strategy. Some of my friends kept searching for the perfect topic and never completed a degree or took too many years to finish.

The downside, however, was a period of demoralization and insecurity as I searched for direction.

I was saved by the Council of Economic Advisers. Joe Peck, one of my Yale professors who had always been supportive, was appointed to Lyndon Johnson's council. He hired me as a junior staff economist, an ambiguous position between senior staff economist and research assistant. Although the council is often thought to focus on macroeconomic policy, during my stay it was also immersed in a multitude of regulatory and programmatic issues. I developed an interest in using economics to study domestic policy during my year in Washington.

My academic career began the next year in the fall of 1969 with an appointment in the Department of Finance of the Wharton School of the University of Pennsylvania. An odd choice, one might think, but the department was trying to increase its stock of applied microeconomists. I began balancing marriage, family, and career. My husband, Bruce Ackerman, is a legal academic who started teaching at the University of Pennsylvania Law School in the same year. We had married two years before when he began two years of clerking for federal judges, and I began working on my dissertation in earnest. I came to my job at Penn pregnant. I felt awkward about announcing the fact in my first meeting with the chairman, but I do not think there is an optimal time to have children. A baby is always time consuming. I remember a young male economist telling me that a senior colleague had advised him to wait until he had tenure before having children. That way childbearing would not interfere with the early years of his career. I did not feel that I had that luxury. I could not be confident that if I worked hard for a few years, I would be a strong candidate for tenure. So we just went ahead and had children, and I made the compromises necessary to be both mother and scholar. For me that meant years of part-time work and not much traveling. But it was worthwhile. Suddenly one day, our son and daughter were both in college, and I realized how busy I had been.

My husband and I and our children bounced about between Penn and Yale, finally ending up with two tenured professorships at Columbia in 1992. After five years in New York we were back on the Yale faculty to stay in 1997. Meanwhile I had followed a rather circuitous scholarly path. By the time I finally received tenure at age forty, I was very tired of the years of insecurity, but I cannot be sure that a more conventional pattern would have been ultimately more satisfying. Maybe in scholarship, as in other things, I was just a late bloomer. Maybe the delays imposed by motherhood were a stroke of good fortune. I will never know, but it is at least possible.

My research agenda has evolved in such peculiar directions since graduate school that I am not even a member of an economics department faculty. I have a joint appointment in the Law School and Department of Political Science at Yale and participate in an undergraduate major in ethics, politics, and economics. I am a maverick economist trying to convince noneconomists to value the tools of economic inquiry. Given my own criticisms of the discipline, this is a strange position to be in. Economics is balanced between formal elegance and relevance. Mathematics has imbued economics with a level of rigor absent from other social sciences, but it can be a trap. Formal analysis can be done for its own sake without much sense for interesting economic problems or worthwhile results. Welfare economics and public finance can be remarkably sterile fields of inquiry, lacking both normative breadth and a sensitivity to democratic choice processes. Political science and law, in contrast, although rich in institutional detail, lack rigor. Thus I am part of a group of scholars trying to bring analytic thinking to these subjects without overlooking the insights of those immersed in the subject matter of law and politics. Although the effort is sometimes dizzying, for me it has been a productive tightrope to walk.

I began, however, as an applied microeconomist. Nevertheless, the topics that attracted me were out of the mainstream of the profession. I like cool, logical analyses of hot subjects like racism, pollution, and corruption. I never took to macroeconomics. It always seemed too aggregated, and I never really understood what was behind the standard models. I like problems with lots of institutional structure and multiple market failures. Topics on the edges of several disciplines are often the most interesting, although they do require an investment in trying to understand what others are talking about. Pure economic imperialism is seldom very productive.

I try to find relatively undeveloped subjects of inquiry. I do not like the feeling of rushing to make a marginal contribution in a field crowded with contestants. I am easily bored, so I change fields frequently to keep myself interested. I like to master esoteric subjects that most economists would not spend their time on. I once spent a whole summer reading the fund allocation reports of various United Ways. When my daughter was a baby, I spent hours in the park rocking her carriage and reading consultants' reports on regional sewage treatment plants along the Delaware Estuary. When I wrote a book on corruption, I clipped *New York Times* stories for several years. I learned German a few years ago so I could read articles about German environmental law and policymaking.

My interests in domestic policy and government structure developed slowly. The finance department of the Wharton School at Penn had, in a power play, taken over the course numbers vacated by a defunct department of real-estate economics and finance. The only problem with this empire-building effort was the lack of anyone in the finance department qualified to teach these courses. By volunteering to fill the gap, I became an urban economist at a time when the field was very dynamic and interesting. Urban economics is a wonderful course to teach. You induce your students to write about their hometowns, and suddenly you have learned about the range of urban patterns in the United States. Teaching led to writing about housing markets with racial prejudice, about multiple government systems, and about federalism.

My early work on environmental policy developed in a similarly opportunistic way. The head of a small foundation called the dean of the University of Pennsylvania Law School looking for someone to study the Delaware River Basin Commission, a joint federal-state body that regulated pollution and water supply in the river. My husband volunteered, and the two of us joined with another economist and an engineer to study the DRBC. The book we produced, *The Uncertain Search for Environmental Quality* (New York: Free Press, 1974), was a baby-to-baby book. It was begun just after the birth of our daughter and handed into the publisher just before the birth of our son three and one-half years later.

My interest in urban and environmental economics led to an interest in public finance, a subject I had never studied in graduate school because the course offerings were weak. Even a passing acquaintance with urban affairs and environmental policy was enough to convince me that normative public finance was not sufficient. One also needs to study how government works and how social choices are made. My interest in corruption dates from that time. Bribery was pervasive in some federal housing programs, and a little thought suggested that the law's drafters had inadvertently built economic incentives for payoffs into the programs.

I also became fascinated by the formal modeling of social-choice processes. Luckily Robert Pollak of the Penn economics faculty had also developed similar interests, and I spent a semester in a seminar he taught working through A. K. Sen's *Collective Choice and Social Welfare* and John Rawls's *A Theory of Justice.* The combination of social-choice theory and anecdotes about corruption in politics and in public programs led to a book, *Corruption: A Study in Political Economy* (New York: Academic Press, 1978). Corruption is an obvious first topic for a budding political economist since it involves the study of monetary incentives in politics. The book is an effort to understand the conditions that produce corruption within political and bureaucratic institutions. Bribery is a response to the monopoly power of officials. I argue that moral transformations are not necessary to fight corruption. It can be limited by redesigning public institutions to reduce monopoly rents.

After moving to Yale in 1974, my growing interest in politics led me to teach courses with a political theorist, Jim Fishkin, at the intersection between public finance and social choice. The Institution for Social and Policy Studies at Yale helped foster interdisciplinary work under the leadership of Ed Lindblom and Richard Nelson. My appointment was jointly with ISPS and the Department of Economics, but ISPS was my real home. Ed and Dick encouraged my efforts to cross boundaries and work on unusual topics. ISPS also sponsored a new research project on the nonprofit sector, and I soon became a part of its diverse collection of researchers. Working on charity was a departure after my prior emphasis on pollution, bribery, and racism. I made the transition by teaching a seminar on gifts and bribes. Without dismissing the importance of charitable and generous motives, I found ways to bring my own ironic and skeptical perspective to the study of altruistic organizations. In fundamental ways my work on nonprofits had close links to my other research in its emphasis on the importance of institutional form and on the economic incentives imbedded in organizational structure.[1]

The step from those interests to law and economics is a short one. Although most modern work in law and economics focuses on the private-law fields of torts, contracts, and property, for me the most interesting connections involve the public-law fields of administrative law and regulation. That is where social choice, public finance, and the new institutional economics overlap with law. When I began to teach administrative law at Columbia Law School in the mideighties, I had the good fortune to be in on the ground floor of this development. I organized one of the first conferences at which political scientists working on rational-choice models of American policies met professors of administrative law. Subsequent meetings followed elsewhere in the country, and several collaborative projects developed. I learned my administrative law from Peter Strauss at Columbia and Jerry Mashaw at Yale. Whatever their own skepticism about my rationalizing enterprise, they were always generous in helping me master a new field. Changing directions in this way proved productive. However difficult I found the case method as a way of learning and teaching, the payoff in new ideas and fruitful interdisciplinary efforts was worth it.

Nevertheless, within the field of law and economics I was fighting a stereotype engendered by the Chicago school of law and economics. This was a view of the field as a conservative branch of legal scholarship with close ties to libertarian thought. Students would sometimes refuse to enroll in law-and-economics courses for fear of being branded right wing by their peers. Distress at this state of affairs led me in an uncharacteristically polemical direction, defending the view that one can be a liberal and a lawyer-economist at the same time. My book *Rethinking the Progressive Agenda: The Reform of the American Regulatory State* (New York: Free Press, 1992), is my attempt to articulate this position. Although I cannot take credit for the transformation, the field today is much less dominated by political conservatives than in the past.

As middle age sets in, I have begun to reap some psychic rewards from my checkered career. About ten years ago, after years of doggedly focusing on domestic American policy, I began to be invited to Europe. These invitations were part of a new interest in law and economics outside the United States. For me — the intellectual tourist — these visits were a delight. Travel that combines interesting conferences with visits to foreign countries is the perfect way to combine business with pleasure. Finally, with a year in Germany in prospect, I decided in the early nineties to do serious comparative work on environmental policy and administrative law. This project involved learning German — not a delight — but the result was a richer knowledge of the range of possible regulatory strategies and a new way to keep boredom at bay. My book *Controlling Environmental Policy: The Limits of Public Law in Germany and the United States* (New Haven: Yale University Press) was published in the spring of 1995.

The other rewards are more subtle. With my law school appointments and my moves from school to school I have never had many graduate students. Thus it is with pleasure that I am beginning to discover that my research has been of use to others. At a recent Allied Social Sciences annual meeting young scholars kept reading my nametag and commenting that "my article" had helped them get started on their dissertations. The articles were all different ones, and some of them were written ten or fifteen years ago. During my year in Europe, I discovered several economists writing dissertations on corruption for whom my 1978 book was a starting point. I felt truly grownup when a young scholar at Harvard commented that the economic analysis of corruption "goes back" to Professor Rose-Ackerman's 1978 book. In the fall of 1994, writing a review article on the economics of the nonprofit sector for the *Journal of Economic Literature,* I discovered that several empirical studies had found my theoretical work useful. The advantage of writing on unconventional topics is that your work has a long half-life. You do not get pre-empted right away by the next eager batch of graduate students. Even if the number of readers is small, the audience is spread out over time.

I used to think the rhetoric of affirmative action overemphasized the importance of female mentors to the success of women graduate students. Obviously, I would have never finished my degree if I had to depend on such advisers. In recent years, because of advising a number of female graduate students, my view has changed. Of course, both men and women starting an academic career are full of doubts and insecurities, but I have the impression of being especially helpful to women as they seek to develop research topics, deal with their other advisers, and set out on the job market. I hope that they think so too.

I doubt if my career path can be a model for anyone, but it does produce a few lessons. I expect that I will sound a bit like Polonius's spouse, but here goes anyway. Marriage, children, and a career are compatible, but do not expect the balancing act to be easy. Marry someone who is supportive and not threatened by an intelligent spouse. Give yourself enough time to play multiple roles, and be sure your employer will go along with this plan.

Do not stay in blind alleys and dead ends. Work on problems that interest you and know when to switch topics. Paying a nanny to take care of your children is a spur to productivity. How can you possibly justify the cost of a good childcare worker or day care center if you are not using the time away from home productively? Find a balance between patience and discipline on the one hand, and flights of originality, on the other. Especially if you have children or other family responsibilities, set aside particular times to work. Since I am a morning person, I pretend to have a regular nine-to-five job, but that is just one solution.

Do not write anything that does not have an idea in it, and do not be too influenced by this year's "hot" topic. It will fade. Use teaching as a way to learn. If you are lucky enough to be in a department or school that encourages innovation, teach a course on a topic you know nothing about. Students need to find out that their professors don't know everything, and you will learn a lot. Do not lose sight of the reasons why economics interested you in the first place. If you are bored by your work, your readers and your students will know it, and you ought to consider a change of career or at least a change of topic.

NOTE

1. See Susan Rose-Ackerman, ed., *The Economics of Nonprofit Institutions: Studies in Structure and Policy* (New York: Oxford University Press, 1986); and Estelle James and Susan Rose-Ackerman, *The Nonprofit Enterprise in Market Economics,* Fundamentals of Pure and Applied Economics, no. 9 (Chur, Switzerland: Harwood Academic Publishers, 1986).

RICHARD SCHMALENSEE

Ways I Have Worked

Perhaps because I had essentially no idea what academic life was like before I began graduate school, I came late to the realization that being a professor would suit me well. Even now, I find it almost impossible to explain to nonacademics exactly how I fill my days or why I enjoy what I do. My life does bear some resemblance to my father's when he ran a small business. Like his days, mine involve many choices, much hard work, and a variety of activities. I have a few more constraints on my actions (including meetings I can't avoid), but I have tenure, and he had to meet a payroll. An important difference is that I have the chance to do research that may have an impact on how others understand the world.

On the whole, I don't think that I've managed my research career particularly well. I have compensated by being lucky, personally as well as professionally,[1] and I have enjoyed myself. I have learned a few things over the years about how to practice my craft, though, as this essay will reveal, I don't always do what I know I should.

Starting Out
As far back as I can remember, I have sought variety and enjoyed figuring things out. The latter inclination was strongly reinforced in a calculus class I took in high school. It was taught by Kenneth Pyatt, a commanding figure who had taught both my parents and was said to

This essay was previously published in *American Economist* 40, no. 2 (fall 1996): 37–43.

have moonlighted as a professional wrestler in those days. Our text was full of formulas, but Mr. Pyatt insisted that we *not* memorize them. He taught us instead to derive formulas as needed from a few first principles and, more importantly, showed us that we could do this. As an MIT undergraduate, I was taught over and over again that I could and should figure things out from first principles.

I went to MIT from my small southern Illinois hometown mainly because almost all the adults I knew told me firmly that my talent for mathematics pointed to a career in engineering and that MIT was the best place to become an engineer. Even though I enjoyed the rigor of math and science at MIT, however, I discovered in fairly short order that I wasn't really interested in spending my life in a laboratory. I drifted into a major in economics because I had enjoyed the combination of rigor and policy relevance in the introductory sequence and because the MIT economics major gave me considerable freedom to take courses on subjects like philosophy and statistics about which I was curious. Economics also seemed like a natural field for somebody who had good, but not great, mathematical skills and good, but not great, verbal abilities, along with interests in business and politics.

As I learned more about economics, my interest in it deepened. Michael Intriligator, then a graduate student, provided a clear and elegant introduction to micro theory, and Ed Kuh quickened my interest in extracting information from data. Paul MacAvoy's industrial-organization course brought economic theory and econometrics together with the interest in business I had brought to MIT from Illinois.

In my senior year, I decided that I would like to be a management consultant, so that I could work on a variety of challenging problems involving people rather than electrons and earn a decent living in the bargain. I applied to a couple of M.B.A. programs, to the Ph.D. program at MIT's Sloan School of Management, and to economics Ph.D. programs at MIT and Yale. (In the mid-1960s it was not yet customary for students to acquire work experience before entering M.B.A. programs.)

In retrospect, I am glad that my parents could not afford to support my graduate education. This kept me from attending the M.B.A. programs to which I applied, since they offered no financial aid. The Sloan Ph.D. program did not offer enough aid to live on. Yale's economics program made a more generous aid offer than MIT's and seemed the dominant choice: I could afford to eat while learning more than in an M.B.A. program and then, I thought, go into consulting with a Ph.D. behind my name. But Evsey Domar, chair of MIT's graduate economics admissions committee and from whom I had taken a fascinating course in comparative systems, quickly matched Yale's offer. Paul MacAvoy, who was advising my undergraduate thesis on firm size and growth in the beer industry, then pointed out that I might want more female companionship than New Haven could offer, and I wound up at MIT.

In graduate school I observed that my teachers seemed to be working (hard!) on a variety of interesting problems while earning decent livings. Moreover, I found I really enjoyed learning the tools of economics from masters of the trade. The idea of being a professor for a few years began to grow on me.

Like many economists, my first serious lessons on how to do research came in the process of writing my dissertation. I spent some months preparing to do theoretical and empirical work with Ed Kuh on the dynamics of price, production, and inventory decisions at the industry level. That project ended abruptly and painfully when the Census Bureau firmly denied me access to the unpublished disaggregated data I needed.

Walking through the economics department shortly thereafter with no idea what to do next, I saw a small notice to the effect that Evsey Domar and Frank Fisher would be interested in having a student work on the economics of advertising. Though I had not previously thought much about this area (it had not figured importantly in Morrie Adelman's industrial-organization course), I decided to see if I could find a dissertation topic within it.

I talked with Frank and Evsey to learn what they had in mind, and I went to the library to learn a bit about the literature on advertising. It struck me fairly quickly that most writers had implicitly treated advertising as exogenous, even though it is plainly the endogenous result of decisions made by market participants. After a good deal of hard work exploring the implications of this point and numerous important lessons from Frank Fisher on how to execute and present both theoretical and empirical work, I had a Ph.D. and the tools necessary to begin a research career.

By the time I started looking for a job, I had decided to try academic life for a while unless a consulting firm made an offer I couldn't refuse. None did, and I left Cambridge for the University of California, San Diego, in the summer of 1970 planning to try academic life until something more interesting came along. After seven productive and enjoyable years in San Diego, I accepted an offer to return to MIT. Being a professor has suited me better than I had ever imagined it would, and I can't imagine that anything more interesting will ever come along.

Generating Topics

Since finishing my thesis, I have written on advertising and related subjects, but I have also worked in other areas and produced theoretical, empirical, and policy papers on a range of topics. As an academic I enjoy and take pride in teaching, but I really enjoy learning.

Every research project must begin with the generation of a topic: a specific question or idea that can productively be studied using intellectual tools that are available or can readily be learned. This is a critical stage in the research process and, for me, the most difficult to manage. Beginning with my dissertation topic, I have gotten good ideas from diverse sources in seemingly random ways.

I have always found it valuable to spend time at home, where interruptions are less frequent than at work, reading widely in economics. Mostly I skim for interesting ideas, data, tools, results, whatever. I read closely only when I find something either directly related to my current work or unusually interesting. Ideas for new research projects come to me mainly when I am not concentrating on my current agenda but am rather contemplating economic issues and ideas in a relaxed, open state of mind. To most people this looks like goofing off, but it involves sustained mental effort.

This sort of intellectual grazing produces no visible output except for illegible scrawls on yellow pads, but I have always found it highly productive. During 1973–74 I was a research fellow with minimal responsibilities at the University of Louvain in Belgium. I had no writing plans, and when not traveling around Europe I spent most of my time reading, attending seminars, and chatting with colleagues. This relaxed and unstructured year produced wonderful experiences, enduring friendships — and ideas that ultimately resulted in about a half-dozen published papers!

In seminars and in conversations, colleagues have given me many good research ideas, and I have gained from productive collaborations, particularly with Tracy Lewis on resource economics and with Paul Joskow on a range of topics. I have also gotten good topics from students' questions to which "I don't know" is a correct but unsatisfying answer. Mostly, though, I have found teaching valuable because it regularly requires me to organize, distill, and evaluate a body of literature. A number of my better papers address problems uncovered while preparing lectures. In all these activities, the key to generating good research topics is to maintain a receptive state of mind.

I have been involved in consulting on antitrust and regulatory issues more or less continuously since leaving graduate school, and I spent 1989–91 as a member of the President's Council of Economic Advisers. These and other nonacademic professional experiences have been valuable sources of research ideas. Indeed, my most-cited paper (Schmalensee 1978) grew directly out of my work on an antitrust case involving the ready-to-eat breakfast cereal industry, and my experience in Washington has given rise to a major research interest in energy and environmental issues.

Most consulting or policy work does not produce worthwhile research ideas, however. Like teaching and administration, it has other private and social payoffs. Moreover, while research ideas generated by nonacademic work usually have the merit of being about something real, they are often of narrow interest or involve unanswerable questions. I believe that most of my nonacademic work has made me a better economist, and I do not believe that research is always even the socially best use of my time on the margin.[2] An academic economist's life typically involves choices among a variety of activities; it is important to be clear about what one does for love, what one does for money, and what one does because of obligations of various sorts.

While good research topics can appear from many directions, I have found it useful to be careful about three common sources. The first is organizers of academic or near-academic conferences and collections of essays who suggest topics and, often, offer compensation. These papers have usually taken me at least twice as long to write as I had expected and are not my best work. Even though I write fairly quickly, the implicit wage has rarely been competitive. I now agree to write on a topic suggested by an organizer only when I have actually been looking for an excuse to write on that topic.[3]

I have also found it useful to be careful about questions suggested mainly because of their social importance. Most such questions are, unfortunately, too hard to be answered fully. Research that produces no answers is time wasted. I like to do work that matters outside universities as well as inside them, but I have found it more productive to use intellectual interest and feasibility to screen topics than to focus on social impact.

Finally, I have personally found it worthwhile to be careful about topics that either stem directly from my own past work or are totally unrelated to it. There is often much to be gained by building on the unique expertise developed in one's own past research. The problem is that sticking too closely to what one knows well runs the risk of focusing on questions that interest only a few others who have done very similar work. I believe that I, at least, am capable of producing only a certain number of good ideas in any single area and that I will produce stale, uninteresting stuff if I don't move on, at least for a time. Creative research seems to me to require a certain amount of bravery: only by venturing away from the security of one's own past work can one have a chance of doing something truly novel.

One must also avoid being foolhardy, of course. Several publications on which I worked particularly hard have sunk without a splash because they were in areas I did not know well enough. On the other hand, I enjoy learning, and I don't believe I or anybody else can impose discipline on the topic generation process. Moreover, apart from wasted time, the negative consequences of taking moderate risks in academic research generally pale beside risks routinely borne in other professions. In this regard, I speak as someone who has survived having his first published paper shown in print to have been fatally flawed.

From Topics to Projects

Most research topics I have come up with have been bad, in the sense that on close examination they did not lead or did not seem likely to lead to interesting research projects.[4] Thus while I try to be open and accepting while searching for topics, I also try to be fairly ruthless and systematic about winnowing unpromising topics quickly and assigning priorities to the ones I tentatively decide to pursue. Sometimes an apparently attractive topic can be eliminated after a few minutes of thought; other topics have remained with me for years as I've waited for the insight necessary to transform them into projects. (I still return from time to time to an unsolved pricing problem posed in a paper I published in the early 1980s.)

The first question I try to ask about any research idea is "If I can do it, will anybody care?" That is, if the idea pans out well and the work is presented well, will the resulting publication attract and interest readers? This is always a hard question to answer, particularly in fields you do not know well. For example, a few years after I moved to San Diego I became convinced on intuitive grounds that two F-tests in a random coefficient regression model I had used for empirical work must be closely related. My careful demonstration that the relation was less close than my intuition had suggested was greeted with a profound yawn by referees from the econometrics community. They made it clear that nobody in their community was at all interested in the basic model I was using and that, accordingly, nobody shared or cared about my intuition. I did not send the manuscript to a second journal.

I am not arguing that one should try only to work on topics in which others are clearly interested. That sort of herd behavior maximizes the risk of being preempted or writing small papers, and it substitutes others' opinions for one's own creativity. I have always tried to work on topics that are a bit off the mainstream but in which I think I can persuade others to share my interest. Of course the risk of misjudging how one's work will be received rises as one moves off the mainstream and away from familiar territory, as does the risk of making an embarrassing error. On the other hand, it is particularly hard to produce innovative research if one studies only familiar topics using well-known tools.

I am also not arguing that one should work only on topics that seem to have the potential to produce a fundamental advance. I know an economist who for many years would discard a topic unless he could persuade himself that James Tobin, whom he idolized, would consider it worth writing up. Since he, like most of us, lacked Tobin's talent, his vita grew more slowly than it should have.

Personally, I have been more prone to waste time writing on unimportant topics than to underestimate the value of my work.[5] But I have made the latter mistake as well. While preparing a lecture soon after my arrival in San Diego, I discovered that a standard textbook description of the effects of vertical integration by a monopolist was valid only for fixed-proportions production. I discovered quickly that I could say some interesting things about the general case, but even after considerable effort I could not sign the integration-induced changes in output or welfare. Convinced I didn't have anything worth publishing, I put my notes aside. While they were gathering dust, the *Journal of Political Economy* published a paper presenting only the first steps in my analysis. The *JPE* subsequently also published the paper (Schmalensee 1973) I hastily wrote from my dusty notes; later work showed that the changes I couldn't sign could be positive or negative in general. I never again kept an almost-finished paper in my files because I thought it wasn't good enough to publish.

An important winnowing question to ask early is "Has this been done before?" Waiting for a definitive answer to this question can induce paralysis, however, particularly in graduate students. If a few days' search doesn't turn up work that clearly preempts a project I've been thinking about, I usually go ahead. There is always a chance that more searching will turn something up, but the odds that it will be so close to what I am planning as to preempt my work and that it will turn up only after I have made a substantial investment of time are low. The longer you wait to work on a promising topic, the greater the chance of being preempted.

It is clearly also important to ask, "Can I do it?" Sometimes the initial idea consists of the solution to a puzzle, and thus itself provides an immediate affirmative answer. In all other cases, I generally find it worthwhile to spend some time explicitly on the issue of feasibility. Sometimes this means working out an example or special case; sometimes it means beating on a general problem until it is possible to decide whether a solution is likely to appear; sometimes it means exploring the properties of a new model long enough to see if it has obvious flaws.[6]

In the case of empirical work, answering this question usually involves starting with a problem and checking the availability of adequate data and/or appropriate methods of estimation and testing. At least in my experience, the quality of the final product is much more closely correlated to the quality of the data and the importance of the question asked than the originality of the econometrics. In my most successful empirical projects — including particularly my 1985 paper on the importance of firm, industry, and market share effects in determining business unit profitability — I have not known what to expect from the computer and would have found almost any pattern of statistical results interesting.

I believe it is important to be tough on the issue of feasibility. The world is full of fascinating questions that nobody can answer, and one can waste a lot of time trying to answer them. On the other hand, I have kept topics on my mental agenda for years because some instinct kept telling me that the key insight would come eventually — and it often has.

My final winnowing question is, "Is it worth the effort?" Most research involves a fairly high ratio of perspiration to inspiration. I have walked away from projects that I thought would produce interesting results because they seemed likely to have an unacceptably low intellectual return per unit of effort. I have never been particularly good at lining up the sort of research support that would let me throw an army of graduate students at complex data collection tasks, for instance, and I have intended to avoid projects that involve such tasks.[7] Similarly, while I enjoy learning new things, my appetite for new mathematical technique has declined over the years, and I am less eager than I once was to learn difficult new tools in order to write papers on topics in which I am not unusually interested.

Executing Research Projects

Good ideas can result in mediocre research; less commonly, good papers can be written on mediocre topics. I am often frustrated at how long it takes to go from what seem to be final results to a completed manuscript, but whenever I try to rush this part of the research process I am unhappy with the final product. Unforeseen delays often reflect the surprises that occur during even what seem to be straightforward and well-structured projects. (After all, if there weren't surprises, we could hardly call it research!) Such delays also reflect my propensity to underestimate substantially the work necessary to produce a well-crafted final product. Unfortunately, at least among my publications, the quantity of embodied labor seems at best weakly correlated with importance or influence.

It is of course sometimes hard to separate project execution from topic winnowing. Figuring out whether a conjectured theoretical result is correct, for instance, may be both the first logical step after forming the conjecture and the hardest step in the whole project. I have usually found that my subconscious mind is better than my conscious mind at solving problems that don't yield to straightforward approaches. That is, on more than a few occasions the solution to a problem has come to me unbidden in the shower or in some other relaxed setting after I've ended a period of intense work on the problem. The solution to one problem (devising an index of competitive localization) that I had pursued intensively for several weeks came to me in the middle of a movie in the old Orson Welles theater in Cambridge. If a moderate amount of intense effort doesn't get me past an important intellectual barrier, I tend to take a break and work on something else — or on nothing at all — for a while.

After the conceptually difficult work on a research project is apparently done, a lot of less interesting but critically important craft work is often required to clarify exactly what has been learned. In empirical analysis, this involves anticipating criticisms of both data and method and either reacting to them (perhaps by refining the data or employing additional tests or estimators), rebutting those criticisms, showing empirically or theoretically that they do not affect the main results, or limiting what is claimed. In theoretical work, this involves seeing which assumptions can be relaxed and making a case for the class of models and/or set of real situations to which the results are intended to apply. In both cases, it is necessary to make clear to readers exactly how the final product contributes to the relevant literature, and attempting to do this may suggest more work.

In both empirical and theoretical research, it is important not to let the best be the enemy of the good. If one decides to work on almost any project until it is perfect, one will never finish anything. A project should be declared done when only small gains in quality seem possible and when these would require significant effort better devoted to other projects.

In talking about the economist's craft, it is almost impossible to overstate the importance of clear and persuasive writing. Most well-known and well-respected economists are good writers and take writing seriously. While rigorous, deductive, model-based analysis is properly at the center of most published economic research, and truly pathbreaking results will usually be published and noticed even if presented terribly, the quality of exposition generally has a major impact on which papers are read and which are persuasive and influential. One attracts and persuades readers not by claiming too much but by being as clear as possible about what has been done and why it is of interest — as well as by making it possible for a reader to work through the analysis as easily as possible. I have only moderate gifts as a writer, but I work hard at it. I spent almost as much time turning my dissertation into a book as I spent writing it in the first place. Much of that time was devoted to improving the exposition, and, because the book did well, I don't regret a minute of it.

After a research report is in nearly final form, it is important to seek criticism and to use it constructively. I have always found seminars very helpful, both because giving them forces me to work on exposition and because I can learn immediately how persuasive various parts of the work are. The reports of journal reviewers, who are generally sent papers they should be especially able to appreciate, are almost always useful. Their judgments and suggestions generally deserve to be taken seriously, and their misunderstandings generally point to problems in exposition that must be fixed because they will stop most other readers cold.

There are, of course, exceptions to these generalizations. The *Quarterly Journal of Economics* once rejected a paper of mine, which argued that brand loyalty was not in itself a barrier to entry, because a referee asserted that it was wrong. In response to my request for some support for that assertion, the editor wrote that I should learn to respect those older and wiser than myself.[8] The *Journal of Political Economy* then rejected the same paper because a referee asserted that my results were well known. I do not believe I received a reply to my request for a citation. The paper (Schmalensee 1974) was finally published in the third journal to which I sent it.

Implications(?)

On the whole, my research has moved from area to area in a way that might appear haphazard, but I don't think I could have been nearly as productive working any other way. Although economic research is not poetry or sculpture, it does have an important creative component. I believe that most scholars do their best work when they follow their personal muse where it leads, and I wouldn't advise anybody to take my history of research topics — or anybody else's — as a model.

A successful research career requires more than good ideas, of course: one must try to avoid wasting time on uninteresting or infeasible topics and do a good job of executing and presenting research projects. While I'm not sure that I've gotten better at generating good topics, I believe I do a better job of discarding bad ones and executing good projects than at the start of my career — though I still don't think I'm as efficient or effective at these tasks as I could be.

Many of my better ideas have popped into my head without much obvious effort, but all of my better publications have required hard work. I have almost always found that work satisfying. I enjoy practicing my craft well, even when I know that I am not working on a great topic.

That experience seems to generalize. I have had the pleasure of knowing many able economists — past and future Nobel laureates, teachers at many colleges and universities, civil servants, corporate economists, and private consultants. Almost all seem to get satisfaction from practicing their craft well, whether working on research that cuts to the foundations of our discipline, executing a routine application of a familiar technique, or presenting an economic concept as clearly as possible to an introductory class or the president of the United States. Thus I firmly believe that the old song's advice is sound: "Do what you do do well!"

NOTES

1. I have been very happily married since graduate school and have two terrific sons. My wife, Diane, has pursued her own successful career in marketing and quality improvement while helping me to pursue mine. She has done a wonderful job of keeping me from taking my work or myself too seriously.

2. I was once asked by a person who was being recruited as a possible member of the Council of Economic Advisers whether I felt that my time on the council had enhanced my career or whether, on the contrary, spending two years in the White House had reduced my lifetime research output. I responded that it had enhanced my career even though it had likely reduced my lifetime output because being on the council was an important part of my career. I believe my policy work on the council had at least as high a social product as most of my academic research.

3. Why did I, then, agree to write this essay? At some level, I suppose I am vain enough to have been looking for an excuse to write about myself. Also, I underestimated the requirements of the task by an even larger percentage than usual.

4. For present purposes, a project is a set of apparently feasible steps that will lead to a publication. I usually have a rough outline for the final publication near the start of a project, and I often have a particular journal or other outlet in mind.

5. I have, however, consistently refrained from writing comments on others' articles, though I will defend my own work when appropriate. The social and private payoff from doing something right has always seemed to me greatly to exceed the payoff from pointing out that someone else has done it wrong. I serve as a discussant, referee, and occasional reviewer because I feel obliged as a professional economist to do so.

6. When I was on the Council of Economic Advisers, I had almost no time for research. But I did spend almost an entire trip home from Greece enjoying

working intensively on a signaling model that seemed to have a great deal of potential. Some months later I found time to look through the notes from that trip, and the model's fatal flaw became apparent almost immediately.

7. I have never been good at writing grant proposals. When I'm not certain that I can execute a research project, I'm reluctant to make a promise I'm not sure I can keep. I'm usually certain I can do a project only after I've done most of the interesting work, and I have a hard time proposing to do what I've already done — though such proposals are not uncommon.

8. This, by the way, is the worst possible advice for a young researcher: science advances only when old authorities are deposed. As they used to say in my youth, "Question Authority!"

REFERENCES

Schmalensee, Richard. 1973. "A Note on the Theory of Vertical Integration." *Journal of Political Economy* 81 (March/April): 442–49.

———. 1974. "Brand Loyalty and Barriers to Entry." *Southern Economic Journal* 40 (April): 579–88.

———. 1978. "Entry Deterrence in the Ready-to-Eat Breakfast Cereal Industry." *Bell Journal of Economics* 9 (autumn): 84–111.

———. 1985. "Do Markets Differ Much?" *American Economic Review* 75 (June): 341–51.

HAL R. VARIAN

How to Build an Economic Model in Your Spare Time

Most of my work in economics involves constructing theoretical models. Over the years, I have developed some ways of doing this that may be worth describing to those who aspire to practice this art. In reality the process is much more haphazard than my description would suggest — the model of research that I describe is an idealization of reality, much like the economic models that I create. But there is probably enough connection with reality to make the description useful — which I hope is also true for my economic models.

Getting Ideas

The first step is to get an idea. This is not all that hard to do. The tricky part is to get a *good* idea. The way you do this is to come up with lots and lots of ideas and throw out all the ones that aren't good.

But where to get ideas, that's the question. Most graduate students are convinced that the way you get ideas is to read journal articles. But in my experience journals really aren't a very good source of original ideas. You can get lots of things from journal articles — technique, insight, even truth. But most of the time you will only get someone else's ideas. True, they may leave a few loose ends lying around that you can pick up on, but the reason they are

This essay was previously published in *American Economist* 41, no. 2 (fall 1997): 3–10.

loose is probably that the author thought about them a while and couldn't figure out what to do with them or decided they were too tedious to bother with — which means that it is likely that you will find yourself in the same situation.

My suggestion is rather different: I think that you should look for your ideas outside the academic journals — in newspapers, in magazines, in conversations, and in TV and radio programs. When you read the newspaper, look for articles about economics . . . and then look at the ones that aren't about economics, because lots of the time they end up being about economics too. Magazines are usually better than newspapers because they go into issues in more depth. On the other hand, a shallower analysis may be more stimulating: there's nothing like a fallacious argument to stimulate research.[1]

Conversations, especially with people in business, are often very fruitful. Commerce is conducted in many ways, and most of them have never been subjected to a serious economic analysis. Of course you have to be careful not to *believe* everything you hear — people in business usually know a set of rules that work well for running their own business, but they often have no idea of where these rules come from or why they work, and this is really what economists tend to find interesting.

In many cases your ideas can come from your own life and experiences. One of my favorite pieces of my own work is the paper I wrote called "A Model of Sales." I had decided to get a new TV, so I followed the ads in the newspaper to get an idea of how much it would cost. I noticed that the prices fluctuated quite a bit from week to week. It occurred to me that the challenge to economics was not why the prices were sometimes low (i.e., during sales) but why they were ever high. Who would be so foolish as to buy when the price was high since everyone knew that the item would be on sale in a few weeks? But there must be such people, otherwise the stores would never find it profitable to charge a high price. Armed with this insight, I was able to generate a model of sales. In my model there were two kinds of consumers: informed consumers who read the ads and uninformed consumers who didn't read the ads. The stores had sales in order to price discriminate between the informed and uninformed consumers.

Once I developed the model I had a research assistant go through a couple of years' worth of the *Ann Arbor News* searching for the prices of color TVs. Much to my delight the general pattern of pricing was similar to that predicted by the model. And, yes, I did manage to get a pretty good deal on the TV I eventually bought.

Is Your Idea Worth Pursuing?

So let's assume (a favorite word of economists) that you have an idea. How do you know if it is any good? The first test is to try to phrase your idea in a way that a noneconomist can understand. If you can't do this, it's probably not a very good idea. If you can phrase it in a way that a noneconomist can understand, it still may be a lousy idea, but at least there's hope.

Before you start trying to decide whether your idea is correct, you should stop to ask whether it is interesting. If it isn't interesting, no one will care whether it is correct or not. So try it out on a few people — see if they think it is worth pursuing. What would follow from this idea if it is correct? Would it have lots of implications or would it just be a dead end? Always remember that working on this particular idea has an opportunity cost — you could be spending your time working on a different idea. Make sure that the expected benefits cover that opportunity cost. One of the primary purposes of economic theory is to generate insight. The greatest compliment is "Ah! So that explains it!" That's what you should be looking for — forget about the "nice solid work" and try to become a Wizard of Ahs.

Don't Look at the Literature Too Soon

The first thing that most graduate students do is they rush to the literature to see if someone else had this idea already. However, my advice is to wait a bit before you look at the literature. Eventually you should do a thorough literature review, of course, but I think that you will do much better if you work on your idea for a few weeks before doing a systematic literature search. There are several reasons for delay.

First, you need the practice of developing a model. Even if you end up reproducing exactly something that is in the literature already you will have learned a lot by doing it — and you can feel awfully good about yourself for developing a publishable idea! (Even if you didn't get to publish it yourself . . .)

Second, you might come up with a different approach than is found in the literature. If you look at what someone else did your thoughts will be shaped too much by their views — you are much more likely to be original if you plunge right in and try to develop your own insights.

Third, your ideas need time to incubate, so you want to start modeling as early as possible. When you read what others have done their ideas can interact with yours and, hopefully, produce something new and interesting.

Building Your Model

So let's skip the literature part for now and try to get to the modeling. Lucky for you, all economics models look pretty much the same. There are some economic agents. They make choices in order to advance their objectives. The choices have to satisfy various constraints, so there's something that adjusts to make all these choices consistent. This basic structure suggests a plan of attack: Who are the people making the choices? What are the constraints they face? How do they interact? What adjusts if the choices aren't mutually consistent?

Asking questions like this can help you to identify the pieces of a model. Once you've got a pretty good idea of what the pieces look like, you can move on to the next stage. Most students think that the next stage is to prove a theorem or run a regression. No! The next stage is to work an example. Take the simplest example — one period, two goods, two people, linear utility — whatever it takes to get to something simple enough to see what is going on.

Once you've got an example, work another one, then another one. See what is common to your examples. Is there something interesting happening here? When your examples have given you an inkling of what is going on, *then* you can try to write down a model. The critical advice here is KISS: keep it simple, stupid. Write down the simplest possible model you can think of, and see if it still exhibits some interesting behavior. If it does, then make it even simpler.

Several years ago I gave a seminar about some of my research. I started out with a very simple example. One of the faculty in the audience interrupted me to say that he had worked on something like this several years ago, but his model was "much more complex." I replied "My model was complex when I started, too, but I just kept working on it till it got simple!"

And that's what you should do: keep at it till it gets simple. The whole point of a model is to give a simplified representation of reality.

Einstein once said, "Everything should be as simple as possible . . . but no simpler." A model is supposed to reveal the essence of what is going on: your model should be reduced to just those pieces that are required to make it work.

This takes a surprisingly long time — there are usually lots of false starts, frustrating diversions, and general fumbling around. But keep at it! If it were easy to do, it would have already been done.

Generalizing Your Model

Suppose that you've finally made your model as simple as possible. At this point your model is probably *too* simple to be of much interest: it's likely just an example or a special case. But if you have made your model as simple as possible, it will now be much easier to see how to generalize it since you know what the key pieces are that make the model work.

Here is where your education can be helpful. At last you can use all those techniques you learned in graduate school. Most of the time when you were a student you probably studied various canonical models: things like consumer choice, and producer choice, general equilibrium, game theory and so on. The professor probably told you that these were very general models that could encompass lots of special cases.

Well, it was true. Over the last fifty years economists have come up with some very general principles and models. Most likely your model is a special case of one of these general models. If so you can immediately apply many of the results concerning the general model to your special case, and all that technique you learned can help you analyze your model.

Making Mistakes

This process — simplify to get the results, complexify to see how general it is — is a good way to understand your model. Most of the time that I spend modeling is involved in this back-and-forth process. Along the way, I make a lot of mistakes. As Piet Hein puts it:

> The road to wisdom? Well it's plain and simple to express:
> Err
> and err

and err again
but less
and less
and less.

This back-and-forth iteration in building a model is like sculpting: you are chipping away a little bit here, and a little bit there, hoping to find what's really inside that stubborn block of marble. I choose the analogy with sculpting purposely: like sculpture, most of the work in building a model doesn't consist of adding things, it consists of subtracting them.

This is the most fun part of modeling, and it can be very exciting when the form of the idea really begins to take shape. I normally walk around in a bit of a daze at this stage; and I try not to get too far away from a yellow pad. Eventually, if you're lucky, the inner workings of your model will reveal itself: you'll see the simple core of what's going on and you'll also understand how general the phenomenon really is.

Searching the Literature

At this point you can start doing your literature search. Tell your professors about what you've discovered — nine times out of ten they'll tell you to look in the 1983 *AER* or *Econometrica 77* or some textbook (maybe even one of mine). And lots of the time they'll be right. You'll look there and find "your" model — but it will be much better done, much more fully developed, and much clearer.

Hey, no one said research would be easy. But this is a point where you really have a chance to learn something — read the article(s) carefully and ask yourself "Why didn't I do that?" If someone started with the same idea as you and carried it further, you want to see what you missed.

On the other hand, if you really followed the advice I gave you above to keep it simple, you may have come up with something that is much clearer than the current treatments. Or, maybe you've found something that is more general. If so, you may have a worthwhile insight. Go back to your adviser and tell him or her what you have found. Maybe you've got a new angle on an old idea that is worth further exploration. If so, congratulations — you would never have found this if you did the literature search right away.

Maybe what you've figured out is not already in the literature. The next possibility is that you are wrong. Maybe your analysis isn't right, maybe the idea is just off the wall. This is where your adviser can play a big role. If you've really made your analysis as simple as possible, it is (*a*) less likely to contain an error, and (*b*) any errors that remain will be easier to find.

This brings me to another common problem. When you've worked on a topic for several months — or even several weeks — you tend to lose a lot of perspective . . . literally. You're just too close to the work to really get a picture of what is going on. This lack of perspective takes one of two forms: first, you may think something is obvious when it really isn't. It may be obvious to *you*, but you've been thinking about this issue for several months — it probably isn't so obvious to someone who doesn't have the benefit of that experience.

The other possibility is that you may think, something is complicated when it is really obvious — you've wandered into a forest via a meandering path. Maybe there's a nice clear trail just a few feet away that you've totally missed.

So at this point you've got to start getting some independent judgment of your work. Talk to your adviser, talk to your fellow students, talk to your wife, husband, girlfriend, boyfriend, neighbor, or pet . . . whoever you can get to listen. And here's what you'll find: they've got no idea what you are talking about (especially your pet). So *you* have to go back to trying to figure out what you really are talking about: what *is* the fundamental idea of your model?

Giving a Seminar

After you've bored your friends, relatives, and pets to death, you should give a seminar. This is a really important phase: the more you can talk about your work, the better the final paper will be. This is because a talk forces you to *get to the point*. If you want your audience to listen to you, you've got to make your idea clear, concise, and organized — and the experience that you gain by doing this is extremely useful for writing your paper.

I listen to a lot of stupid ideas — but that's what I'm paid to do. Lots of people listen to stupid ideas from me, too: my colleagues get paid to do it, and the students get examined on it. But most people don't have to listen to you. They don't have to read your paper. They won't even have to glance at the abstract unless they have a reason to.

This comes as a big shock to most graduate students. They think that just because they've put a lot of work and a lot of thought into their paper that the rest of the world is obliged to pay attention to them. Alas, it isn't so. Herb Simon once said that the fundamental scarcity in the modern world was scarcity of attention — and brother, is that the truth. There are demands for everybody's attention, and if you want someone to pay attention to you, you have to give them a reason to do so. A seminar is a way to get them to pay attention, so be sure to exploit this opportunity to get people to listen to you.

The useful thing about a seminar is that you get immediate feedback from the audience. An audience won't put up with a lot of the things that authors try to write in papers: turgid prose, complex notation, and tedious details. And, believe it or not, readers won't put up with these things either! The trick is to use the seminar to get all those things out of your paper — that way, it may actually get read.

Controlling the Audience

I've seen it claimed that one of the greatest fears that most people have is speaking before a group. I imagine that most assistant professors have this problem, but after many years of giving lectures before several hundred students it goes away.

In fact, lecturing can become downright addictive (as my family often reminds me). As the mathematician R. H. Bing once said: "When I was young, I would rather give a lecture on mathematics than listen to one. Now that I am older and more mature I would rather give *two* lectures on mathematics than listen to one." Giving lectures is a bit like eating oysters. Your first one requires some courage, but after you develop a taste for them, it can be hard to stop.

There are three parts to a seminar: the introduction, the content, and the conclusion. My advice about introductions is simple: don't have one. I have seen many seminars ruined by long, pretentious, contentless introductions. My advice: say a few sentences about the big picture and then get down to business: show them what you've got and why it's important. The primary reason to get down to business right away is that your audience will only remember about twenty minutes of your talk — and that is usually the *first* twenty minutes. So make sure that you get some useful information into that first twenty minutes.

As for conclusions, the most common problem is letting the

seminar trail off into silence. This can ruin a good talk. I always like to spend the last couple of minutes summarizing what I accomplished and why the audience should care. After all, this is what they will walk away with, so you might as well tell them what they should remember rather then make them figure this out for themselves.

Nowadays everyone seems to use overheads for their lectures. The downside of this is that the seminar isn't very spontaneous — but the upside is that the seminar is usually better organized. My advice is to limit yourself to one or two slides for an introduction and one for a conclusion. That way you will be forced to get to *your* contribution sooner rather than later. And make your overheads *big;* use large type and don't try to say too much on each one.

There are two things to avoid in your presentation: don't let your audience go to sleep, and don't let them get too lively. You want the audience to hear what you have to say. They won't hear your message if they are sleeping, and they won't hear your message if they are talking more than you are. So don't lose control of your seminar!

The key to maintaining control is to establish credibility early on. The way to do so is to go into great detail in the presentation of your first result — a theorem, a regression, a diagram, whatever. Spell out each aspect of your result in excruciating detail so no one can possibly misunderstand. When you do this you will certainly get questions like "Will this generalize to n agents?" or "Have you corrected for heteroskedasticity?"

If you know the answer to the question, go ahead and answer it. If you don't know the answer — or the question is totally off the wall — say, "That's a good question; let me come back to that at the end of the seminar." (Of course you never will.) Don't get sidetracked; the point of going through the initial result in great detail is to establish credibility.

Once you've presented your result and you see that the audience has understood the point — their heads are nodding but not nodding off — you can go on to the generalizations and elaborations. If you've done a good job at establishing your credibility initially, now the audience will believe anything you say! Of course you shouldn't abuse this trust, but it is useful to exploit it in the rest of your presentation. This is the fundamental reason for starting simple: if you start out with a delicate argument, it will be hard for the audience to understand and you will never establish trust.

When you are done with your talk you should take a few minutes to jot down some notes: What was difficult for people to understand? What questions did they ask? What suggestions did they make? What references did they give you? You may think that you will remember these points, but quite often you won't. The audience is a very useful resource for clarifying your thoughts — make sure you use it well.

Planning Your Paper

Almost everyone writes on computers these days. I know that computers are great time savers: I get almost as much work done now as I got done before I started using computers.[2]

I thought that I would spend a bit of time talking about how I use computers, not because it is all that important, but because no one else in this collection will discuss such mundane matters. Since I am well known as a computer nerd, people always ask me what I use, and I figure I can save time by pointing them to this article. Undoubtedly this will all look incredibly archaic in a few years, but that's the cost of being on the bleeding edge of technology.

I currently use a UNIX machine, but most of what I say applies equally well to other environments. I have a directory on my computer called `Papers` and when I start to work on a new topic I create a subdirectory under papers. (For example, this paper is in a directory `Papers/how-I-work.`) When I create the directory I create a `notes.txt` file: this contains my initial ideas, a rough outline, whatever. For example, the `notes.txt` file for this paper initially had entries in it like:

```
*read the newspaper

*simplify

*write and talk

**if you don't grab them in the first page, they
won't read it
```

I create a notes file like this when I first start to work on a topic — I jot down the initial ideas I have, which are usually pretty sketchy. In the following days and weeks I occasionally take a look at this outline. When I look at it I move things around, add material, and so on. I rarely take anything out completely — I just move material to the end of the file. After all, I might want those notes again.

After organizing these ideas for several weeks or months I am ready to write the first draft on paper. I usually try to do this in a day or two, to keep it all fresh. I normally put the notes in one window and the paper in the other and write the paper while I refer back and update the notes to keep them in sync with the paper.

Once the paper is written I put it aside for a couple of weeks. Papers need to age like fine cheese — it's true that mold might develop, but the flavor is often enhanced. More importantly, it gives your subconscious mind a chance to work on the idea — maybe it will come up with something your conscious mind has missed.

When I come back to the paper I try to read it with a fresh mind, like someone who has never seen it before.[3] On rare occasions I like what I read, but usually I have lots of criticism. Whenever I have to pause and think "what does that mean?" I rewrite — I add more explanation, change the notation, or whatever is necessary to make the paper clearer. When I'm done with this process I have a first draft.

I next check this draft into a revision control system. This is a piece of software that keeps track of the revisions of a paper. It documents all of the changes you make and allows you to restore any previous version of a paper. I use the UNIX utility rcs but I know there are many other systems available. Revision control systems are especially valuable if you are working with a coauthor since they keep track of which person made which changes when.

I then repeat the process; let the paper sit for a few more weeks or months, then come back to it, read it with a fresh mind, and revise it accordingly.

It is particularly useful to do a revision right after you give a seminar. Remember those notes I told you to write after your seminar ended? Sit down with the paper and go over the questions the audience had and the suggestions they made. Can you answer their questions in your paper? Can you incorporate their suggestions? Be sure to modify the notes/outline/slides for your talk when you incorporate the audience's suggestions.

Bibliographic Software

One very useful computer tool is a bibliographic system. This is a piece of software designed to manage a list of references. There is a master database of references that is stored in your computer. You assign a key to each article like Arrow70 or ArrowRisk. When you want to refer to a paper you use the key, by saying something like \cite{Arrow70}. The bibliographic program then looks up the appropriate citation in your database and puts it in the list of references at the end of your article.

I use the system called BibT$_E$X, since it works well with T$_E$X. However, there are many other systems available that work for other word-processing packages. It's a good idea to get in the habit of using a system like this. Over the years you will build up a comprehensive bibliography for the areas you work in.

But where do you get your references in the first place? Well, one way is to ask people: your adviser, your colleagues, your friends, and so on. This is still one of the most reliable ways. But nowadays there are a number of computerized databases available online or on CDs that allow for easy search. You can open the CD for *Journal of Economic Literature,* type in a few key words like *price discrimination,* and get the last ten years' worth of abstracts of published articles that contain the words *Price discrimination.* As you look at these articles you will see a few "classic" articles cited. When you identify these classic articles, go to the *Social Science Citation Index* and search for all the recent papers that have cited these classics. This process should give you an up-to-date bibliography pretty quickly. Often you can download the citations you get directly into your bibliography database program.

The Structure of the Paper

There's an old joke about academic papers. They are all supposed to have three parts. The first part, everyone can understand. The second, only a handful of readers can understand. The last part no one can understand — that's how the readers know it's a serious piece of work!

The big mistake that authors make these days is to leave out the first part of the paper — that part that everyone can understand. But the introduction is the most important part of the paper. You've got to grab the reader on the first page. No matter how brilliant the rest of the paper is, it won't be noticed if no one reads it. And no one will read it if you don't get their interest in the first few paragraphs. If you really know what your paper is about, you shouldn't find it hard to explain this to your reader in a couple of paragraphs.

My basic advice is to make your paper look like your talk. Get to the point. Use examples. Keep it simple. Tell people why what you did is important after you've done it. Put the tedious stuff in the appendix. End with a summary of what you have accomplished. If you have really written a good paper, people won't have to listen to your seminar to find out what you have done: they can just read it in your paper.

When to Stop

You can tell when your work is getting ready for publication by the reactions in the seminars: people stop asking questions. (Or at least, the people who have read your paper stop asking questions.) If you've followed my advice, you've already asked their questions — and answered them — in your paper.

Once you've made your point, stop. Lots of papers drag on too long. I said earlier that people only remember about twenty minutes of your seminar (if you're lucky), and they only remember about ten pages of your paper. You should be able to say most of what you want to say in that length.

Once your paper is written, you can submit it to a journal. I don't have too much to say about this; Dan Hamermesh has written a nice article that describes the procedure better than I can.[4] All I can say is to echo his advice that you go over the article with a fine-tooth comb before sending it in. Nothing turns off an editor or a referee more than to find typos, missing references, and sloppy editing in the articles they deal with.

Writing Textbooks

Most of what I've had to say so far has to do with writing articles. But I suppose I really should say a bit about the other kind of writing I've done: textbooks.[5]

My first text, *Microeconomic Analysis,* really wasn't planned; it just happened. When I first started my professional career at MIT in 1973 I was asked to teach the first-year graduate micro course. The text, such as it was, consisted of about twenty pages of notes written by Bob Hall, maybe forty pages of notes from Don McFadden and Sid Winter, and a few journal articles. The notes were awfully sketchy, and the journal articles were much too advanced for first-year students. So I had to write my own notes for the students.

The first year I wrote about fifty pages; the next year another fifty, and the year after that another fifty. The students who used them were great. They read them carefully and told me what was wrong: where the obscurities were, where the errors were, what was too advanced, and what was too simple. I owe much of the success of that book to the fact it was class tested before a highly critical audience.

During this period I happened to meet Richard Hamming, an electrical engineer who had written several texts. He gave me a key piece of advice: "Get together the problems that you want your students to be able to solve after they've read your book — and then write the book that will teach them how to solve them."

This was great advice. I followed it to some degree with the graduate text, but later, when I wrote the undergraduate text, I followed it religiously — but more about that below.[6]

One day a publisher came into my office and asked (as they often do), "Are you writing a book?" I said that would be a silly thing for an assistant professor to do — but as a matter of fact, I did have some class notes that I had been working on for a few years.

Next thing I knew, I had several publishers interested in my notes. I spent a semester at Berkeley in 1977 and used that opportunity to hammer them into shape. Much to my surprise the notes eventually became a book and ended up being very widely used. I did a second edition in 1983 and I *should* have done a revision in 1987 or so — but instead I decided to write an undergraduate text.

I wanted to write an undergraduate book because I was fed up with the books I had been using. I had tried several different ones, but couldn't find any I really liked. I remember one semester I sat down and tried to write a midterm exam — but the book I had been using was so vapid that I couldn't think of any problems that the students could solve using the tools that had been presented in the book! At that point I figured I could produce something better.

About the same time one of my undergraduates had picked up a workbook by Marcia Stigum called, I believe, *Problems in Microeconomics*. The student found this very helpful in understanding the concepts of economics, and I remembered what Hamming had told me about how to write a textbook. So I asked my colleague Ted Bergstrom if he would like to work with me to create a serious workbook.[7] Ted created problems as the text was being written, and I had to make sure that the text contained everything necessary to solve the problems he created. I created the problems too, but those were automatically coordinated with the textbook — the external stimulus imposed by Ted's problems was much more important in shaping the contents of the book. If the students weren't able to solve the problems, I had to add explanations to the text until they could — and if we couldn't create a problem to illustrate some point, the point probably wasn't important enough to put in the text.

It's a pity that most workbooks are created as afterthoughts. Creating the workbooks really should be an integral part of the writing process, as Hamming suggested. You want the students to be able to *use* the material you teach them, so the first order of business is to figure out what it is that you want them to be able to do. The latest buzzword in education is "learning by doing," but as far as I'm concerned, that's always been the only way to go.

The undergraduate text turned out to be pretty successful as well. And the workbook has ended up selling two or three times as much as any of its competitors — which goes to show that there still is a market for a quality product in the textbook market.

Summary

I said that every talk should have a summary — so I suppose I have to follow my own advice. Here are the points to take away:

Look for ideas in the world, not in the journals.

First make your model as simple as possible, then generalize it.

Look at the literature later, not sooner.

Model your paper after your seminar.

Stop when you've made your point.

And now my points have been made, so I'm duty bound to stop. Go forth and model!

NOTES

1. But which sources to read? I read the *New York Times,* the *Wall Street Journal,* and the *Economist;* these are probably good places to start.
2. If a train stops at a train station, what do you think happens at a work station?

3. This is much easier once you reach middle age.

4. Daniel S. Hamermesh, "The Young Economist's Guide to Professional Etiquette," *Journal of Economic Perspectives* 6, no. 1 (1992):169–80.

5. The reader may recall Disraeli's warning: "An author who speaks about his own books is almost as bad as a mother who talks about her own children."

6. The general principle that I followed (and still follow) with the graduate text is that it should give the student the information they need to know to read a microeconomics paper in the *American Economic Review*. Every now and then I go through a few issues of the *AER* and note topics that should go in the next edition of the book.

7. As it turned out, it wasn't quite as serious as I had expected—in fact, I think it is quite funny, but that is due to Ted's unique sense of humor rather than my intentions.

DAVID WARSH

Knowing vs. Proving: Working as an Economic Journalist

In my set, there's a story about a reporter for the *Wall Street Journal* blowing into Seoul's airport during one of the periodic South Korean coups in the 1970s. An anxious immigration clerk, stamping the journalist's passport, asked him what he thought was going to happen. "I'm a reporter," came the reply. "What I think doesn't matter."

This is a little like a viola joke; only the insiders laugh. The gag has to do with the baldness of the lie, the reporter's automatic adoption of the standard rhetorical pose in that moment of high drama; for everybody, including immigration clerks, knew that each coup rose or fell at least partly on the strength of what the Western press had to say about it.

In real time, we simply cannot afford to dwell on our involvement in the process, or even to admit it, for reasons that I think are obvious: nobody likes a reporter who does the Hamlet thing. But too often, we are reluctant to think hard about our efforts even long after the event. I'm a journalist too, economics correspondent for the *Boston Globe.*

Who cares how I work as a commentator around the edges of a learned community? The editor of this book.

After all, what exactly was the real story about Seoul in those days? Political instability? Fast economic growth? Growing inequality? Reporters are accustomed to forming their own opinion after consulting widely. But our scribe would have come away with one view if the economist to whom he turned for guidance was Anne Krueger, who in those days was counseling the government of Turkey to loosen up its hold on its economy, and quite another if the economist he had consulted was Joan Robinson, in whose expert opinion North Korea was the real success story and South Korea a sham. Even today, these matters are still far from agreed upon, although it seems clearer than ever that the transformation of the economy was the really interesting aspect of events. Robert Lucas has been studying South Korea recently. "These economic miracles are still extremely mysterious," he says. "I mean, how did South Korea pull it off?"

The interesting questions have to do with how journalists form their convictions. How do they decide which expert to trust? What measure of trust to assign to any expert? Surely it is worth knowing something about the deep-down convictions of journalists who seek to interpret economics and economists to a wider public. My hunch is that the answer boils down to life experiences.

I will take my assignment literally, and write about my own working history, rather than the more neutral topic of how economic journalists operate as a class. Economists are well known to each other because they go to school together all their lives. Not so with journalists: we come up in many different ways. The reader will perhaps prefer that I briefly introduce myself.

What the News Is

I am a midwesterner by temperament. My father was an accountant for the Bureau of Public Roads; my mother was a writer-turned-schoolteacher. I am the first of their four children. Life is high school, they say: it is where you find out you're not going to be a basketball player or a chemist. I was the beneficiary of a good science education at Lyons Township High School in LaGrange, Illinois, during the years immediately after Sputnik. I liked science, but I was no scientist, and this became clearer when I went off to Harvard College, where the list of possibilities expanded to include economics and the competition stiffened considerably. I did have a good seminar with Nieman Foundation curator Louis Lyons on how to read a newspaper, and I left college after a year and became a reporter for the City News Bureau of Chicago, a wire service owned by the four dailies in the city.

The life of a journalist is not much less full of tournaments than is the life of an economist, but for reporters these are of a different sort, less well organized than the seminar or the refereed journal submission, but no more ambiguous in their outcomes. Did you get the story or didn't you? Even in the 1960s, a beloved story at City News had to do with its scoop on the Iroquois Theater fire of 1903, when reporter Walter Howey, first on the scene, paid boys to put pins discreetly through the wires of all the telephones in the neighborhood but his, shorting them out and insuring the exclusivity of his report. The second most famous story had to do with the initial City News bulletin on the St. Valentine's Day massacre: "Six men are reported to have been seriously injured in a fight in a poolroom at 2122 N. Clark St." Only the address was correct.

As a kid at City News, I learned the importance of background knowledge. As in science, so in news, chance favors the prepared mind. The great teacher there was A. A. Dornfeld, who chopped wood on the edge of the prairie during the days and came in to the city in the evenings to put the fear of The Desk in reporters who might otherwise be intimidated by an array of hard-bitten cops, firemen, coroners, judges, aldermen, and other characters on whom they depended for the news. Dorny would send us out with a pocket full of dimes and dire warnings about the need to stay on speaking terms with deputy coroners and desk sergeants at a dozen police stations. "Spare me the bullshit, laddie," he would say when we phoned in to dictate our breathless accounts, following up with a string of probing questions born of seventy-five years of accumulated collective experience with fires, murders, bodies found floating in the river, stolen elections, and the rest.

News, in this case, was what Dorny wanted to know. What time had the fire been discovered, and what time had the alarm been called in? How many alarms were sounded, and how many battalions turned out? (And how do you spell *battalions,* anyway?) How much damage was done? Who says so? Dorny preached a gospel compounded of equal measures of empiricism and skepticism, in which salvation was achieved through attribution and verification. "If your mother says she loves you," he would say (at least according to legend), "check it out." Scoops were possible in this wire-service world but they were extremely uncommon; if a finding was novel, if a story was sufficiently interesting, reporters from the big dailies would be assigned. Dorny knew who the customers were, that it was the dailies who were paying the bills. If there was a Big Story to be told, other guys would be along to tell it, and the City News reporter would return to his list of coroners' cases.

In Vietnam, which was my graduate school, I practiced (for *Stars and Stripes* and *Newsweek*) this doctrine of simultaneously trusting and mistrusting expert opinion and learned from watching others practice it. Good reporters were everywhere in Saigon. (There were some bad ones too.) Next to Henry Kamm, who brought his experience in Eastern Europe to the beat in Southeast Asia, I admired no man more in this wonderful circle than Stanley Karnow, who was better than anyone at producing accounts that could reasonably be described as first drafts of history. His book on China's Cultural Revolution was the first to get in historical perspective that remarkable event; his eventual book on Vietnam was magisterial. The reporter's tools were nothing more elaborate than background knowledge and skepticism, Karnow would say.

Reporters are most useful when they are not beholden to particular interests contending in a complicated swirl. They must be the agents of their readers, perpendicular and not easily swayed. They should be able to imagine the various points of view in a controversy, but not be very quick at all to identify with one at the expense of the others. In other words, they should run a fair game. The key thing here has to do with leaving room for doubt; the nature of the truth of any particular story should be painstakingly negotiated with editors and other newsmen; it should not be entailed by some theory learned from experts. The celebrated cautionary tale of the Vietnam era illustrates this principle: in Graham Greene's *The Quiet American,* the diplomat Pyle, the well-intentioned villain/victim of the story, permits a tome by a scholar named York Harding titled *The Role of the West* to guide his every decision — a perfect example of the intellectual capture we reporters were supposed to resist. How proud we were that we did!

Yet even then, it was clear that the press was itself caught up in collectively telling a tacit story about what was at stake in Vietnam. We all made our assumptions about the shape of history; somewhere in our intellectual baggage, we all had our own equivalents of the mythical Professor Harding. We were embedded in informal hierarchies based on shared tastes and skills. Little of this could be brought to the surface, but it was with this discovery in mind that I returned to Harvard College.

Social Studies

My undergraduate concentration was a program that Harvard College calls Social Studies. Here we read passionately and sometimes deeply in the history of social theory: in the course of the solemn sophomore tutorial year when I was there, hardly more than Tocqueville, Marx, Durkheim, Weber, and Freud, in the expectation that these writers comprised a sufficient list to have covered all the relevant approaches to social thought. These were the deep thinkers, it was felt, who uncovered the dramas in which we all play out our lives. They were the real York Hardings, known mainly to persons who were themselves somehow outside the system. These persons were no longer the international press corps but instead members of the university-based elite that Karl Mannheim had labeled the "free-floating intelligentsia."

Down the street in one direction, the great MIT economics department was at (or maybe just a little past) its zenith; the Harvard economics department was in the early stages of its rebuilding. But all that had little to do with us, for we were in social studies. About all I noticed at the time was that the Harvard department had declined to grant tenure to Samuel Bowles, and that Wassily Leontief advertised his disillusion first in a memorable presidential address to the American Economic Association, later on the front page of the *New York Times.* An introductory economics course was recommended, but, since it wasn't required, I didn't take one.

Instead, I plunged deeper into what was known as "the main line of social inquiry" with Daniel Bell, who then was writing *The Coming of Post-Industrial Society* — Bergson, Simmel, Sorel, Mannheim, Burnham, that sort of thing. In the end it didn't seem very useful stuff in hands less deft than those of Bell. My mind wandered. I undertook a thesis on Joseph Alsop and Henry Adams as exemplars of men living in changed times. The thought of graduate school barely came up as I finished college. I couldn't wait to get back to the news business — to the *Wall Street Journal,* as it happened, and then to *Forbes.*

My conversion to economic journalism lay just over the horizon.

It occurred when Jim Michaels, the editor of *Forbes,* asked me to write a story about inflation, on the eve of the 1975 recession. I phoned up a number of people including Philip Cagan and interviewed him over brunch — at Maxwell's Plum, if I remember correctly. It dawned on me that we were speaking completely different languages. Pretty quickly I realized that, whatever background knowledge I possessed about the fathers of sociology, I knew next to nothing about prices and taxes and money. So, under the tutelage of E. L. Minard, a fellow reporter who happened also to be a doctoral student in economics at the New School for Social Research, I went back and, for the first time, read Adam Smith, David Hume, David Ricardo, and Alfred Marshall.

The effect was electrifying. I felt, quite literally, just as Smith intended: like a groundling who had finally been permitted to go behind the scenes at an opera house to see the machinery there at work for the first time. Alternatively, I felt as though I had been misled by the architecture of the social-studies curriculum, but no longer! (Anomalies are catnip to reporters.) Not only did the history of social thought make far more sense than before, but so did the world itself. Minard and I formed a lasting friendship. I bought the first of many economics textbooks (though I continued to prefer reading the history of thought). I've worked around the edges of economics ever since — university-based economics mainly, for it was clear that the creation of most new knowledge and the destruction of old takes place there. *Forbes* was uninterested in a disciplined reconnaissance of this sort, so in 1978 I moved to the *Boston Globe.*

In retrospect, it is interesting to consider what the Committee on Social Studies of the late 1960s thought they were doing by leaving Montesquieu, Smith, Ricardo, and Malthus off their reading lists, however briefly, in those days. These were very smart people, after all: Stanley Hoffmann, H. Stuart Hughes, John Rawls, Barrington Moore, David Riesman, and Michael Walzer. Presumably they had their reasons. I am certain that they had read their Smith, just as Karl Marx, Emile Durkheim, and Max Weber had read theirs in their day. Or maybe not — looking back at the influential survey Consciousness and Society, I find no reason to think that Stuart Hughes had any feeling whatsoever for economic explanation. In any event, if you want to remember what the world looked like when seen from a certain angle in the late 1960s and early 1970s, I think this scrap of evidence — the existence of this potted curriculum — affords a good insight into the times.

This angle of vision, the one that omitted Smith, eventually changed for the Social Studies committee, as it had for me. It would be fascinating to know exactly how. By the early 1980s, the college's introductory economics course, Economics 10, renamed itself Social Analysis 10 as if to underscore the conviction that it, too, had something to say about the topics that Social Studies took to be its own. The economist and historian David Landes subsequently took over the leadership of the Committee on Social Studies, and courses in economics and statistics were integrated into its curriculum. It was all part of the emergence, both from the universities and from the essentially grassroots processes of politics, of a broader consensus about the appropriate framework for economic, political, and social analysis that was perhaps the most striking development of the past quarter-century.

It was during these years that Latin America began its transformation; that China took the capitalist road; that the industrial democracies had their tax revolts; that the Berlin Wall fell and the Soviet Union came apart. By the early 1990s, the common themes were so unmistakable that it was possible to speak of an "economic revolution" of the twentieth century reaching to the farthest corners of the globe, much as historians had delineated a worldwide "democratic revolution" of the eighteenth century. I sometimes wish I had covered a bigger piece of this story. I wish the economic journalists who covered it had been more numerous. But I consider that I was in some sense there, near the very beginning of the story, before a much smaller piece of it captured my interest.

Knowing and Proving

As it happened, early in the course of preparing that first story about the prospects for inflation, I had become interested in the quantity theory of money. It was not the practical policy debate at the time surrounding "monetarism" that fascinated me, but rather the analytic framework and vocabulary. In particular, I was intrigued by the use of the word *inflation* to describe a rise in prices, by the way that this language glossed over what I and most other newsmen who were covering the economic stories in the 1970s took to be the most important aspect of the phenomenon: the intricate interdependence between the financial and real inflation. Once again, I had the sensation of having been gulled somehow. I became that convinced that implicit in the apparatus of the quantity theory was what the historian of ideas Arthur O. Lovejoy long ago had called "the principle of plenitude": a peculiar assumption, embedded in many disparate doctrines over the centuries, that (as Lovejoy put it) the world is "complete once and for all and everlastingly the same in the kinds of its components." Long before Arrow-Debreu there was Spinoza! Eventually I wrote a book, *The Idea of Economic Complexity*. It was published in 1984.

In 1983, I started writing a column for the *Globe* about economists and others of their ilk. I called it "Economic Principals," and set about an open-ended week-to-week description of what economists actually did. My model was Leonard Silk, the great economics columnist of the *New York Times,* though my line of inquiry was different from his. Appropriately, the first piece was about Frank Fisher: both his stature as a thinker at the top of his profession and the sotto voce censure he had suffered because of his neglect of teaching and disinterested research in favor of antitrust advocacy on behalf of IBM. "The Nobleman Who Stooped to Trade," read the headline. The next few columns were devoted in turn to Rosabeth Kanter, Edward Tufte, Theodore Levitt, Roger Brinner, Arjo Klamer, John Meyer, Seymour Melman, and an ebullient quack businessman named J. Morton Davis (he has turned up in many guises since, most recently as investment guru to Mrs. Newt Gingrich) — pretty much laying out the reconnaissance I have kept to ever since. The *Globe* carries the column every Sunday, as does the *Chicago Tribune.* For a few years it ran in the *Washington Post,* until a mutual-funds column displaced it. It is distributed by the New York Times Wire Service. And, naturally, it is available on the World Wide Web.

The title *columnist* permits me to do pretty much what I like with the space. The basic idea behind "Principals" is to give readers some insight into how technical economics is really done: to illuminate the social structure of the profession, to demonstrate why some ideas succeed and others fail, to consider issues when they aren't being considered elsewhere. Most of the really interesting stuff I see seems to come from universities, after all; some of my favorite columns are simply accounts of really good papers, after they reach the National Bureau of Economic Research but before they actually appear in a journal. Other columns involve a fair amount of reporting.

No book has been more useful to me over the years than John

Ziman's little classic *Public Knowledge: An Essay concerning the Social Dimension of Science* (Cambridge University Press, 1968); I recommend it to every economist. Ziman is my own York Harding, I suppose, except that he espouses views that I believe to be widely shared among practitioners in the community of news. The epigraph to his book is a quotation from the physicist Richard Feynman: "A very great deal more truth can become known than can be proved." I don't know of any principle that yields a richer distinction between journalism (including journalism as practiced by economists) and professional technical economics than that between knowing and proving.

What's the difference? For Ziman, the answer has to do mainly with the character of the audience and the extent to which consensus is sought. Scientific knowledge is recognized as "true" because it has been so widely tested as to remove all doubts among those considered qualified to judge — the members of a small expert community. Formulating questions so narrowly that they can be answered "yes" or "no" is the essence of this process: it was Sir Peter Medawar who called science "the art of the soluble." Measurement, experiment, the passive and impersonal voice of the scientific article: all are designed to persuade readers of the dependability of the account.

In this sense, the enterprise of science is the polar opposite of the endless succession of judicious snap judgments that journalists are expected to make. News and economics are both investigative undertakings, "truth disciplines," in Jack Fuller's phrase. The values of news and science are mostly the same — skepticism, disinterestedness, openness, and all that — but with respect to the trade-offs between relevance, certainty, and timeliness, their ambitions are entirely different. News is the best answer to broad questions that can be obtained quickly and, if possible, exclusively (recall the reporter Howey, who paid the urchins to sabotage his competitors' phones). Science is the best answer, period, to far less sweeping propositions, which are framed in such a way that all can participate in the enterprise of proof. Knowing — which includes some of journalism, I suppose — lies somewhere in between.

Some years I concentrate more heavily on developments in economics, other years on politics at the borderline of economics, industrial organization, management — virtually anything that involves dollar signs. (I write a second column for the *Globe* that is more often concerned with institutions and events in Boston.) Readers and editors tell me that the trick is to vary the mix. Some columns read more like feature stories, others are straightforward political commentary. I know from experience that the real rewards come from reporting something new. (I published a representative collection in 1993.)

Occasionally I try something more ambitious. When at last the significance was borne in upon me of the reorientation of economics toward growth instead of redistribution that took place during the 1980s — thanks to the successful formalization of increasing returns in general equilibrium models — I wrote up the developments in a forty-part series in the newspaper in 1994. It has taken more than three years to finish a subsequent book, but I'm glad I made the effort.

Aside from such an occasional long patrol, I find that I work today much the way I learned to work thirty years ago at City News, with a pocket full of dimes and an automobile. I call economists now instead of desk sergeants, I visit campuses instead of detective areas, I work for a great-hearted newspaper instead of a wire service, but the method is the same. I ask the economists if anything is going on and, with varying degrees of candor, they tell me; they ask me what I have heard and, with varying degrees of candor, I tell them; and by dint of what I put in the paper, I seek to create relationships that make it likely that they will tell me when there is news and not attempt to sell me a bill of goods when there is not and argue with me when opinions differ.

True, the relations between cops and reporters are in some sense more nearly equal than those between reporters and research scientists. Covering economists, sometimes I have felt like a scribe who has wandered into a dressing room of professional athletes: although the joy of participating in economics through journalism is very great, it is not the same as actually playing the game. But this is not quite the right analogy either to capture the role of reporter, interpreter, and critic; after all, we all play sports. So I usually return to the cops. Law and order is a social construction. So is economics (not to mention economic justice!). Journalism is a completely natural outgrowth of these enterprises — necessary, too. And as a journalist who occasionally has been skeptical of the way economists do economics, I feel all the more entitled to say when I think they are doing a good job.

So whenever I feel a tendency to awe coming on, I remind myself that deep down I'm still a reporter and that the essence of the news business is still the same, whether its subject is cops, firefighters, soldiers, economists, or politicians. I'm there to find out what Dorny wants to know about what the experts say (and say among themselves), not to solve the crime or win the war or prove the theorem. I bring my own sense of what constitutes an explanation. It has been fashioned over the years by the broad community of those who write the news and those who read it. And when I'm done, I'll go home to a roomful of reporters, which is itself a truly wonderful thing.

GAVIN WRIGHT

How and Why I Work on Economic History

When an economic historian sets out to describe his work routine to an audience of general economists, he might be wise to establish first that this hybrid subdiscipline really does have something important to offer to the larger profession. Notwithstanding the Nobel Prizes awarded to Douglass North and Robert Fogel in 1993, economic history remains peripheral for most economists today. Few rising graduate students believe that knowledge of history will contribute significantly to their advancement in the profession, just as they also doubt that familiarity with institutions and experience in applied areas will be of great value. The deeper problem is less neglect of historical facts than an absence of historical thinking: Economists somehow feel that the remote past is indeed remote, too distant from their own concerns to be of practical relevance; yet they are deeply reluctant to specify the historical context within which their *own* empirical findings or theoretical propositions actually pertain. Like the student who once asked me when in history rational expectations had come into effect, most economists are content to believe that modern economics simply describes the modern economy, which came into being at some imprecise but surely remote time in the historical past.

Fortunately, there are signs that this attitudinal iceberg is beginning to thaw. Influenced perhaps by the spectacle of emerging nations trying to build market economies from the ground up, economists are showing renewed interest in the nature and significance of *institutions*. In international economics, for example, the dominant tradition starts from the premise that mutually profitable exchange is as natural as falling off a log. But as Avner Greif points out, in the face of long communication lags and imposing risks, and in the absence of effective transnational commercial law, the rise of long-distance trade required supporting institutions. Greif's analysis of medieval trading institutions, such as the merchant guild, the patron system, and the law merchant, has attracted considerable attention.[1] Although the concept of institutions is subject to no end of refinement and debate, their core property is that they develop historically and are not subject to ready invention nor reversibility.

A second area in which "history matters" is technology, particularly the evolution of technological systems featuring "network externalities." Because technological progress is a form of cumulative learning, and because technical adoption decisions are frequently interdependent, the analysis of such dynamic systems implies that outcomes may be *path-dependent* (i.e., not uniquely determined but affected by the sequence of previous choices). The QWERTY typewriter keyboard is a favorite example, but others ranging from railway gauge to videorecorders to the English language have come in for discussion.[2]

Probably the primary development pushing economists toward renewed awareness of history, however, has been the stumbling performance of the American economy over the past quarter-century. British economists have long since been led to ponder when or whether their economy began to slip. But Americans have only recently begun to think seriously about the historical origins of their country's economic success, as that success has come under threat. Perhaps my perspective on this issue is skewed, since it happens to be my own primary research topic at present. This choice has surely been influenced in some degree by a desire to show the relevance of history for the present day. But even more, I would like to think, by the thought that the historical background really does matter, for the ways in which we think about the state of the American economy and its performance. This is a view, however, that I have come to only over a considerable stretch of time.

How I Became an Economic Historian
I grew up in a Quaker family with a strong social conscience. My father and mother worked at settlement houses in various northeast-

ern cities during the 1930s and 1940s, before our family moved to Minneapolis in 1953 when I was ten years old. There, my mother taught school and my father worked for the Community Chest and Council (later to be the United Fund). My midwestern upbringing was comfortable and wholesome, but certainly did not point me in any particular intellectual direction.

When I enrolled at Swarthmore College in the early 1960s, the Civil Rights movement in the South was in full swing. In what would prove to be a formative experience, I spent the summer of 1963 on a voter registration project based in Warrenton, North Carolina, a little town in one of the black-majority counties of the old tobacco belt. The trip south was eighteen hours via un-air-conditioned bus, into what was then as remote and unfamiliar a place as I had ever seen. Our little group of college students had no doubts about the rightness of our cause, but seeing racial prejudice deeply entrenched in the attitudes of the white South, we had no inkling that the structures of segregation would crumble within a few years time in the wake of federal legislation. I felt then and still feel that this nonviolent revolution stands as one of the great achievements of American history, its stature now enhanced by successful emulation in South Africa. This sense of fulfillment was further augmented some thirty years later with the election to Congress of Eva Clayton, a local cosponsor of our Warrenton group, who today serves with distinction as one of the first black representatives from North Carolina since Reconstruction.

Despite the thrill of joining in a movement of historic significance, the summer in the South also led to some disquieting reflections on my part, about my lack of understanding of the context in which these struggles were going on. One pang came out of the endless discussions we had about the nature and causes of racial segregation. When asked whether racism was evil, I of course replied yes, without hesitation. But when asked again whether segregation had not developed from slavery, and thus from elements of historical chance, I had to agree that this also was true, admitting to myself that my knowledge on these subjects was underdeveloped. A second misgiving had more immediate bite: While interviewing local businessmen in the Warrenton area (perhaps propagandizing would be a more appropriate term), I had a minor confrontation with the manager of a sawmill just outside of town. When asked what he would do if he were black, the man quickly answered that he would get a job and better himself. Before we had time to scoff at this insensitive reply, he pointed out the window at a group of workers both black and white, noting that his firm employed both in goodly numbers at good wages. To this visual evidence I could hardly respond, but made a mental note that I wanted to understand the perspective of both sides in the South better than I did at that moment.

The following summer gave me the chance to act in response to one of the taunts often heard in the South: "Why don't you do something about the racial problems in your own backyard?" A group of students and faculty at Swarthmore put together a program to bring minority teenagers (and others from "culturally deprived" backgrounds, in the language of the day) to the campus for instruction and enrichment, in hopes of preparing them to enroll at Swarthmore or other colleges. From the vantage point of the 1990s, it may be hard to recall that there was virtually no minority presence at leading American colleges before the mid-1960s, even at liberal schools like Swarthmore. This effort produced practical results within a few years time, as several summer alumni went on to become successful students at the college, and projects of this type served as models for the federally sponsored Upward Bound program. One further lasting effect was that I met my future wife Cathe, who also served on the summer staff and stayed on to work for Wade House, the cosponsoring community center in Chester, Pennsylvania. The experiences of these years gave us the strong sense that concerted collective efforts at social improvement can work, a conviction we have held onto despite the many disappointments and setbacks that such aspirations have experienced between then and now.

But I knew that my education was deficient, and it was with the goal of improving my understanding of the economic background behind social problems that I entered graduate school at Yale in September 1965. Economic factors were surely more fundamental as a source of human suffering, it seemed to me, than pure prejudice and racial hostility. The notion that economics as a discipline could be helpful came from my teachers at Swarthmore, especially Joseph Conard, whose economic-theory seminar was known for its demanding rigor. Conard was himself a Quaker, fully sympathetic to the student movements of that day, yet one who consistently urged us to confront economic realities as opposed to the "easy assumptions of idealism." Sadly, Conard died of leukemia shortly before my graduation, so that I have not had the benefit of his counsel over the years.

Like many students who pursue economics full of curiosity about the real world, I found graduate school at first disappointing. Theory was primarily a more technical version of the same analysis I had already been exposed to. Econometrics was new, but its main message seemed to be how difficult it was to conclude anything from real-world data. In macro, James Tobin was an inspiring figure, whose scientific work was infused with concern for the human consequences of economic policy. But at that time macroeconomics seemed to be mainly fine-tuning, lacking new frontiers to challenge the aspiring student. International economics, taught by Bela Balassa, looked to be engaged in progressive refinement of the basic model handed down from Ricardo with little interaction between theory and events. I recall being struck by an article by Jaroslav Vanek on the optional reading list, showing that between 1900 and 1955, the United States had moved from major exporter to major importer of natural-resource content in international trade.[3] It was astonishing to me that this article and its implications were never discussed in class nor in any of the assigned readings. Evidently something about that subject stuck in my subconscious, to reemerge years later.

Of course, most of these impressions about fields in economics were radically out of date very soon thereafter, but that is the way they looked to me at the time. Then there was the course in economic development taught by Lloyd Reynolds, who was certainly broadminded and open to diverse approaches; but there was nothing I could get a real grip on as an object of closer study. I recall a comment by Duncan Foley, who was in that class and tended to be brutally critical, that the topics were like the glittering goods on the shelf in one of the *Alice* books, rich and enticing until you actually looked at them up close, whereupon they shriveled away. The most memorable parts of the course were the guest lectures by Hla Myint, who interpreted historical trade expansion in developing countries in terms of the classical "vent for surplus," and thus questioned the contribution of trade to productivity growth in those countries.

Hoping to find something different in the midst of this somewhat frustrating year, I requested and received permission to take economic history as an overload. This quasi-required course was taught by Bill Parker, who over the years became one of the most beloved figures at Yale and my own close mentor and friend. His teaching was often humorous and exciting, but the course itself was all over the map, and few of us came away with any very coherent view of economic history. But when Parker asked me to join the research project on the southern cotton economy, on which he was collaborating with Robert Gallman, I jumped at the chance. Cathe and I spent the summer of 1966 at Chapel Hill, where work on the now-famous Parker-Gallman sample (from the 1860 census) was nearing completion. The excitement of the New Economic History was then in the air, a self-conscious effort to apply theory and econometric methods to historical topics. For me, it was a chance to come back to the questions that had originally motivated me to go into economics, while making use of my grad-school training on a cutting-edge branch of the field. Because of delays in the computer work, we did not actually get into the quantitative analysis that summer. But it gave me a chance to explore my old haunts from three years before (taking note of, though not sufficiently appreciating, the remarkable changes in segregation practices over that brief time), and to read widely in and around the topics of slavery and the South, exchanging ideas almost daily with Bob Gallman and the other members of the research team. From that time forward, I was an economic historian.

How I Became Committed to Economic History

But perhaps not a committed economic historian. It turned out to be not so easy to apply theory and econometrics to history and thus come to a deep understanding of the nature of slavery and the roots of poverty. As I struggled to come up with something meaningful back in New Haven, the Vietnam War turbulence of the late 1960s often intervened. Current events seemed more pressing and significant than the historical economics of the cotton South, and it was probably only a subliminal self-protective urge that led me to keep any research going at all. I did publish one statistical study of wealth distribution in the antebellum South, perhaps prompted by a vague desire to show that the slave system was inequitable for poor whites as well as for slaves. Another econometric article on cotton markets was prompted by nothing more than a desire to make use of simultaneous-equations methods on something historical. A third publication, joint with Peter Passell, came out of a discussion we had about the politics of territorial expansion under slavery. This was a chance to apply my econometric apparatus to a more specific and interesting problem, and we were able to show that the effects of added acreage on slave prices were ambiguous. There was some achievement here, but little sense of self-expression or creativity, and I entertained thoughts of easing out of economic history into more policy-relevant work — as Peter himself has in fact done, in his distinguished career at the *New York Times*.

In an effort to find new directions, I spent 1971–72 on a postdoc at the University of Chicago, where Bob Fogel and Don McCloskey were supervising a lively workshop in economic history. Fogel was in the early stages of his work with Stan Engerman on the economics of slavery, a topic of obvious interest to me. But I was not directly involved in their project and had recently started a new study on the political economy of New Deal spending. This one was prompted by an article by Leonard Arrington, presenting some previously untouched data on federal spending during the 1930s, showing remarkably wide differences among the states in their per capita levels. Reflecting the influence of my surroundings, and chasing what looked like a good, quick one-shot publication, I took up the hypothesis that these spending decisions could be interpreted as an attempt to maximize expected electoral votes. This supposedly simple idea ended up consuming the entire year at Chicago, in searching out and analyzing additional sources of data and reading government documents, and in the end produced exactly one publication, in the *Review of Economics and Statistics* (1974). Although this article has generated a steady flow of citations and commentary over twenty years time, I was not altogether happy with it even then. The style of analysis was unhistorical, and I did not feel that it opened windows to further understanding of the New Deal and its legacy. When I tried to move the argument in a more historical direction, suggesting that the logic of New Deal politics had changed over the course of the decade, George Stigler objected that this amounted to "explaining away failures" of the hypothesis. Because the new "economics of politics" field seemed to take these very properties as its core objective — setting out to show that self-interested behavior always prevailed, in political as well as economic life — my interest was not sustained. But looking through history for evidence of idealism and altruism did not seem like a viable agenda either, and I had little idea how else one might approach these issues.

At about that time, a series of unexpected developments helped me to begin pulling things together in a different way. At Chicago I made the acquaintance of Howard Kunreuther, a decision science specialist at the business school, who was trying to adapt the "safety-first" model to interpret the planting choices of Bangladeshi peasants. The idea that poor farmers were risk-averse was hardly novel, but Kunreuther found that those on the smallest plots actually had riskier crop portfolios than the rest. He argued that in light of their extremely limited resources, these peasants had to take on more risk in order to have any prospect of meeting their subsistence targets. We discussed whether this idea might help to explain a puzzle in southern economic history, the apparent "overproduction" of cotton by small farmers and tenants. We found that the same U-shaped pattern of cash-crop specialization was present in farm-level data for 1880, and proceeded to build a series of articles around this theme. For me it was a turning point, because I saw that one could interpret economic behavior more richly than mere "response to price signals"; individual circumstances (such as wealth) also mattered. These studies also opened the prospect of making econometric work more historical, by placing it in the context of the attitudes and institutions of the times, as best we can understand them from historical sources.

Midway through the year at Chicago, a call came in from Gary Saxonhouse (whom I knew as a fellow graduate student at Yale), asking if I were interested in coming to Michigan, where the department was trying to build up economic history as a field. It seemed to be a good time for a move, and so Cathe and I (and our two-year-old son Anders) arrived in Ann Arbor in September 1972. Shortly after, I attended a seminar given by Sid Winter entitled "New Thinking and Old Confusions on the Theory of the Firm." This was an early version of the ideas that led to Nelson and Winter's *Evolutionary Theory of Economic Change,* and for me it was another eye-opener. Rigorous economic theory did not have to be tied to "profit maximization," a concept that slides into vacuity when closely scrutinized. The ferment at Michigan in the 1970s was suggestive to me in many ways. On the one hand, useful economic analysis could be plugged in to microlevel thinking and practices, which meant that there was real value in a diversity of source materials — some of which economists are well practiced in ignoring, such as the "business press." On the other hand, larger systems may follow an evolutionary logic over time, developing in ways that are not well understood or perceived by operators at the grass roots. All this was food for thought.

The third catalyst was an early draft of the introduction to Paul

David's *Technological Choice, Innovation, and Economic Growth,* later published in 1975. David argued that the New Economic History was misdirecting its energies in concentrating on *applying economics to history:* if economic history is merely applied economics using old data, one would have a hard time justifying the field as anything but a narrow subspecialty. But if economic structures change through time, and if the impact of particular stimuli is different between one economic epoch and another, and if the apparent stability of a system is subject to background conditions that ultimately shift — then economic history is fundamental and indeed constitutes not a subspecialty but a distinctive approach to the study of economic life. This message was persuasive to me, quite possibly because I was looking for just such a formulation at that time. What I took from it was not just the idea that economics could be intellectually flexible and open-ended, but the invigorating thought that I was already in a field ideally positioned to develop this potential.

That is about where I was intellectually when the storm broke over Fogel and Engerman's *Time on the Cross* (1974). The book was a bombshell, contending that contrary to previous thinking, American slavery had been an extremely efficient and productive economic system, and that the material conditions of the slaves compared reasonably well to those of free workers in either North or South. Although I had some prior knowledge of the research and had picked up a sense of its novelty and appeal, like many readers I was jolted by the provocative way in which the arguments were put forward in the book. In any case, I could hardly sit out the debate, since for the mostly fortuitous reasons just reviewed, I was perhaps the only person in the country with a sufficient background knowledge on the economics of the cotton South to be able to offer a plausible alternative view. I was already at work on a synthesis, but the particular components of my interpretation were undoubtedly shaped by the prominence of *Time on the Cross* as a point of reference.

In brief, my argument was that the apparent efficiency of slave plantations in 1860 was largely attributable to allocative effects rather than the personal effort-levels of the slaves. Adapting a model developed by Heywood Fleisig, I argued that plantations grew large, not because of scale economies, but because slavery provided an elastic labor supply at the micro level, in contrast to the family farm. The big slaveowning operations allocated a much larger share of their resources to cash crops (mainly cotton) than did the smaller farms. They also allocated much more of the family labor force to market as opposed to nonmarket production, primarily by assigning slave women to fieldwork and thus overcoming the constraints of the prevailing intrahousehold division of labor. Together, these two effects had a high payoff in terms of the value of output per person, which was particularly accentuated during the census year 1859–60, when both demand and supply conditions were extraordinary. The high growth rates over the preceding decades were derived from the South's unique role as supplier of raw cotton during the first great wave of demand expansion associated with the Industrial Revolution. This interpretation, summarized in *The Political Economy of the Cotton South* (1978), has the feature that the dimensions of slavery are viewed as aspects of the historical setting rather than as timeless performance properties of a particular management system. In this respect the book expressed my intellectual priorities at the time, priorities that I have retained ever since.

One Thing Leads to Another
The work on slavery had only an indirect bearing on the issues of southern backwardness and racial segregation, which I still wanted to pursue. Responding once again to conversations with colleagues, I began a collaboration with Gary Saxonhouse on the history of the textiles industry. Saxonhouse, a Japan specialist who had also studied economic history at Yale, was in constant demand as a policy expert and thus was always looking for ways to stay active in economic history. Textiles was a logical industry for us to work on, because it formed the core of industrialization in the South after the Civil War, and there were suggestive parallels between the pattern of regional competition within the United States, and Japan's encroachment on the historic British industry before World War II. Why had textiles served as a springboard for successful industrialization in Japan, but not in the South? (Here was an illustration of Stephen Potter's advice on how to deflate a pompous windbag holding forth on any country, any century. Wait until he finishes and then say: "Yes, but not in the South." It works every time.) The southern industry was doubly interesting for me, because it had maintained a rigid lily-white color barrier into the mid-1960s, an apparent defiance of economic rationality that had not been satisfactorily explained. So the two of us sought and obtained NSF funding for a comparative project, collect-

ing firm- and industry-level data on production, machinery, labor, and markets.

As in every good economic-history project, the research led us in directions that were unexpected and that would have been hard to predict. We had some preliminary hypotheses about positive links among learning, labor force experience, and productivity, and we found much supporting evidence in each of our two cases. But in contrast to Japan, the southern sources were so scattered and incomplete that we were unable to compile a measure of productivity that we felt happy with. As we read further in the trade press, it emerged that "productivity" in the conventional sense was not at the heart of interregional competition anyway. Instead, at any point in time the South held a virtual monopoly on certain product lines; developmental progress took the form of expanding the range of products successfully produced in the South, moving the frontier of competition along a quality dimension. This led to a reformulation of the basic model as a moving-equilibrium system within the national market, which I was able to estimate with available data. This version was published in the *Quarterly Journal of Economics* in 1981.

We also found that despite their broad similarities as cheap-labor competitors, the Japanese and southern textiles industries had fundamentally different labor systems. The Japanese hired young girls who typically stayed only a short time, often running away before their contracts were up. Southern firms recruited entire families to live in the mill village, expecting nearly all family members to work in the factory. These descriptions sounded familiar, and it did not take long to trace the source. The alternative models were self-conscious descendants of the two main branches of the early New England industry: the "Lowell-Waltham," or dormitory system, and the "Rhode Island" or "Slater" family system. We could hardly have hoped for a better illustration of historical processes at work. To be sure, there were contextual reasons for the initial choice of one system or the other. But our main finding was that once chosen, the two systems were shaped over time by very different internal dynamics. Work experience had a positive payoff in both cases, but the southern system accumulated worker experience so rapidly that it was (in some sense) excessive by the 1920s. Since this type of analysis linked econometric history to the older institutional tradition, we were pleased to offer it as the lead essay in our coedited festschrift for Bill Parker, our teacher.[4]

Interesting as they were, these studies had still not provided answers to my original question: why was the South economically backward? What happened to this apparently promising development path for the textiles industry? One part of an answer poked its way out of the data on real wages, an unexpected observation that stared me in the face for too long to be ignored. In this supposedly low-wage industry in a labor-surplus economy, the real hourly wage increased by 50 percent between 1914 and the 1920s. Statistical testing confirmed that compositional effects explained no more than a small fraction of this jump. Demand-side pressures did not seem to explain it either, since the contemporary accounts were full of stories of severe underemployment, as desperate, displaced, poor tenant farmers came to the mill villages begging for work. (Interestingly, these accounts made virtually no mention of an increase in real wages.) Evidently the level of real wages had simply been dislocated by rapid inflation during World War I and the sharp deflation of prices afterward, and employers found it difficult to reverse this upward jump after the fact. So I put this down as an interesting case of nominal and real wage stickiness in the absence of labor unions or legislation. Simulations showed that the wage increase was a significant factor in the deceleration of southern textiles growth during the decade of the 1920s.

It was disappointing to encounter widespread skepticism about this claim. Historically knowledgeable critics had trouble believing that southern textiles could possibly have been slowed down by excessive wages, since this contradicted everything they had heard and read about the heartless and exploitative mill village. Unknowledgeable economists were just as dubious, suggesting that if you don't have a really good analytical explanation, then it couldn't have happened. I was quite ready to take my stand with Oliver Wendell Holmes, who wrote: "Upon this point a page of history is worth a pound of logic." But economists often seem to prefer ignorance to a challenge to their worldviews, confirming in my mind their subservience to what Veblen called a "trained incapacity" to think in historical terms.

Yet in retrospect this skepticism was useful, because it forced me to continue to ponder these phenomena in more depth. What I came to see was that impressions of the South were derived from evidence passed through the highly selective filter of politics. One of the factors behind wage stickiness in the 1920s was the spotlight of national public opinion, and that spotlight was being directed by interested parties, especially the New England workers and firms who were suffering from southern competition. Their powerful desire to push southern wages upward could be seen even more clearly in the 1930s, when the industry took quick advantage of the wage-setting authority of the National Industrial Recovery Act (passed in 1933), and then reestablished these wage norms through the Fair Labor Standards Act of 1938, after the NIRA was declared unconstitutional. This insight led to an interesting reinterpretation of the practice of night work in the South and the campaign against it. Although night work was widely condemned as an example of ruthless profit-seeking and exploitation in the South, we came to see it differently, as a response to the labor-surplus conditions that were aggravated by continuing increases in the real wages of southern textile workers. This interpretation, miles away from anything considered when we launched the research project, was summarized in a 1983 article in *Explorations in Economic History,* coauthored by Martha Shiells (formerly a graduate student of Michigan).

These findings suggested a broader view of southern backwardness, which was that this historical phenomenon was intimately bound up with the regional character of the labor market. To some degree, the apparent backwardness of the region was a simple matter of aggregating the data in a particular way. Skilled and professional Southerners had long enjoyed a standard of living not much below that of their northern counterparts, but the South also contained large numbers of poor people of both races, and despite high rates of population growth, they did not leave the region. But there was a more truly regional element in the structure, in that southern workers were not "immobile"; migration rates were in fact quite high, even for black sharecroppers. But by and large they moved from east to west within the South, an example of a labor market process that was "path-dependent" in more ways than one! Though growing out of relatively conventional quantitative and econometric research, this larger view was more venturous, so I wrote it up in more expansive terms in book form, in *Old South, New South,* published in 1986.

Regionalism and the labor market brought me back to segregation, in a sense back to the puzzle with which I started in North Carolina in the 1960s. Was segregation irrational and costly, part of the reason for regional backwardness? Was segregation inherently discriminatory? Or was it instead the case, as the theories of Gary Becker and his followers maintained, that a competitive labor market would generate wages equal to the marginal product of labor even under segregation? (Indeed, segregation might facilitate this result, by minimizing the costs of friction between the races.) These topics were extremely difficult to study historically. It was fine to be led along by the data, but data from textiles would not offer direct information about the impact of segregation, because there were virtually no black workers in the industry. A handful of southern industries did employ blacks (on a segregated basis) prior to the 1960s, but aside from a few scraps, there seemed to be no surviving information on wages by race. To remedy this situation, Warren Whatley and I obtained NSF funds for what was largely a data-search operation. Warren, now at the University of Michigan, was one of a remarkable cohort of graduate students that I met during a visiting year at Stanford in 1977–78, several of whom are now practicing economic historians (besides Whatley, there were David Weiman, David Weir, and Avi Cohen, plus several others who were not specialists but had a lively interest). Warren had a special interest in this topic, since he was himself one of the first African-Americans to earn an economics Ph.D. at Stanford, and this topic was a logical sequel to his dissertation on the mechanization of cotton agriculture in the South.

Even after extensive search, we still had to make do with highly imperfect information. My part of the hunt followed up a source used by Robert Higgs, the early reports of the Virginia State Labor Bureau, giving firm-level wage rates by race for some industries for the years 1900 and 1909. The industry and historical coverage was quite incomplete, as the bureau had changed its report format completely (to simple industry-level wage summaries) after 1920. Far from being led by the data, I had to pound the prewar and postwar figures into comparability, making use of auxiliary information on segregation practices by industry and job. The quality of the resulting racial wage distributions would be scoffed at by today's labor economists, but as this was an important subject area on which there was almost no quantitative knowledge, I thought the payoff might still be high. There were two striking empirical findings: (1) prior to World War I, there was no racial wage differential in the unskilled labor market despite pervasive segregation (this in fact confirmed and extended Higgs's conclusion); (2) during the 1920s and 1930s, a wide gap between the races did emerge, even when the industry mix was held constant. In other words, the economic character of segregation changed over time, from a relatively innocuous horizontal separation at first, to enforcement of a wage differential between the races at a later point, a practice widely seen and rationalized as an expression of "traditional" southern values. This discovery threw new light on the earlier evidence on rising real wages in textiles over the same historical period.[5]

The previous debate had largely revolved around the impact of schooling and the power of the human-capital model, as discussed by such writers as Higgs, James Smith and Finis Welch, and Robert Margo. As Whatley and I came to see the matter, the issue was not the equilibrium point but the nature of the adjustment process. There surely were severe racial inequalities in access to schooling, but these were not exogenous to the prior fact of segregation and to the emerging political economy of "modernization" in a segregated society. Partly in response to outside pressures, but partly as an outcome of the region's own dynamics, "the South" was catching up to the rest of the nation, but this regional abstraction meant the white South (as indeed it always had in terms of consciousness and sense of identity). Increasingly from the 1930s to the 1960s, one finds statements by knowledgeable observers (including economists) to the effect that "the South" was not really backward, the apparent gaps being mainly due to the presence of large numbers of poor blacks who happened to reside in the region. A good example of misreading the evidence for lack of historical perspective. All of this points to quite a different interpretation of the massive black outmigration from the South after 1940, and of the conditions giving rise to the Civil Rights movement of the 1950s and 1960s. We took some satisfaction from the appearance at the end of the 1980s of studies by the distinguished labor econometrician James Heckman and coauthors, showing that as of the 1960s, segregation in textiles did indeed support an "unjustified" racial wage differential, and that integration was an important avenue of black economic progress during that decade.[6]

The Origins of American Economic Success

Having had such a rewarding visit at Stanford in 1977–78, I was pleased to accept the offer of a permanent position there a few years later, arriving in the fall of 1982. We had many misgivings about leaving friends and colleagues in Ann Arbor, where our second son Nicholas was born and the family felt at home, for the land of sun and fun on the West Coast. But there was also an interest in trying something new, and Stanford was a top department, with particular strength in economic history in the persons of such people as Moses Abramovitz, Paul David, and Nate Rosenberg. My first few years there were devoted to completing the agenda on the South, but southern economic history was not an area that was easy to sustain at that distance, and anyway I had never set out to be a regional specialist. Possibly in contrast to the view that a traditional historian might take, for me the South was interesting primarily as a locus of backwardness in the midst of prosperity, a chapter in the larger American national story. As the continued success of that national economy came into question, it seemed timely to rethink the historical sources of America's rise to economic preeminence. This too was largely unexplored territory. Little in American economics seemed even to entertain the notion that the country's leadership position had a history; it was just a simple fact, more a divine benefaction than an anomaly of world history. (As put by the authors of *1066 and All That:* "America became top country and history came to a full stop.") More remarkably, this issue — the performance of the U.S. economy in a world context — was not even the central topic within the field of American economic history itself, which concentrated instead on such matters as the timing of growth and the impact of particular technologies such as the railroad.

As part of a program sponsored by the Center for Economic Policy Research at Stanford, Paul David suggested a study of "American technological leadership." Having little background in the economics of technology, I embarked on an exploratory statistical analysis of factor content in U.S. manufacturing trade, reasoning that elements of national distinctiveness ought to be visible in patterns of exchange with other countries. Perhaps it was the ghost of Vanek still lingering somewhere, but to the surprise of my conscious self, easily the most striking feature of U.S. exports was their intensity in non-renewable natural resources. Not only that, but this high level of resource intensity was actually *increasing,* over the very period (roughly 1880–1920) that U.S. industry surpassed that of Great Britain and other industrial nations. Vanek was certainly right in pointing to the decline in the resource content of net U.S. exports after World War II. But he had missed this earlier phase of rising resource intensity, a development that seemed to defy all received economic intuition, from Ricardo to the Club of Rome. On looking more deeply into likely causes, I discovered that as of 1913, the United States was in fact the world's leading producer of virtually every one of the major industrial minerals of that day, from petroleum through coal, copper and iron ore, to phosphate, molybdenum, zinc, lead, salt, and tungsten—by a wide margin. The evidence seemed conclusive that resource abundance had played an important part in America's rise to industrial leadership. This surprising interpretation was the theme of an article I published in the *American Economic Review* in 1990.

But what exactly was the meaning and significance of this redis-covery of natural resources? When I summarized the argument in an op-ed piece in the *Wall Street Journal,* the caption read: "U.S. Success Due to Luck, Not Skill." This misinterpretation was understandable, but nonetheless quite wrong. The availability of cheap minerals was undoubtedly vital in that era of high transport costs and resource-using technologies, but mineral abundance was not mainly a matter of luck. In follow-up research that Paul David and I have conducted, we show that the United States was exploiting its geological potential far ahead of most other parts of the world. This precocious development was the result of extensive investment in the infrastructure of geologic knowledge, in both public and private sectors; advanced training of mining engineers and geologists; an accommodating legal framework (not quite the same as a set of well-defined and secure property rights); and what we call an "ethos of exploration," a conviction that ongoing exploration would bring forth a continuing flow of new finds, a belief that turned out to be true. In a word, natural resources were not natural, they were historical.[7]

The main relevance of this research is not to offer a recipe for growth in the future, but to provide perspective on growth in the past, and the impossibility of returning to the "good old days" of American preeminence. One objection I have heard dozens of times is: "How could growth depend on resources, when Japan has done so well with no resources at all?" The question is a clear sign of a missing historical sense, because the answer is, that was then, this is now. The U.S. advantage in resources disappeared after World War II, with the onset of exploration and discoveries all over the world and with dramatic declines in the cost of transportation. In the mod-ern world economy, *all* industrial countries import most of their re-sources, and new resource discoveries do not provide much of an advantage to the home country in industrial competition. (More likely, the country may suffer from the so-called "Dutch disease," as resource exports crowd out manufactured goods in the country's trade balance.) Further, modern industry draws upon a broader range of science-based technologies, much less tied to locational imperatives than they used to be. The United States had an early postwar lead in most scientific fields, but as Richard Nelson and I argue, there is little reason to expect that a single country will retain an indefinite leadership position in this type of technology.[8]

Nor is this discussion meant to suggest that resource abundance is the *only* important factor or vehicle for two centuries of U.S. economic growth. It may serve, perhaps, as a kind of metaphor for the historically specific character of American economic distinctiveness. For me, it shows that the value of knowledge on the subject is high enough to mark it as a prime research area for the future. My utterly unanticipated involvement in the history of mining and metallurgy is also an example of the adventures in store for those who allow themselves to follow the paths suggested by their evidence, wherever they lead.

Reflections

My account suggests that the topics and issues dealt with in my research have been influenced by all manner of accidents and impulses, ideas, opportunities, and interests. But there have also been some continuities and coherence amid the chaos and randomness. Some of the common threads reflect the need in economic history for considerable investment in knowledge of the time and place under study, including not just assembly of quantitative data sets, but also familiarity with the original sources of these data, and extensive reading in the secondary literature and contemporary materials. Within the setting provided by this background work, the inspiration for particular studies or interpretations can come from just about anywhere, from current events to parallel historical cases, from conversations with colleagues to debates with students — this last being especially valuable in my own case, the best way to get responses from engaged and motivated individuals with up-to-date training in economics. But you cannot do good work in economic history without the infrastructural investment, and in a single academic career there may not be time for more than a handful of such undertakings. The range can be extended somewhat by collaborations and team projects, but even here, it is not prudent to rely excessively on secondhand readings by research assistants and collaborators, when it comes to key interpretive works and historical materials. The chance to return to earlier topics and enthusiasms years later, with new approaches and presumably more mature insights, is an added bonus. These considerations perhaps explain the common observation that career trajectories are more protracted in economic history than in fields like mathematics or theory.

There is not much resemblance here to the classical scientific method in posing hypotheses and designing explicit tests of competing theories. Before launching a major project, one certainly should have some explicit questions in mind, to motivate the enterprise and shape the research design. Invariably, the questions themselves will mature and evolve as the study unfolds, sometimes reemerging as unrecognizable descendants of the originals. This is not "cheating." The openness to this sort of inductive, exploratory learning is one of the most rewarding and hopeful features of economic history as a subdiscipline and subculture of economics. In reality, the rest of economics does a lot more of this than it admits, and would be better off doing more. My views on these issues have been reinforced by the methodological writings of such people as Paul David, Deirdre McCloskey, and Phil Mirowski, to name three with whom I have maintained conversation and friendship over the years. Though an avid reader of this literature, my own role has been more on the practical side, in hopes of alerting economists to the importance of history by presenting a compelling historical account of how past events contrived to bring us to where we are today.

I do feel strongly that economic history is fundamentally a constituent part of economics. No one could argue that work on current policy design should be replaced by historical studies, but a deeper understanding of history would enrich and enhance the teaching and practice of contemporary economics in countless ways. Even when the message is, "How different things were back then," this too is a valuable lesson on the fleeting character of economic structures. For these reasons, slavish imitation of current economic techniques would be a serious mistake for economic history. The early enthusiasm of the New Economic History arose from the vistas opened by the application of explicit economic theories and econometric methods to history, and it was essentially for this inception that the Nobels were awarded to Bob Fogel and Doug North. It is interesting to note, however, that both of these formidable figures have moved quite some distance from their original methodological positions, and are now much involved with the historical study of institutions, ideologies, and evolutionary dynamic systems.

However one may have arrived at a particular interpretation, it is essential to be able to articulate it in terms of the concepts and vocabulary that economists use. Conveying the results in econometric form is that much better, and doing so need not imply subservience to the false gods of methodological positivism. Econometrics, however, is only one of many tools in the economic historian's kit. Ultimately, the important thing is not econometric rigor but integrity in the search and honesty in the presentation to a readership.

Finally, it should be evident that there is passion as well as cool-headed analysis in much of this work. If I ask myself frankly whether the discipline has fulfilled the motivations that caused me to enter it in the first place, I might have to acknowledge that thirty years of study have mainly taught that economics does not have the answers I was looking for in those days. But so much has changed over that time, that the question itself is hardly meaningful. For my part, I have no complaint. Having the time, freedom, and opportunity to pursue one's own education over this extended period is a rare privilege that I am grateful for. My observation is that graduate students who have a passion for their topic and adapt their method to the problem at hand, rather than the other way round, not only enjoy their work more but actually do better than those who merely knuckle under to what they take to be the expectations of the profession. But conveying this view to the young is never easy. For the most part, those who are open to this outlook will have to come to it in their own way.

Passion for what then? I still feel that the underlying reason for these pursuits is that, directly or indirectly, they contribute to understandings that can enhance the welfare of the society and its members. This conviction justifies the essentially national focus of my research, even though the pathways of inquiry have sometimes led to distant corners of the globe. If you ask an American what it means to be an American, the answer may be muddled, but very likely it will have something to do with human rights and freedoms. A country that has this as part of its legacy has a lot going for it and should have the good sense to cultivate and augment this heritage. Economic history can contribute to this enterprise, not by Whiggishly glorifying the past nor by cataloging the record of oppression and suffering, but by advancing our understanding of where the country has come from, what it has accomplished in the past, and what a realistic program for its future might be.

NOTES

1. Avner Greif, "Contract Enforceability and Economic Institutions in Early Trading: The Maghribi Traders' Coalition," *American Economic Review* 83 (June 1993): 525–48.

2. W. B. Arthur, "Increasing Returns, Competing Technologies, and Lock-in by Historical Small Events," *Economic Journal* 99 (March 1989):116–31; Paul David, "Understanding the Economics of QWERTY: The Necessity of History," in W. N. Parker (ed.), *Economic History and the Modern Economist*, ed. W. N. Parker (Oxford: Basil Blackwell, 1986); Nathan Rosenberg, *Exploring the Black Box: Technology, Economics, and History* (Cambridge: Cambridge University Press, 1994). True to form, skeptical economists have focused almost exclusively on the question of market failure or path-inefficiency as a feature of such models. This is not the main point, because the domain within which such inefficiency can be defined precisely is quite limited. See S. J. Liebowitz and Stephen E. Margolis, "Network Externality: An Uncommon Tragedy," *Journal of Economic Perspectives* 8 (spring 1994): 133–50.

3. Jaroslav Vanek, "The Natural Resource Content of Foreign Trade, 1870–1955, and the Relative Abundance of Natural Resources in the United States," *Review of Economics and Statistics* 41 (May 1959): 146–53.

4. *Technique, Spirit, and Form in the Making of the Modern Economies: Essays in Honor of William N. Parker,* Research in Economic History, Supplement 3 (Greenwich, CT: JAI Press, 1984).

5. Our analysis is summarized in "Race, Human Capital, and Labour Markets in American History," in *Labour Market Evolution,* ed. George Grantham and Mary MacKinnon (London: Routledge, 1994). Whatley had better success locating firm-level data for the cities of Atlanta and Cincinnati, and the results of his comparative study are consistent with the conclusions presented here. See "Getting a Foot in the Door: 'Learning,' State Dependence, and the Racial Integration of Firms," *Journal of Economic History* 43 (1983): 913–26.

6. J. Heckman and B. Payner, "Determining the Impact of Federal Antidiscrimination Policy on the Economic Status of Blacks: A Study of South Carolina," *American Economic Review* 79 (1989): 138–77; J. H. Donohue III and J. Heckman, "Continuous versus Episodic Change: The Impact of Civil Rights Policy on the Economic Status of Blacks," *Journal of Economic Literature* 29 (1991): 1603–43.

7. Paul A. David and Gavin Wright, "Increasing Returns and the Genesis of American Resource Abundance," *Industrial and Corporate Change* 6 (December 1997).

8. "The Rise and Fall of American Technological Leadership: The Postwar Era in Historical Perspective," *Journal of Economic Literature* 30 (1992): 1931–64. Our analysis pertains to the literature on "convergence" in productivity levels, which we argue is not a general rule but a development facilitated by postwar circumstances.

Contributors

Francine D. Blau is Frances Perkins Professor of Industrial and Labor Relations, Cornell University, and Research Associate, National Bureau of Economic Research.

David Colander is Christian A. Johnson Distinguished Professor of Economics, Middlebury College.

William Darity, Jr. is Cary C. Boshamer Professor of Economics, University of North Carolina at Chapel Hill.

Avinash Dixit is John J. F. Sherrerd '52 University Professor of Economics, Princeton University.

Benjamin M. Friedman is William Joseph Maier Professor of Political Economy, Harvard University.

Claudia Goldin is Professor of Economics, Harvard University, and National Bureau of Economic Research.

David M. Gordon was Professor of Economics, New School for Social Research, at the time of his death.

Elhanan Helpman is Professor of Economics, Harvard University, and Fellow, the Canadian Institute for Advanced Research.

Paul Krugman is Ford International Professor of Economics, Massachusetts Institute of Technology.

William M. Landes is Clifton R. Musser Professor of Law and Economics, University of Chicago Law School.

N. Gregory Mankiw is Professor of Economics, Harvard University.

Deirdre N. McCloskey is John F. Murray Professor of Economics and Professor of History, University of Iowa.

Rachel McCulloch is Rosen Family Professor of International Finance and director of the Ph.D. program in International Economics and Finance, Brandeis University.

Philip Mirowski is Carl E. Koch Professor of Economics and Fellow, Reilly Center for Science, Technology and Values, University of Notre Dame.

Roger B. Myerson is Harold L. Stuart Professor of Decision Sciences; Professor of Economics; and Professor of Political Sciences, Kellogg Graduate School of Management, Northwestern University.

Susan Rose-Ackerman is Henry R. Luce Professor of Jurisprudence, Yale Law School, and Professor of Political Science, Yale University.

Paul Samuelson is Institute Professor Emeritus, Massachusetts Institute of Technology, and the 1970 winner of the Nobel Prize in economic science.

Richard Schmalensee is Gordon Y. Billard Professor of Economics and Management, Massachusetts Institute of Technology.

Hal R. Varian is Dean, School of Information Management and Systems; Professor of Economics; and Professor of Business, University of California, Berkeley.

David Warsh is a syndicated columnist, the *Boston Globe*.

Gavin Wright is Professor of Economics, Stanford University.

Index

Loury, Glenn, 66
Lovejoy, Arthur O., 279
Lucas, Robert, 74, 183, 273

MacAvoy, Paul, 244, 245
Machiavelli, 10
Machlup, Fritz, 55n
MacIntyre, Alisdair, 223
Malthus, 277
Mankiw, N. Gregory, 12, 176–86
Mann, Thomas, 19
Mannheim, Karl, 276
Manson, Charles, 216
Marglin, Stephen A., 120
Margo, Robert, 297
Marshall, Alfred, 277
Marx, Karl, 10, 13, 60, 222, 276
Massachusetts Institute of Technology, 13, 41–46, 59, 60, 62, 66, 68, 139–40, 144, 154,177–80, 195, 202–3, 244–46, 268, 276
Maxwell, James Clerk, 16n
McCloskey, Deirdre, 12, 99, 110, 184, 187–98, 289, 301
McCulloch, Rachel, 8, 12, 199–212
McFadden, Daniel L., 268
McNeill, William, 194, 195
Meade, James, 64
Medawar, Peter, xi, 280
Melman, Seymour, 279
Meyer, John, 190, 192–95, 279
Meyer, Leonard B., 15n
Middlebury College, 53, 54
Mill, John Stuart, xvii, 7, 10
Mills, Wright, 196
Mincer, Jacob, 107, 163
Mirowski, Philip, 12, 213–26, 301
Mirrlees, James A., 74
modeling, 90, 144–54, 158, 256–62
Modigliani, Franco, 62
Montesquieu, 277
morality and imagination, 9–11
Morgenbesser, Sidney, 47
Morgenstern, Oskar, 221, 228
Mormon Genealogical Society, 100
Mosley, Oswald, 16n
Mosteller, Frederick, 1, 15n
Moyers, Bill, 6
Mozart, xii, 215

Mundell, Robert, 188, 203, 208
Mussa, Michael, 203
Myerson, Roger B., 12, 227–33
Myers, Sam Jr., 63, 66
Myint, Hla, 287

NAFTA, 153, 216
Nalebuff, Barry, 74
Nash equilibrium, 221, 228–29
Nash, John, 227–29
National Archives, surveys, 100, 103–5, 111n
National Bureau of Economic Research, 157, 162–63, 177, 180, 279
National Economic Association, 63–67
National Humanities Center, 61
National Science Foundation, 128–30, 163, 292, 296
Nelson, Richard, 239, 290, 300
Neumann, John von, 76, 221, 228
Newsweek, 275
New York Times, 125, 238, 270, 276, 279, 289
Nobel Prize, xiii, 14, 53, 73, 169, 171, 194, 227, 283
Nordhaus, William, 144
Norman, Victor, 70, 139, 146
North, Douglass, 283, 301
Nussbaum, Martha, 173n

Oates, Joyce Carol, 196
OCED, 92
Okun, Arthur, 50
OPEC, 86, 204
Oppenheimer, Robert, 14
Oxford University, 51

Paderewski, 80
Paris Review, xii, 196
Parker, William, 287, 288, 293
Passell, Peter, 288, 289
Pasteur, xii, 98
Peck, Merton J., 236
Pelikan, Jaroslav, 4, 15n, 18n
Peltzman, Sam, 167
Perkins, Frances, 21
Picasso, Pablo, 6

Piore, Michael, 116
Planck, Max, xi
Plato, 1, 8
Pollak, Robert, 239
Porter, Roger, 16n
Posner, Richard, 163–66, 168, 170, 172, 173n, 175n
  Economic Structure of Tort Law, The, 166
Potter, Stephen, 292
Poulenc, Francis, 16n
Powers, Thomas, 19n
Princeton University, 109, 177
  Institute for Advanced Study, 195
productivity, 119–26
Progressive Alliance, 122–23, 132n
Pryor, Frederick, 62

Quarterly Journal of Economics, 253, 293
Quesnay, 219

Raaheim, K., 17n
Rabi, Isidor Isaac, 4
Raiffa, Howard, 228
Rawls, John, 239, 277
Razin, Assaf, 136–37, 140, 142n
Reagan, Barbara, 24
Reagan, Nancy, 74, 81n
Reich, Michael, 116
Research in Economic History, 62
research, progress, 89
Review of Black Political Economy, 66, 67
Review of Economics and Statistics, 289
Review of Economic Studies, 79
Reynolds, Lloyd, 287
Ricardo, David, 13, 60, 277, 287, 298
Riesman, David, 277
Rilke, Rainer Maria, 3
Roberts, Sylvia, 66
Robinson, Joan, 15n, 273
Romer, David, 178
Roosevelt, Franklin D., 21
Rorty, Richard, 214, 223
Rose-Ackerman, Susan, 12, 234–42
  Controlling Environmental Policy:

  The Limits of Public Law in Germany and the United States, 240
  Corruption: A Study in Political Economy, 239
  Rethinking the Progressive Agenda: The Reform of the American Regulatory State, 240
  Uncertain Search for Environmental Quality, The, 238
Rosen, Harvey, 177–78
Rosen, Sherwin, 167
Rosenberg, Nathan, 298
Rosenfield, Andrew, 169–70, 174n
Roth, Henry, 8, 17n
Rousseau, 214
Rubinfeld, Daniel L., 174n

Samuels, Warren, 217
Samuelson, Paul A., xi, xv, xvi, 7, 10, 62, 77, 133, 141n, 151, 182, 195
Sargent, Tom, 219
Schmalensee, Richard, 12, 243–55
Schrödinger, Erwin, 5, 17n
Schultz, Theodore, 8, 10, 17n
Schumpeter, Joseph, xiv, 13, 60, 79, 80, 143
science, art, economics, and econometrics, 213–26
Scott, Robert, 166
Selten, Reinhard, 227, 229
Sen, A. K., 239
Sent, Esther-Mirjam, 219
Shakespeare, 192
Shapley, Lloyd, 227–28
Sharpe, William, 72
Shattuck, John, 15n
Shavell, Steven, 173n
Shelley, Percy, 9
Shell, Karl, 202
Shepherd, George B., 212n
Silk, Leonard, 279
Simms, Margaret, 67
Simon, Herbert A., 263
Simon, Julian L., 17n
Simons, Henry, 163
Singer, Isaac Bashevis, 3, 6
Skinner, B. F., xvii
Sklar, Lawrence, 217

slavery, 62–63, 100–101, 288–92
Smith, Adam, xii, 10, 13, 18n, 60,
    179, 277
  Theory of Moral Sentiments, The,
    18n
  Wealth of Nations, The, 18n, 60,
    179
Social Science History Association,
    193
Solow, Barbara, 63
Solow, Robert M., 11, 18n, 42, 144,
    153, 183, 194
Southern Economic Journal, 63, 65
Southern Methodist University, 24
stagflation, 117, 120–21
Stanford University, 70, 296–98
Stern, Robert M., 211
Stewart, James, 63, 67
Stigler, George, 42, 99, 159, 163, 165,
    173n, 208, 289
Stiglitz, Joseph E., 144, 151, 182
Stigum, Marcia, 269
Summers, Lawrence H., 177–78
Svensson, Lars, 76
Swarthmore College, 62, 285–86
Szenberg, Michael, xiii, 16n, 17n, 213
  *Eminent Economists: Their Life Phi-
    losophies,* xiii, xv, 13, 15n–17n

Tarphon, Rabbi, 89
Taylor, Lance, 62, 64, 67
Tel Aviv University, 133, 135, 137,
    142n
Telser, Lester G., 99
Temin, Peter, 195
Temple University, 189
Thompson, Ed, 62
time management, 33–36, 75
Tobin, James, 249, 287
Tocqueville, 276
Tolstoy, Leo, 5
Trinity University, 175n
Twain, Mark, 16n

Ulam, S. M., 196
Union for Radical Political Econom-
    ics, 120
United Fund, 285

University of California, San Diego,
    245
University of Chicago, 8, 99, 107,
    162–64, 166–67, 172, 173n, 174n,
    188, 191–93, 195, 201, 203, 205–
    6, 209, 289, 290
University of Illinois, 22, 24
  Institute of Labor and Industrial Re-
    lations, 22
University of Louvain, 246
University of Maryland, 24, 61, 210
University of Michigan, 215, 290, 296
University of Munich, 14
University of North Carolina, 61, 63,
    64
  Institute of Arts and Humanities,
    61
University of Pennsylvania, 105, 109,
    202, 236, 238
University of Rochester, 78, 137, 138
University of Texas, 59, 61, 63
University of Virginia, 166, 192
Uzawa, Hirofumi, 203

Valéry, Paul, 12
Vanek, Jaroslav, 287, 298, 303n
Varian, Hal R., 12, 74, 256–71
  Microeconomic Analysis, 268
Verne, Jules, 225
Vickrey, William, 46–48, 231
Viner, Jacob, 40, 55

Wallace, Phyllis, 66
Wallich, Henry, 49, 50
Wall Street Journal, 270, 272, 276, 299
Walters, Barbara, 15n
Walzer, Michael, 277
Warsh, David, 12, 272–82
  Idea of Economic Complexity, The,
    279
Washington Post, 279
Watson, James D., 28, 79
Webb, Beatrice, 16n
Weber, Max, 276–77
Weiman, David, 296
Weintraub, Roy, 219
Weintraub, Sidney, 49, 50
Weir, David, 296

Michael Szenberg is the Director, Center for Applied Research, and Professor of Economics at the Lubin Graduate School of Business, Pace University. He is author of *Economics of Israeli Diamond Industry*, with an introduction by Milton Friedman, which won the Irving Fisher Monograph Award, and editor of *Eminent Economists: Their Life Philosophies*, which was translated into several languages. A recipient of the Kenan Award for excellence in teaching, Szenberg also serves as editor-in-chief of the *American Economist*.